Affective Encounters

Against the background of China's rapidly growing, and sometimes highly controversial, activities in Africa, this book is among the first of its kind to systematically document Sino-African interactions at the everyday level.

Based on sixteen months of ethnographic fieldwork at two contrasting sites in Lusaka, Zambia—a Chinese state-sponsored educational farm and a private Chinese family farm—Di Wu focuses on daily interactions among Chinese migrants and their Zambian hosts. Daily communicative events, e.g. banquets, market negotiations, work-place disputes, and various social encounters across a range of settings are used to trace the essential role that emotion/affect plays in forming and reproducing social relations and group identities among Chinese migrants. Wu suggests that affective encounters in everyday situations—as well as failed attempts to generate affect—should not be overlooked in order to fully appreciate Sino-African interactions.

Deeply researched and with rich ethnographic detail, this book will be relevant to scholars of anthropology, international development, and others interested in Sino-African relations.

Di Wu is a Departmental Lecturer in the School of Anthropology and Museum Ethnography at the University of Oxford, UK. He gained his PhD at the London School of Economics, UK and previously worked at SOAS, UK and Sun Yat-sen University, China.

London School of Economics Monographs on Social Anthropology

Managing Editor: Laura Bear

The Monographs on Social Anthropology were established in 1940 and aim to publish results of modern anthropological research of primary interest to specialists. The continuation of the series was made possible by a grant in aid from the Wenner-Gren Foundation for Anthropological Research, and more recently by a further grant from the Governors of the London School of Economics and Political Science. Income from sales is returned to a revolving fund to assist further publications. The Monographs are under the direction of an Editorial Board associated with the Department of Anthropology of the London School of Economics and Political Science.

Affective Encounters

Everyday Life among Chinese Migrants in Zambia

Di Wu

LONDON AND NEW YORK

First published 2021
by Routledge
2 Park Square, Milton Park, Abingdon, Oxon OX14 4RN

and by Routledge
52 Vanderbilt Avenue, New York, NY 10017

Routledge is an imprint of the Taylor & Francis Group, an informa business

© 2021 Di Wu

The right of Di Wu to be identified as author of this work has been asserted by him in accordance with sections 77 and 78 of the Copyright, Designs and Patents Act 1988.

For legal purposes the Acknowledgements on pp. viii–ix constitute an extension of this copyright page.

All rights reserved. No part of this book may be reprinted or reproduced or utilised in any form or by any electronic, mechanical, or other means, now known or hereafter invented, including photocopying and recording, or in any information storage or retrieval system, without permission in writing from the publishers.

Trademark notice: Product or corporate names may be trademarks or registered trademarks, and are used only for identification and explanation without intent to infringe.

British Library Cataloguing-in-Publication Data
A catalogue record for this book is available from the British Library

Library of Congress Cataloging-in-Publication Data
A catalog record has been requested for this book

ISBN: 978-1-350-10243-9 (hbk)
ISBN: 978-1-003-08439-6 (ebk)

Typeset in Minion Pro
by Deanta Global Publishing Services, Chennai, India

For my parents and for J. A. L

Contents

Acknowledgements		viii
Introduction		1
1	The tone of encounters: Strangers, anxiety and everyday exclusivism	43
2	Interactional affection: Suspicion and sustainability of voluntary cooperation	73
3	Emotional labour: Leadership, dependency and everyday work relations	103
4	Ethical qualia: Role ethics and the moral transformation of young Chinese migrants	133
5	Speaking with affect: Speech capital, situational affect and daily (mis)communication	159
Conclusion		193
Notes		211
Bibliography		216
Index		231

Acknowledgements

This book would not have been possible without generous help from many people. First and foremost, my greatest debt is to my hosts in Lusaka, Zambia. It was their hospitality that helped me overcome my loneliness during fieldwork and made me feel at home even though I was thousands of miles away from it. My special thanks go to the staff at the China-Zambia Agricultural Technology Demonstration Centre. They provided me with a base to carry out my research, introduced me to the local community and offered me many insights into the daily routines of a Chinese state project in Zambia. I am also truly grateful to the Zou family. Father and Mother Zou received me like their own son and looked after me just as my parents would have done. They shared many fascinating personal stories with me. Their own son, Xiao Zou, often drove me around Lusaka to visit farms, companies and interviewees. It was their generosity, their tender care and their unconditional support that partly oriented my research interest towards questions of emotion and affect. I also warmly thank Mr Mbozi, farm manager of the University of Zambia Farm, and the many Zambian friends I got to know at the China-Zambia Agricultural Technology Demonstration Centre. Through sharing *shima* (a local staple) with them, our afternoon chit-chats and visits to a local church I started to understand their concerns and began to see the 'China-Zambia' relationship from a very different perspective.

This book is based on research partly funded by the Newby Trust. For this support I am very grateful. Several draft chapters were presented at the writing-up seminar at the LSE Department of Anthropology. I have benefited enormously from the comments and suggestions made there, and I appreciate the help of all the members of this seminar. I also feel deeply grateful to the Department of Anthropology at Sun Yat-Sen University, where a post-doctoral position granted me more time and resources to further polish this manuscript for publication.

Acknowledgements

I am indebted to those who read and commented on parts of this book at various stages: Eona Bell, Hsiao-Chiao (Evie) Chiu, Ana Paola Gutierrez, Andrea Pia, Hans Steinmuller, Tan Tongxue, Johanna Whiteley, Matthew Williams, Mag Wong and Qiu Yu. I also need to thank the series editor, Professor Laura Bear, for her kindest help while I was revising the manuscript for publication.

I also want to thank my supervisors, Professor Charles Stafford and Professor Stephan Feuchtwang, for their endless help since I began the doctoral programme at LSE. I appreciate their prompt and insightful feedback on my drafts. I have learnt a great deal from them. They have shown me not only what a serious scholar ought to be but also how caring a supervisor can be. Specifically, I want to thank Charles for his perceptive advice and steady encouragement that kept me going through some tough phases across the years, and also for his kind help with my book manuscript. Equally, I benefited enormously from my discussions with Stephan, who has been exceptionally inspiring and understanding. I am deeply indebted to them for their guidance and support.

Last but not least, I would like to thank my parents for their unfailing support and love.

Introduction

On my British Airways flight from London to Lusaka, my mood was unsettled as questions flew through my mind. What was fieldwork going to be like in Zambia? How would I be treated? Lonely, uneasy and worried, being the only Chinese person on the aircraft did not help me either. The moment I stepped out of the plane, the bright sunshine half-blinded me. I could vaguely make out the symbol for the 'Bank of China' not far from me on a big advertisement board near the terminal exit. As I approached, the picture became clearer: Chinese people dressed in red and navy blue uniforms and smiling broadly. 'Bank of China welcomes you' (*zhongguoyinhanghuanyingnin*), proclaimed a line of Chinese characters above the image. I was immediately aware of very complex feelings. As an anthropology student trained in Britain, I automatically connected the scene unfolding in front of me to questions of economic imperialism and domination – questions that have, of course, been routinely raised in relation to China's recent Africa initiatives; meanwhile, being Chinese, the familiar images, symbols and their placement around me as I passed through the airport offered me some vague reassurance and slightly eased my tension. Following the herd of 'white travelers' just off the British Airways flight, I very quickly passed immigration control without being questioned or checked. (Only months later, after I had several times helped my Chinese interlocutors to meet their friends from China at the airport, I realized that not all flights or passengers could enjoy such a smooth transit.) Walking past the luggage check, I spotted a young Chinese guy at the other end of the barrier holding a sign with my name.

'Hello, I am Liu Danhan. Director (*zhuren*) Lu asked me to pick you up today. He is waiting for you at the hotel. How was the journey? You must be tired now', Xiao Liu greeted me after I introduced myself. Then he took my luggage, turned around and passed it to the Zambian following behind him, saying, 'Thomas, get the car. We go back to the hotel'. No formal introduction whatever was made between Thomas and me.

En route to the hotel, Xiao Liu told me that the China-Zambia Agriculture Technology Demonstration Centre farm, where we would all be working, was still a couple of months away from completion, so the staff were all staying at Mother (*dama*) Liu's hotel in western suburb of Lusaka. Then he briefly told me the story of Mother Liu, a well-known businesswoman in Zambia, whom I had already heard of from other researchers in the UK and read about in Chinese newspapers even before my fieldwork. He suggested I should interview her if I was interested in Chinese businesses in Zambia. While we were talking, the car approached a checkpoint, but Thomas clearly had no intention of slowing down. Instead, he drove past the queuing cars and, to my surprise, one of the police officers even saluted us. Seeing my astonishment, Xiao Liu explained that the priority came with the car and its registered plate: 'Only government ministers in Zambia use a Toyota SUV. Plus, the plate shows the car is registered with the Ministry of Education, so they think the Minister of Education must be inside. This plate saves us a lot of trouble.'

Almost an hour later, we drove through an iron gate and into a courtyard surrounded by high stone walls. I still had not been introduced to Thomas the driver or spoken directly with him. An older man and woman were chatting and laughing while we were parking the car. Seeing our arrival, they stopped their conversation to greet us. 'How was your flight, Little Wu?', the older man asked me, using the diminutive although we had never met.

'This is Director Lu', Xiao Liu immediately told me. Realizing that this older man was the person who had permitted me to do fieldwork at the farm, I thanked him and presented a small gift that I had brought from London.

Director Lu thanked me: 'Aiya, you are too courteous [*keqi*]', to which I replied, 'I am afraid that I will give you extra trouble [*tianmafan*] when I am here'.

Pointing to the woman beside him, Director Lu said,

> Oh, this is Mother Liu. She is a true 'Old Zambian' [*laozanbiya*].[1] She has been here for decades. If you need anything while I am away, just ask her. The conditions [*tiaojian*] in Zambia are not as comfortable as in China, especially the food. Come here sometimes when you are really hungry [*chan*]. I am sure she will feed you well. Isn't that right, Mother Liu?

Director Lu turned his body slightly towards Mother Liu, who answered, 'Sure. Come along anytime. I will host you with the nicest meals and then Director Lu will pay the bills!' Director Lu and Mother Liu both laughed out loud.

Director Lu then asked me what I was studying. When I told him, 'Anthropology' (*renleixue*),[2] he responded: 'Zambia is the right place to study that. They [Zambians] have not evolved yet! They sleep on the ground with a piece of cloth and pick up fruits from the trees when they are hungry. Isn't that right, Thomas?'

Thomas took several steps forward once he heard his name called; however, as Director Lu was speaking Chinese, he could not understand. Thomas asked Xiao Liu to translate but Xiao Liu ignored him. Considering it was my very first encounter with Director Lu, who is senior to me with regard to age as well as office, I felt I had little choice but to listen in silence.

Mother Liu spoke next: 'Hmm … there was a girl here before who studied anthropology.' She suddenly stopped smiling and looked rather distracted and a bit concerned.

Director Lu filled the silence: 'Teacher [*laoshi*] Bao is inside. Drop your luggage first then say hi to him. We are going to meet the South African sprinkler supplier this afternoon. Xiao Liu has other things to do so we need you to come with us after lunch to translate.'

I followed Xiao Liu to the accommodation building while he explained to me that the anthropologist who previously stayed with Mother Liu had caused her a few problems and the Chinese embassy, in the end, had intervened – so Mother Liu was a bit sensitive to the term 'anthropology'.

As it happens, this was the very first ethnographic vignette I documented in my fieldwork notebook. Looking back now, it encapsulates and represents many characteristics of my subsequent research experience: Chinese migrants coming from various backgrounds (official/private, senior/junior, male/female, researcher/informants, etc.); initial friendly contacts between Chinese and then the everyday social interactions that follow on from these first contacts; and the revelation in the flow of conversation of 'Chinese perspectives on Zambian society' – with the Zambians themselves, in many if not most contexts, standing by at an awkward remove.

Into Africa: The new Chinese arrivals

In recent decades, Chinese engagement with Africa has expanding enormously, not only in terms of the quantity of capital and the speed of investment but also with respect to the variety and scale of activities. In 1999, the value of bilateral trade between China and African countries was only US$6.5bn; by 2008, the total investment was fifteen times greater, and in November 2009, the Chinese government announced another new project in Africa that included a further US$10bn of financial investments (Raine 2009). Sino-African trade had reached a historical record high of US$198.5bn in 2012, and had enjoyed an average annual increase of more than 30 per cent in the previous ten years. In 2012 alone, direct investment from the Chinese government to African countries increased by more than 20 per cent (*Xinhua*, 29/08/2013)[3] while Chinese financial loans to Latin American countries dropped from US$17.8bn in 2011 to US$3.5bn in 2012 (*China-Latin America Finance Database*).

Historically, modern Sino-African relations start with the Bandung Summit of 1955[4] and Chinese Communist Party policy guided by Mao's theory of the 'Third World'. The main focus then was predominately political: namely, to set up and enhance political alliances – the so-called South-South Cooperation – against colonialism. While China was assisting African countries with liberation and independent political movements, African countries were helping the newly founded People's Republic of China (PRC) to step onto the international diplomatic arena (Mwanawina 2008). This guideline was the foundation of China's foreign policy towards African countries and, later on, the discourse of Sino-African brotherhood and friendship based on shared colonial history against the West was repeatedly invoked in mutual diplomatic activities (Alden, Large and De Oliveira 2008).

This focus on an anti-imperial political alliance shifted to economic cooperation after Deng Xiaoping's 'Open Door' policy emerged in the 1980s and the 1990s. The main basis for cooperation was made clear by Jiang Zeming in 1996: seeking mutual economic benefits and common development. There has been frequent emphasis on equality with regard to political relationships, which are said to be defined by 'mutual respect for each other's sovereignty, and non-interference in each other's internal affairs' (Waldron 2008: xii). Under Jiang's further policy of Chinese enterprise 'going out' (*zouchuqu*) into the world in the late 1990s, Chinese enterprises began setting up business in Africa, and a huge number of people started migrating there. As Alden reported in the mid-2000s, 'over 800 Chinese companies are doing business in 49 African countries' (Alden 2007: 16). In South Africa, there were 4,000 Chinese in 1946, but the number rose to between 300,000 and 400,000 by 2006. Alden (2007: 52) notes that 'the Chinese community in Nigeria is estimated to be 100,000 while Ethiopia and Kenya are host to 5,000 and 4,000 Chinese respectively'.

The Forum on China-Africa Cooperation (FOCAC) Summit in 2006 further upgraded Chinese engagement in Africa and opened a new chapter in Sino-African relations. The forum was held under the new guideline of Hu Jintao's government to establish Chinese 'soft power' in the twenty-first century, so the focus of Sino-African cooperation turned to strengthening mutual communication and promoting 'Chinese culture' in Africa. By the end of 2009, sixteen Confucius Institutes had been established in thirteen African countries (Raine 2009: 85). As of 2012, 350,000 Chinese experts (in agriculture, engineering, medicine and education) had been assigned to Africa and 53,700 Africans had been granted Chinese government scholarships to study in China. In his visit to Africa, Premier Li Keqiang further confirmed the importance of communication between China and Africa and pointed out that China and African countries could learn from each other's culture (*wenhuahujian*) and developmental experiences (*People's Daily*, May 2014).[5]

The relationship between China and Zambia has followed the current of Sino-African relations stated earlier. Nevertheless, Zambia enjoys a unique position as the showpiece of the success of Sino-African relations as well as the 'experimental region' for new Chinese diplomatic policies in Africa. First of all, Zambia is one of the African countries that has long-standing diplomatic relations with the PRC. Not only did China help Zambia in the independence movement against British colonialism but it also actively assisted the reconstruction of the Zambian economy in the 1960s. Of all Chinese aid to Africa, the Tanzania-Zambia railway construction in the 1960s and the 1970s has been the most significant project. It took more than ten years from planning to completion and involved around 12,000 Chinese migrant workers in total. To this day, it remains the symbol of 'Sino-African friendship' (Yu 1971; Raine 2009). Indeed, this symbol makes Zambia a well-known and popular African country at the grassroots level in China and attracts more migrants because of the image of Zambia, promoted by the Chinese government, as a 'safe, politically stable and friendly' country.

Moreover, because of this historically close relationship between the two countries, Zambia is the African nation most dependent on China. According to statistics from the Zambia Development Agency, China occupied 47 per cent of total Zambian foreign direct investments in 2007, in areas including agriculture, mining, manufacturing, construction, health, communication and transport (Mwanawina 2008: 7). Furthermore, Zambia has secured all of the most up-to-date Chinese projects since the 2006 FOCAC. These include two Special Economic Zones, one agricultural technology demonstration centre, two rural schools and one hospital (Raine 2009; Rotberg 2008). Zambia's strategic position in Chinese policies towards Africa has also brought more and more Chinese professionals, experts and labourers to work in the country.

Nevertheless, this historical image of a 'healthy Sino-Zambian brotherhood' and Zambia's central position in China's African policy has been seriously brought into question by anti-Chinese political campaigns that have surfaced there since 2006. Anti-Chinese sentiment has grown in part due to everyday accusations of low wages and ignorance of safety procedures among the Chinese businesses operating in Zambia, and was accelerated by anger over several high-profile shooting incidents during protests (Hare 2007). The anti-Chinese political campaign reached its peak during my fieldwork (2010–12) when Michael Sata, the leader of the Patriotic Front Party, was elected president of Zambia. Sata's election added to the uncertainties that Chinese migrants faced and forced many of them to reconsider their initial plans of long-term migration to the country, a point I will discuss further in the next chapter.

These historical trends in Sino-African relations (Sino-Zambian relations specifically in the case of my research) provide the backdrop for the individual trajectories of Chinese migrants. In general terms, Chinese migration into Zambia has gone through three major phases. Although in each period migrants themselves had distinctive motivations, the Chinese state has always played a major role in shaping what actually took place on the ground. The first phase was during the construction of the Tanzania-Zambia railway that, as mentioned earlier, involved about 12,000 Chinese workers. No official statistics record how many Chinese workers stayed in Zambia after the project was complete; however, when visiting the Leopards Hill Memorial Park in Lusaka, one learns that hundreds of Chinese workers died in Africa when building the railway. During my fieldwork, I did not encounter any Chinese migrants or descendants of migrants who came to Zambia in this historical phase.

The second phase was after the implementation of the Chinese government's 'Going-Out' (*zouchuqu*) policy to improve the Chinese market economy in the 1990s. Hundreds of state enterprise and other organizations flooded into Africa to work on 'national projects', followed by tens of thousands of Chinese workers. The majority of the workers were recruited in China under short-term contracts and brought to their country of employment (e.g. Zambia). They were normally either employed to construct buildings and roads, maintain dams, cultivate the land and exploit natural resources or assigned to carry out domestic services (usually cooking) for a work team. Once a particular project was finished, the company would relocate, either to another African country or back to China.

Most workers simply followed their companies when they left Zambia, but some chose to stay and start their own businesses, especially if they had secured enough capital or social networks during their employment. Those who did choose to stay longer in Zambia are, like Mother Liu, described by other migrants as *laozanbiya* or 'Old Zambians'. After a few years, the families of such migrants would typically join them in Zambia to contribute to their private businesses; meanwhile, they would also often bring over their friends, usually from the same region. At my field sites in Lusaka, there were fewer than thirty *laozanbiya*, a small group well-known due to their senior position among migrants. But, although they have settled in Zambia for more than two decades, theoretically, *laozanbiya* still need to be considered as first-generation migrants because none of them were born outside China.

The real boom in China-Zambia migration came after the 2006 Summit and intensified in 2009 when the worldwide economic crisis hit the Chinese domestic market. There has been no official survey of Chinese migration to Zambia, but according to the 'Old Zambians', the number of migrants rose from thousands in the early years of the new millennium to about 30,000 in 2010 and is still increasing rapidly. The trajectory of migration is continuing in the pattern of the 1990s but the migrants have diversified: the majority of new arrivals are still workers on Chinese 'national projects'; however, more migrants from various professions are appearing due to the shift of Chinese foreign policies towards Africa – from predominately achieving economic cooperation to encouraging cultural communication. During my fieldwork in Lusaka, among the Chinese I met were professors of agriculture, adventurous backpackers, language tutors from the Confucius Institute, volunteers, exchange students, and Chinese martial arts artists and acrobats: certainly not all were officials or private entrepreneurs. Another new trend is that more and more young Chinese are migrating to Zambia as pioneers. These Chinese were mostly born between the mid-1970s and the 1980s. Instead of relying on a chain of social networks (based on government employment of family connections) in order to migrate, they usually come to Zambia by themselves, either as individuals or in groups of two or three friends. With the advantage of good English language skills, they set up small joint ventures and start businesses, mostly doing international trade in petty commodities. Compared with the mass of migrants who follow the state to Zambia, the number of independent young Chinese business people is very small, but they are beginning to show distinctive characteristics when interacting with Zambians (Dobler 2009; Arsene 2014).

The historical shifts and diversifying trends behind Chinese migration patterns to Africa have made the 'Chinese in Africa' far more homogeneous than in the past. Although all my interlocutors are from mainland China, in reality, the 'Chinese community' in Africa displays great diversity and complex stratifications. In her study of Chinese migrants in Zanzibar, Elizabeth Hsu (2007) categorizes the 'Chinese community' she encountered into three different groups: the '*huaqiao*' (overseas Chinese) community that can be traced back to the 1930s; government-sponsored teams of experts; and 'come-and-go' Chinese business people arriving from the 1990s onwards. As Hsu points out, inter-group interactions are few, and different groups have variable allegiance to the local community *and* to China – in line with their various socioeconomic backgrounds. Similar categories have been outlined by Ma Mung (2008) who divides Chinese migrants in Africa into three types: temporary workers for government projects, independent entrepreneurs and 'a proletarian transit migration flow consisting of people trying to sell their labor in western countries while waiting in Africa for opportunities to enter those countries' (2008: 95). Because of the great variety of social backgrounds among migrants, Dobler (echoing Hsu) argues not only that 'ethnic solidarity and local ethnic network do not play a significant role for Chinese traders' (2009: 710) but also that social stratification is formed in the migrant community based on the length of their settlement and their degree of integration into the host society.

Nonetheless, in the chain of migration, affinity and locality are still the main motors pulling Chinese private migrants to Zambia in general. Compared with Chinese migrations to other places (mainly Western Europe and North America, see Benton and Pieke 1998; Bell 2011; Christiansen 2003; Pieke 2002; Wickberg 2007), there are three distinctive characteristics worth noting. First, as described earlier, the Chinese state and its policies have played a significant role in bringing people to Zambia. Although most of the workers only remain with state enterprises for a relatively short term, the governmental policy of 'provincial assignment for project construction' (*duikouyuanjian*, see further) provides the base for future private migrants' strategies and their decisions on settlement. Therefore, it could be argued that the state indirectly maps out the demographic spread of Chinese migrants in Africa in the long run. The policy is designed to exploit the comparative advantages among different Chinese provinces in production and construction. Typically, once a new project is agreed between the Chinese central government and African governments, the task will be allocated to several Chinese provinces that have similar experience and particular advantages in carrying out the project. Each province will be assigned to one African country, then a provincial company or organization will be sent to that country to operate and manage the project. Partly under the influence of China's household registration system (*hukou*),[6] provincial companies tend to recruit workers from within the same province. As a consequence, many Chinese from the same region will tend to flow into one particular African country. So in the long run, there is a phenomenon of provincial concentration in different African countries. For example, Lusaka is dominated by Chinese migrants from two provinces, Henan and Jiangxi: they refer to each other as *Henan Bang* and *Jiangxi Bang*.[7] According to my interlocutors, around 3,000–4,000 Jiangxi people had settled in Zambia by 2011.

Another consequence of the policy of 'provincial assignment for project construction' (*duikouyuanjia*) is that the division of profession or area of trading by Chinese migrants in Africa corresponds to their provincial origin. Since the policy concentrates on one type of project, the employees arriving in Africa for the project are usually skilled in specific professions. While under contract to their Chinese employers in Zambia, migrants get to know the local market and establish social networks. Therefore, when they leave the company and decide to settle in Zambia, they setup their own businesses based on prior skills, knowledge and contacts. This phenomenon could easily be observed in Zambia, where migrants often generalize that Henan people are doctors and those from Jiangxi are builders; that is, nearly all of the Chinese clinics in Lusaka are opened by settlers from Henan, and Jiangxi firms occupy the biggest portion of the Zambian construction market. This is because Henan Province took charge of Chinese medical aid to Zambia during the 1990s, and similarly, Jiangxi province was tasked with helping Zambians build infrastructure, and its people stayed afterwards in the construction business.

Second, Chinese migration to Zambia takes place in the context of China's rise as an international power, which impacts on the social status that Chinese migrants enjoy in their host societies as well as their interactions with local people. In studies of past Chinese migration to Southeast Asia, overseas Chinese have been described by scholars as 'pariah capitalists' (Hamilton 1978) or 'middleman minorities' (Bonacich and Modell 1980) in the receiving communities. As Oxfeld (1993: 12) summarized it, 'the key characteristics of all such groups are a fair to high degree of economic success coupled with lack of political power and social status'. Hamilton (1978: 4; cited in Oxfeld 1993: 14) reasons that 'the essence of pariah capitalism … is a structure of power asymmetry which enables an elite group to control and prey upon the wealth generated by a pariah group'. Research on Chinese migration to economically developed English-speaking countries (e.g. Britain, Canada and the United States) shows that Chinese children's choices in education and employment are subject to the local class and racial structures, which may put them at a disadvantage (Louie 2004). To give one example, earlier studies of Chinese children in Britain with a family background in the catering industry (Chan 1986) suggested that they were inclined to anticipate their own failure in competition with their White British counterparts for professional jobs; therefore, they preferred to stay in the catering trade. Invoking Bourdieu, Bell points out that some of the Chinese children she studied in Edinburgh suffer 'internalized limits'; that is, they as 'members of subordinate groups adjust their personal aspirations downwards because of constraints which are really external to themselves' (2011: 59).

By contrast, because of the rapid economic and social development in China, the Chinese migrants now in Zambia hold a much higher opinion of their own status in the host society than they would have had a generation ago. African countries are widely considered by my Chinese interlocutors to be 'backward' (*louhou*), 'poor' (*qiong*), 'remote' (*pianyuan*) and 'chaotic' (*luan*). Migrating to Africa is normally seen as undesirable and would be regarded by most people in China as socially downgrading; therefore, for many people it is the last option. As my interlocutors often told me, only when one could not survive by any means in China does one move to Africa. Similar statements are documented by McNamee in his comparative study of Chinese traders in five African countries: South Africa, Lesotho, Botswana, Zambia and Angola. He claims (2012: 4–5) that

> Africa is the bottom-rung destination for China's migrants. The continent draws the poorest and least educated of the Chinese diasporas. Nearly all are in Africa because they could not make a living in the pressure-cooker that has become China's job market. If they had a choice, they would be elsewhere, but only Africa possesses the minimal entry requirements and light regulations that enable Chinese migrants with limited capital and low levels of skills to compete.

This negative perception of Africa as a migration destination – regardless of its fairness or accuracy – can also be observed in the policy published by the Chinese government regarding the differential allowances to Chinese aid workers in foreign countries. To attract people to work in Africa, Chinese state-owned companies and organizations pay Chinese staff (officials as well as workers) special allowances known as *jiankubuzhu*: an allowance for working in regions of 'poverty and bitterness'. The value of allowance is classified by the Chinese government not only according to the worker's administrative ranking but also according to its projection of a region's level of development and standard of living. The rationale embedded in the classification of the allowance is that the less developed a country, the more a Chinese worker will 'suffer', so the more allowance the government shall grant. According to the policy, there are five classes in total, and as the projected degree of 'bitterness' ascends from Class 1 to 5, so does the allowance (no allowance is granted to Chinese workers working in a Class 1 region). For example, South Africa is in Class 1 and Zambia along with Cuba, Mongolia and so on are Class 2 regions. Sudan is in Class 5 region, and staff working there will get more than twice the allowance of those working in Zambia.

Bearing in mind these negative connotations, Chinese migrants arrive in Africa with a pre-existing sense of their own cultural advancement. In practice, they often perceive themselves to be entitled to amend the 'rule-books' of the host society, especially in certain areas of trade that are dominated by Chinese migrants, for instance, construction in Zambia. Furthermore, as I will discuss later, Chinese migrants in Zambia aspire to send their children to developed countries for education, and Chinese children and young people (at least those I met in Lusaka) do not plan to work in Zambia in the future despite the success of their family businesses there.

Third, because people consider Zambia undesirable for permanent settlement, many migrants who decide to stay in Zambia after a national project has been wrapped up intend to re-migrate in future to economically developed countries; in other words, they use Zambia as a springboard for a long-term strategy of migration towards higher-status places. Their plans were demonstrated by their choices concerning schooling for their children: 'Old Zambians' (*laozanbiya*) tend to support their children in studying abroad, usually in Britain, the United States, Australia or Canada, and hope one day their children will work and form families there so they can join them. If they are educated in Lusaka, the children of Chinese families rarely go to local Zambian schools. Before the age of five or six, they normally attend a day nursery that was founded by six successful Chinese entrepreneurs, and where children are taught in English and Chinese by Chinese volunteers; the nursery does employ local Zambian women to look after the children while playing in the field after class. By the age of six or seven, the children will enrol for formal education in one of three prestigious 'white schools' (*bairenxuexiao*) – ones founded and managed by white settlers. Although the tuition is very expensive – about US$2,000–3,000 per term – Chinese families perceive these schools as a fast track for their children to study in developed countries when they reach the age for high school or university.

Although they have this long-term plan, in reality, some senior migrants do find it difficult to emigrate again, because of age, health or financial considerations, or simply because they are used to the lifestyle in Zambia and worry that they would not fit in elsewhere, either in China or in another country. Nevertheless, they do encourage their children to move out of Zambia.

No matter what their long-term plans may be, if one looks into Chinese migration to Zambia as a whole across history, this significant flow of population is a fairly new phenomenon and still in its early stages. As stated earlier, majority of the migrants are temporary workers who tend to go back to mainland China after their contracts end, and, as I will show in Chapter 1, even for private entrepreneurs, many face great political and social uncertainties that force them to alter their plans of settlement frequently. Thus, the people I studied were *newly arrived, transient, first-generation migrants* whose ties to their host country were always open to question. As I will demonstrate further in the book, due to their characteristics, there is a strong social and cultural continuity when it comes to daily socializing processes among Chinese migrants in Zambia. This continuity, I argue, is often the result of migrants' choices. As James Ferguson (1999) points out when studying Zambian rural-to-urban migration, keeping close ties with one's home society and performing one's cultural identity are strategies of survival employed by migrants when they face great uncertainty for settlement in their host societies. Similarly, to my Chinese interlocutors at the field site, as transient migrants, performing 'Chineseness' (as the way they imagine it) is their strategies to keep choices open for future migrating plans.

China in Africa from the ground up

The rapid expansion of Chinese activities in Africa, as outlined earlier, has attracted a great deal of interest from scholars and other experts in the last couple of decades. The key question so far has been to interpret the nature of this extensive and growing engagement.

Haunted in part by their own historical experiences, Western commentators have, on the whole, been extremely sceptical about the arrival of China in Africa and repeatedly painted a negative picture of this unfolding event. The Western press has frequently referred to 'irresponsible exploitation of raw materials and labour', 'violation of local laws and human rights' and 'support of authoritarian regimes' (for details, see Sautman and Yan 2013). Furthermore, echoing these popular images, certain scholars have begun to depict China as a new imperialist power and to describe Chinese activities in Africa as a form of neocolonialism (see Ferguson 2011; Limos and Ribeiro 2007).

This view of things has, however, been criticized at least in part as an oversimplification by a number of academics from various disciplines. On the one hand, Sautman and Yan (2006) argue that Western powers actually promote these negative images of China in order to safeguard their own economic and political interests in Africa; they further (Sautman and Yan 2013) use statistics to suggest that China's engagements in Africa are, in fact, no worse than those of their Western counterparts. On the other hand, other scholars endeavour to prove that the arrival of China may provide the African countries with an opportunity to challenge the hegemony of the West and suggest that China is simply balancing the structure of international power (Chan-Fishel and Lawson 2007).

Despite their good intention to reveal a more realistic picture of Sino-African relations by presenting counterarguments at the macroscopic level, in my view, such research hardly touches the ground to describe what Sino-African interactions are actually like. In other words, they have not demonstrated sufficiently in what respects Chinese engagements in Africa are intrinsically different from those of the West.[8] Indeed, they arguably re-affirm the negative images of China while criticizing them. As Large's (2008) survey shows, studies on Sino-African relations have predominately been macroscopic and mostly in the field of international relations. Research from this macroscopic perspective, while treating 'China' and 'Africa' as homogeneous categories for analysis, display several inadequacies.

First, in terms of the experience of the Chinese themselves, they overlook some important variations. As mentioned earlier, these variations are not only about Chinese migrants coming from different regions, social status, ages and genders but also about the distinctive contexts, historical as well as social, of the different African countries to which they have moved. Indeed, more and more researchers have been aware of these variations in recent years and have started to present more complicated pictures of Sino-African engagements from different analytical angles (Park 2008, 2010; Dobler 2009; Lee 2009; Giese and Thiel 2012; Monson and Rupp 2013).

Second, the macroscopic perspective also tends to presuppose the passivity of individuals and groups, and largely omit individual agency from the picture. Against this, several scholars have proposed to study China-in-Africa as 'globalization from below' without overemphasizing state power and have, among other things, argued that 'African actors also exercise agency outside the confines of the state, even as these actions are shaped by and in turn shape processes of state formation and function' (Mohan and Lampert 2013). Africans actively influence not only the Sino-African mutual understanding from below but also the agency of Chinese migrants exercised in day-to-day interactions, which I will elaborate later in this book.

Third, macro-level investigation faces the danger of re-enforcing pre-existing stereotypes in the West of both China and Africa (Giese 2014), and, more importantly, of imposing an analytical bias when it comes to interpreting China and Chinese-African relationships. As Park and Hunyh pointed out, 'most media coverage and scholarly studies continue to focus primarily on the economic and political aspects of Chinese activities in Africa', but ethnographic research of 'people-to-people encounters' has been scarce until recently (2010: 208). Other scholars further contend that 'the lack of reliable field research data has not only resulted in dependency upon a macro-level analysis, but has also contributed to the circulation of rumors and distortions' (Monson and Rupp 2013: 23). Consequently, in order to gain a comprehensive and thorough understanding of this new phenomenon, microscopic research is necessary, and this becomes especially urgent when the Chinese activities and Chinese migrants to Africa are intensifying and diversifying. Monson and Rupp have well cautioned that 'the question, therefore, may not be whether "Chinese" actors are better or worse than other actors, but rather how the study of China-Africa entanglements, in all of their complexity and in their multiple, rapidly changing milieus, can lead us to a deeper understanding of the world which Africans and Chinese currently engage' (2013: 40). They further suggest that studies of China-in-Africa should shift the lens from national level to community and individual level, and should engage more with ethnographical specific research on everyday interaction:

> Research on everyday interactions between Chinese and African actors allow us to see 'China-Africa' not as binary partnership premised on political and economic (im)balances that are often viewed as geopolitical complementarities. Instead, such historically grounded

and ethnographically specific research allows us to analyse engagement between China(s) and Africa(s) as *a flexible and emerging process* that links two areas of the globe – including their people, businesses, governments, ideas, networks – in ways that are both fundamentally rooted in historical processes and unfolding before our eyes. (2013: 28, italics added)

This book takes up this call and aims to make an ethnographic contribution to understanding Sino-African relationships through the lens of *everyday interactions and communication* at the micro-sociological level. In the last few years, more and more scholars have begun pursuing this line of inquiry. On the one hand, sociologists and historians concentrate on the impact of local socio-historical contexts (usually one particular African region) on the interaction of Chinese migrants and their host societies. When comparing labour tensions in Zambia and Tanzania, sociologist Ching Kwan Lee (2009) argues that it is the long history of class struggle and trade unionism in Zambia that successfully halts the inclination towards 'casualization' in Chinese workplaces; whereas in Tanzania, due to its own political history on labour relations, casualization is still widely practised. Again in Zambia and Tanzania, historian Jamie Monson (2013) documents how the story of Tanzania-Zambia railway construction is invoked and re-told according to their shared memories of railway building by retired TAZARA African workers in order to achieve recognition and material securities in the process of economic cooperation and liberalization between China and Africa, in which they feel forgotten. Writing about South Africa and Lesotho, sociologist Park (2013) affirms that national geo-demographic differences and their distinctive historical engagements with Chinese immigrants to these two regions shape local people's perception of the Chinese 'other'. As she argues, 'Chinese are generally seen as a friendly and familiar "other" because of their long historical presence in the country (South Africa)'; whereas the fact that 'there are no other significant "others" in Lesotho makes the Chinese vulnerable' (145–6). Even though presented as ethnography (see Monson and Rupp 2013), research of this kind normally relies on interviews, surveys and questionnaires, which are mainly self-reports.

Undoubtedly, this research focus is valuable to highlight the driving force of socio-historical conditions on Sino-African interaction; however, it dims the individual at the same time. It gives very little evidence of how action takes place in *everyday situations* and how the socio-historical constraints are consciously negotiated and manipulated in real world interactions.

While looking into the interaction of Chinese migrants and local Africans at the grassroots level, another aspect that researchers draw on is the life of Chinese traders and private entrepreneurs, particularly their work relationships with the African employees. Compared with studies produced from socio-historical analysis, most of this research concentrates on interpersonal relations, and focuses on cultural dissonance, relational tensions and sometimes conflicts in daily life caused by mismatched social expectations and incompatible interpretations of each other's symbolic actions. In his detailed studies of Chinese in Ghana, for example, Giese documents how tension arises at work due to the conflictive social meanings of and associated cultural practices of certain social roles, such as boss and middleman, as well as in gift exchange. As he clearly illustrates,

> In the Ghanaian context, however, the appearance and behavior of Chinese traders send out contradictory messages. They do not fit into the employee's role expectations, informed by the authoritative and at the same time caring attitudes of fellow Ghanaians in similar positions. Almost every Chinese employer fails to fulfill the role of the responsible elder *vis-à-vis* his young local employees. (2013: 152)

Instead of merely analysing the tension on Chinese shop-floors as a representation of economic exploitation and resentment of class interests, Giese offers an alternative reading of the labour conflicts from the level of interpersonal relations. He further points out that the labour conflicts 'cannot be thoroughly understood without taking into account pervasive cultural and societal norms, customary laws, political struggles and the longstanding convictions of their own societies' (153). This focus on the impact of cultural norms and practices on interpersonal relationships between Chinese migrants and local Africans has inspired many other researchers. In his studies of Chinese shopkeepers in Uganda, Arsene (2014) gives a rich ethnographic account of how Chinese employers' knowledge and acceptance of local notions and practices of *enjawulo* influence the proximity of Chinese migrant bosses and local Ugandan workers. Similarly, Men (2014) shows how Confucian values, such as *renqing* (human emotion) and *mianzi* (face), as an embedded cultural rationale practised by Chinese firm managers in Tanzania mediate perceptions and relationships at work.

In general, I will pursue Giese's methodology for analysis in this book; that is, mainly applying intense participant observation to investigate how embodied social and cultural norms and symbols influence the formation of interpersonal relations at the grassroots level, especially in everyday situations. As Mohan and Lampert have cautioned, overly culturalist explanations and static readings of intercultural relations may potentially essentialize both groups at play and may lose the dynamic and diverse class relations that political economy could illuminate (2014: 14). Taking this warning seriously, in this book, instead of imposing group ethnicities as enduring and essential categories, I treat 'groupness' as a happening event and as being 'embodied and expressed not only in political projects and nationalist rhetoric but in everyday encounters, practical categories, common-sense knowledge, cultural idioms, cognitive schemas, interactional cues, discursive frames, organizational routines, social networks, and institutional forms' (Brubaker 2004: 2). Therefore, in this book, the focus of my discussion is on how social relations or groups can be formed or prevented and on the significant role that emotional proximity plays in the process of group formation. Furthermore, I have no intention to ignore the socioeconomic condition that my interlocutors are acting in but to see it embedded in situations and functioning through individual motivation and conscious choices. As Max Gluckman argued,

> A social situation is thus the behaviour on some occasion of members of a community as such, analysed and compared with their behaviour on other occasions, so that the analysis reveals the underlying system of relationships between the social structure of the community, the parts

of the social structure, the physical environment, and the physiological life of the community's members ... . The shifting membership of groups in different situations is the functioning of the structure, for an individual's membership of a particular group in a particular situation is determined by the motives and values influencing him in that situation ... . Thus the association of certain Zulu with Europeans and their values and beliefs, creates groups within the Zulu which in certain situations across the separation of interests of Africans and Whites, but emphasize the difference between them. (1958: 9–26)

Inspired by Gluckman's approach of situational analysis, I will observe intra-Chinese and Chinese-Zambian interactions in *everyday situations* and will treat them as a dynamic process of negotiation, mutual transformation and ultimate integration. I take 'everyday' here, to follow Hans Steinmuller's usage, not only in the sense of 'ordinary routine' but also with respect to the continuous reflection on and the acute consciousness of 'living in the present' (2013: 13). Nevertheless, at my field sites, this sense of being in the 'everyday' is provoked not so much by a process of modernization, I would say, but rather by displacement through the process of international migration. It is through this ordinary yet problematic 'everyday' that the entanglement of Chinese migrants and Zambians is revealed. I consider that close attention to the relationships that emerge in everyday situations, in this context, can help us avoid the imposition of a researcher's analytical bias. Another advantage of this approach is that it treats interaction and communication as a dynamic process, emphasizing mutual expectation, negotiation, and cooperation (or conflict). Compared with static structural analysis, this approach gives social agency a greater role to play in the process of relationship formation.

Investigating everyday sociality from a Chinese perspective

If one looks at the literature published in recent years on the topic of Sino-African relations, there is a common thread, which is that most of the analysis is based, in the end, on reports from the African side – in other words, the voices of the 'Chinese' are relatively weak. As Giese clearly points out, 'most studies have been conducted on *ventures operating under enclave-like conditions*, and have concentrated on violations of legal labor rights, focusing almost exclusively on the perspectives of African employees' (2013: 139, emphasis added).

This orientation may have arisen for two reasons. The first is the comparative inaccessibility of the Chinese populations who are based in African countries. This may seem surprising. But as more and more negative reports about China's activities and agenda in Africa spread in international media, Sino-African relations are considered by Chinese officials as a topic with high political sensitivity that needs to be handled carefully. The Chinese embassy in Zambia repeatedly reminds Chinese state-owned companies, organizations and even the Chinese Committee of Commerce in Zambia that they are representing China as a nation to the world; their workers are not mere individuals, as their daily conduct could damage the image of 'China' if they do not act with caution. Since almost all the administrative staff and workers are in Zambia for short-term projects and many migrants still have extensive connections back in China, most will choose to 'shy away' when being interviewed. As shown in later chapters, in interviews, words are carefully selected and usually fall into bureaucratic style (*guanqiang*) and 'prepared package-talk' (*taohua*). It is generally becoming extremely difficult to obtain permission from 'gate-keepers' to do intensive fieldwork in Chinese organizations.

Second, most studies are produced from an African perspective, I would suggest, because of the understandable assumptions we hold about power relations in this setting. In other words, many scholars, and perhaps especially anthropologists, will naturally ally with the vulnerable or dominated party in order to balance the relations and to avoid being criticized as an instrument of 'the powerful'. While investigating Sino-African relations and interactions, naturally from the current structure of international power, Africans are presumed to be the vulnerable party and it is their stories that need to be heard and told. This way of selecting interlocutors, however, can run into the danger of reinforcing bias, not matter how understandable it may be. As described in the next chapter, for example, many Chinese migrants actually feel very 'vulnerable' and 'powerless' while living and working in Zambia. If as anthropologists we really want to understand what is going on in this setting, it is surely important to have this kind of information – regardless of the view we may hold about Chinese engagement in the African continent, and about potential Chinese domination of Africans.

In truth, when I arrived in Zambia, my plan was to study how Zambians perceive the arrival of the Chinese. Soon after, I started to talk with Zambians who had previous contact with Chinese, at the University of Zambia (UNZA), Chinese farms, street shops and Chinese restaurants. As time passed, I began to meet other researchers working in Zambia on related topics. One by one, they told me how difficult it was to get into Chinese field sites. Reflecting upon their stories, I realized my 'unconventional' yet fortunate position (being Chinese myself and doing research in Chinese workplaces in Zambia; and being accepted by the Chinese gate-keepers at a very early stage to work, live with the Chinese groups and participate in their daily activities) was an opportunity to offer an alternative perspective on the same topic. It was then that I decided to take the 'unconventional' further – to tell the story from the perspective of the presumed 'powerful'.

Obviously, I appreciate that this move is likely to raise eyebrows, especially in the discipline of anthropology. It is worth clarifying further that the focus of this book is to describe how the Chinese migrants (who come from highly varied social backgrounds) perceive and evaluate their interactions with their Zambian hosts *and*, more especially, the interactions they have within their own relatively isolated community. The main purpose, in short, is to provide an ethnographic account of everyday life of Chinese migrants in Zambia. The narrative that follows is descriptive rather than prescriptive. As readers will certainly notice, some discourses of Chinese migrants about Africans can be derogatory as with the earlier example of Director Lu's comments about Zambians.

But one aim of the book is precisely to unpack and deconstruct comments of this kind by investigating the process of community formation and socialization among Chinese migrants. For example, I will describe how young Chinese workers are actually stopped from forming meaningful bonds of friendship with the Zambians they meet. This 'Chinese perspective' on interactions and relations between China and Zambia should not be taken to imply that I treat Chinese perspectives as the reference system, nor that Zambians should learn from and incorporate them. On the contrary, I consider that interaction is a long process of mutual transformation. To view the situation 'from the Chinese perspective' means to investigate what issues have attracted attention and been put forward for negotiation and reflection by my Chinese interlocutors during the process of communication and everyday socialization, which, as I have explained earlier, has not received equal scholarly attention. Undoubtedly, the study of 'China-in-Africa' is a grand project that needs much cooperation between various researchers from different disciplines to reveal the story piece by piece, and over a long times pan. What I intend to do in this book is merely to contribute by providing a 'thick description' of Chinese migrants' everyday life in Zambia.

As summarized in the previous section, another major phenomenon repeatedly documented in recent studies on Sino-African interactions on the ground is the easily triggered tension and sometimes even conflicts that mostly take place in Chinese shops (see Giese 2013, 2014; Arsense 2014; Men 2014). These studies have been criticized for overlooking the 'convivial relations' that sometimes exist alongside the tension (Mohan and Lampert 2014). Personally, I regard that conviviality and conflict are two sides of the same coin if one sees the intercultural relationship as a process of formation. The question perhaps is no longer about the nature of Sino-African relations, but how the social relationship is formed, from the perspectives of both parties. If the question is framed this way, naturally, it will lead into a precondition: How are social relationships formed for both groups of players *before* they interact together? Considering the conditions of my fieldwork, the main question I will try to answer in this book is how Chinese migrants in Zambia socialize every day, how social relationships are formed among them and what they hold dear in the process of relation-formation. Only having done this, might one understand how tension arises, and ask how convivial relations between Chinese migrants and their host society become possible. As stated earlier, I consider this order of inquiry as crucial, especially in avoiding essentializing migrant groups. As Ferguson and Gupta claim, 'all associations of place, people, and culture are social and historical creations to be explained, not given natural facts … . Cultural territorializations (like ethnic and national ones) must be understood as complex and contingent results of ongoing historical and political processes' (1997: 4). While studying Sino-African relations on the ground, one should not take any group for granted but should try to understand how the groups are (re)produced and affinity is achieved through everyday situations.

A Chinese theoretical model of Chinese sociality

Obviously, there are many theoretical frameworks that might be applied to my fieldwork material, and there are many literatures that can and should be referred to in relation to it. In later chapters, I will take up some of these other frameworks and literatures, but in this Introduction, I want to focus especially on a Chinese social scientific resource that I have found to be very useful.

Arguably, the modern study of Chinese sociality was originated by the anthropologist Fei Xiaotong. In his groundbreaking book *From the Soil* (1992), drawing a contrast with Western individualism, Fei uses an analogy to vividly illustrate the idea that Chinese sociality 'is like the circles that appear on the surface of a lake when a rock is thrown into it. Everyone stands at the centre of the circles produced by his or her own social influence. Everyone's circles are interrelated' (Fei 1992: 62). He categorizes this Chinese type of sociality as the 'differential mode of association' (*chaxugeju*) and further explains that association formed in this mode is not based on fixed groups. Rather it is extendable in scope and size depending, among other things, on the power and authority of the person in the centre.

Later on, in a memorial lecture dedicated to Fei, Stephan Feuchtwang, having compared the 'differential mode of association' with Maurice Freedman's account of Chinese lineages, reinterprets Fei's model as being based on 'social egoism'. As Feuchtwang explains:

> For Fei it was vital to conceive of sociality, starting from the family, as ego-centred, whereas for Freedman and for the studies of kinship in English anthropology in Freedman's time, ego-centred kinship, or as it was called 'kindred', is distinguished from permanent structure. A kindred by contrast to a lineage, is transient just because it is ego-centred. For Fei ego-centred kinship is both transient and permanent. Freedman's lasting organisation is conceived as a group, whereas Fei's lasting organisation has no fixed boundaries. It certainly has rules, law-like customary rules, but it precedes either organisation or institution as a primary conception of sociality. For Fei, 'structure' in the English anthropological sense of something permanent and fixed, would be too abstract. (2009: 5–6)

Based on his comparison, Feuchtwang further claims that the relations built into Fei's 'differential mode of association' (*chaxugeju*) are in fact 'always more flexible than Fei assumed. They were in any case not just relations of consanguinity but also *relations of affinity and friendship, expectations of trust and reciprocity in hierarchical relations*' (2009, italics added). To put this differently, Feuchtwang suggests that Fei's model can and should be understood in relation to the 'relatedness' turn that came much later in anthropological studies in kinship (Carsten 2000), although Fei's model was proposed half a century before the latter was introduced.

Although many Chinese anthropologists have applied and developed Fei's theory to understand social phenomena in China (among others, see Yan 1996, 2009 on Chinese gift exchange and particularistic ethics; Chang 2010 on Chinese reciprocity; and Tan 2010 on the transformation of sociality in rural China), many Western sinologists have more rigidly interpreted Chinese sociality in association with *guanxi* (social networking) and its instrumentality when studying social relationships in the post-socialist era (Jacob 1979; Walder 1986; Yang 1988; Kipnis 1997). As I will discuss further in Chapter 2, *guanxi* has been regarded as the key notion to analyse Chinese social facts in the 1990s. Mayfair Yang (1994) dedicated a monograph to the 'art of *guanxi*' (*guanxixue*), while Andrew Kipnis (1997) considers *guanxi* as the fundamental fact organizing Chinese sociality and Chinese society. Moreover, in parallel with these scholarly debates there has been a public debate in China for some years now about the nature of social ties and the extent to which people may 'selfishly' pursue them in the context of China's market reform era. I argue in this book that the continuous objectification and abstraction of *guanxi* has basically turned it into a technique for utilitarian aims and social manipulation, which has raised acute awareness among Chinese migrants of the instrumentalist tendency embraced in the *guanxi* practice (to put it more simply: they explicitly think of making connections as a goal-oriented and self-interested process). This explicit social awareness has become a central element in the environment where individuals are socializing with others. Consequently, when interacting, my Chinese interlocutors intentionally separate the instrumental side of *guanxi* with its affective side,[9] and *guanxi* is gradually losing its efficacy for forming and sustaining long-term genuine social relationships.

Against this rigid take on Chinese sociality, in this book, I aim to extensively reinterpret Fei's 'differential mode of association' (*chaxugeju*) in light of Feuchtwang's qualifications and clarification, and particularly in line with recent developments in anthropological research on sociality (for an overview, see Moore and Long 2012). Specifically, I will demonstrate through each chapter and theorize in the Conclusion the meaning of 'emotion' in Chinese contexts, the crucial role that 'emotion' (with extensive connotation) plays in the process of forming and sustaining Chinese social relations, and the dialectical relation between sociality and 'emotion'. To analyse everyday practices of sociality in my field sites based on Chinese sociological theory is the second facet of what I refer to in this book as 'the Chinese perspective'.

(To recap, the first facet is to understand Sino-African interaction from my Chinese interlocutors' point of view.)

Reinterpreting 'differential mode of association': Role ethics, situational affect and emotional proximity

In recent years, a group of scholars have proposed to revitalize the theory of human sociality (Moore and Long 2013). In contrast with previous studies, which see sociality as 'formal patterns of social relations' and 'products of either social relations or social interactions', Moore and Long suggest studying sociality as a process. They want to 'conceptualize human sociality as a dynamic relational matrix within which human subjects are constantly interacting in ways that are *coproductive*, continually plastic and malleable, and through which they come to know the world they live in and find their purpose and *meaning within* it' (2012: 41, italics added). While Toren stresses intersubjectivity, which she refers as 'the capacity for recursive thought that makes human learning a micro-historical process' (2012: 64), arguing the fundamental position of sociality in human actions, more intriguingly, Moore (2012) integrates ideas from neuroscience and the so-called 'affective turn' in recent anthropological studies and sees the capacity of affective objects on impacting human interactions and relations. As she observes:

> Any view of human sociality has to take account of these capacities, not just their peculiar propensity for forward and backward projection in space and time (memory, regret, aspiration, hope) – thus extending any notion of 'environment' or 'culturalecology' well beyond the presentism of many theoretical formulations of affect or assemblages of actants – but also crucially their ability to imaginatively ascribe attributes and qualities, and subsequently to form attachments, to things of the imagination.

In light of this revitalization of studies of human sociality, I see potential dialogue between Fei's theory of Chinese sociality and the model of human sociality being proposed by Moore, Long and others, especially in aspects of perceiving sociality as a dynamic process, as entailing intersubjective engagements, as shared recognition of affects, and more importantly as fundamental human condition organizing human actions. In the following section, I will elaborate how Fei's theory could be reinterpreted in this way.

Going back to Fei's original writings, it seems to me that the 'differential mode of association' entails at least another three characteristics of Chinese sociality, distinct from utilitarian *guanxi* (social networking). First, as referred to in his texts, Fei's model is based on the Confucian notion of *lun*:

> *Lun* stresses differentiation … . *Lun* is order based on classifications … . In fact, the basic character of traditional Chinese social structures rests precisely on such hierarchical differentiations as these (abstract positional types). Therefore, the key to understanding networks of human relationships is to recognize that such distinctions create the very patterns of Chinese social organization. (1992: 65–6)

What this notion connotes is not only the classification but also the distinction brought in by various social roles and, more importantly, the impact of social roles on organizing and transforming individuals. In other words, individuality is not *a priori* but is realized and achieved through taking one's place in a hierarchy and interacting with others. In his insightful book *Confucian Role Ethics*, philosopher Roger Ames (2011) brilliantly illustrates this significance of 'social roles' in Chinese cosmology:

> Individuality is not a given; it is the accomplishment of becoming distinctive and distinguished in one's relations with others … . The principle of individuation in this cosmology (Confucius) is not a ready-made and replicable essential identity that constitutes us as natural kinds – a soul, a heavenly-endowed human nature, a rational mind, a virtuous character, a self-conscious self, an independent agency. Rather, it is a qualitatively achieved distinctiveness in the configuring of one's relations within family and community. In

this Confucian model of the constitutive relations of role-bearing persons, then, we are not 'individuals who associate in community', but rather because we associate effectively in community we become distinguished as relationally constituted individuals; we do not 'have minds and therefore speak with one another', but rather because we speak effectively with one another we become like-minded and thrive as a family and community; we do not 'have hearts and therefore are empathetic with one another', but rather *because we feel effective empathy with one another we become a whole-hearted, self-regulating, community.* Indeed, paronomasia – defining and realizing a world through associated living – is the Confucian way of making meaning in a communicating community. (Ames 2011: 74–6; italic added).

He further elaborates that social role-bearing in China is a process of embodiment and the embodiment of roles directs the perception and social valuation of the individual:

> The quality of one's conduct is not mediated by or reduplicated in some notion of a discrete 'agent' or 'character' that would isolate and locate persons outside of the concrete pattern of their social and natural relations. Instead, the identity of persons lies in the achieved amalgamation, the integrations, and the sustained coherence of their continuing habits of conduct within the embodied roles that constitute them. (ibid: 111)

As I will illustrate in the following chapters, the value of social roles and the embodiment of such values in Chinese sociality has a profound impact on everyday interactions between my Chinese interlocutors and their Zambian hosts. Not only could the unmatched recognition of each other's roles (e.g. boss or colleagues or friends) cause misunderstandings, but different embodiments of mutually agreed roles could also often lead into quarrels in practice (Chapter 3). More importantly, as I will argue in Chapter 4 on moral interactions, this recognition of the value of social roles nurtures the everyday practices of 'role ethics', while taking roles in Zambia encourage the self-realization and individual moral transformation of my Chinese interlocutors, particularly younger ones. Potentially, as I will explain, role ethics may offer an alternative understanding of the debates that have taken place within the anthropology of morality and ethics since the last decade or so (for an overview, see Laidlaw (2014)).

Second, social roles are intrinsically dyadic and role-taking is always fluent and situational. As described earlier, individualization is subject to positional social relationships; that is, the realization of the self often needs the assistance of the other. As a result, this dialectic dyadic relation leads to a reactive self; namely, one's role shifts when the counterpart varies, and therefore, one's role is always changing and further defined according to the *particular situation*.

While studying Chinese epistemology, Ames also illustrates the social significance of 'situation' in China:

> Order is the emergent harmony achieved in the always-contingent relationships that obtain among this unsummed totality … . With no 'One behind the many' as the ultimate source of meaning, there is no single-ordered world, no strict sense of *kosmos* that assumes an external orderer; there is only the ongoing evolving harmony expressed as the quality of life achieved by the insistent, co-creating particulars which together make a world for themselves. In this world in which things are constituted by their conditioning relations, meaning does not arise *ex nihilo* from some independent and external source – from some conception of God or Natural Law or Platonic ideas or Muse, or from some audacious, reclusive genius. Instead, increased significance is always situated and situational. Meaning arises *in situ* through the cultivation of deepening relations that we have expressed elsewhere as *ars contextualis*: 'the art of finding optimal contextualization within one's roles and relations'. (2011: 77)

This cosmology, as I will discuss in Chapter 5, impacts on the process of everyday communications between my Chinese interlocutors and their Zambian counterparts. Not only do they construe meanings of action from everyday situations and encounters, and react to them according to their personal projection, but they also expect their Zambian communicative co-operators to have a similar sensitivity to the situation.

This sensitivity to the situation is not just to acknowledge each other's roles at play and the interpersonal power set. More crucially, it is to be sensitive to the 'emotion' embedded in a situation. Note that 'emotion' in this book has extensive connotations. It entails three dimensions – emotion as a personal psychological state, empathy as an intersubjective interaction (for the definition of 'empathy', see Hollan and Throop 2011) and affect in terms of 'energy/spirit' (*qi/shen*) that is embedded in social objects and situations for resonance.[10] The meaning of 'emotion' and its significance in Chinese sociality will be discussed at length in the Conclusion. Here, what I would like to point out is that 'situation' in Chinese is called *qingkuang*, which combines morphologically *qing* (emotion) and *kuang* (shape/status). Pragmatically, this term could be used to mean that one could only comprehend a fact by taking its 'emotional dimension' into account. In other words, in the Chinese understanding, it is actually impossible to talk about affect without simultaneously talking about 'situation' or *qingkuang*; the two are mutually implied. As Ames (2011: 74) writes, '*Qing* then is both the facticity of and the feeling that pervades any particular situation. Any perceived fact/value distinction between "circumstances" on the one hand, and "feelings that are responsive to circumstances" on the other, collapses.' This embeddedness of 'emotion' (*qing*) especially in objects and situation (I will term this 'situational affect'), despite being 'invisible' and easily omitted, makes 'emotion' pervasive and crucial in Chinese sociality; that is, only when one is sensitive to the embedded 'emotion', can one comprehend the situation. Only when one appreciates the situation, can one fix the roles to play. Only when one understands the role to take in a situation with embedded 'emotion', does one know how to respond, act and communicate in general.

As I have pointed out earlier, I will try to understand the relationships between my Chinese interlocutors and their Zambian hosts from the Chinese perspective, and mostly in the process of everyday situational interactions. The approach I take will be situational analysis (for more, see Gluckman 1958). The significance of situation in my Chinese interlocutors' sociality offers my research validity, and their sensitivity reminds me that I should not ignore the 'emotional dimension' if I would give an adequate account of their everyday sociality.

Third, Chinese groups are fundamentally (re)produced based on social and emotional proximity achieved in shared understanding after long-term interactions. This goes beyond instrumental *guanxi* networks. This is perhaps the most important message that Fei offers in his theorization of Chinese sociality.

> The force that stabilizes social relationships is not emotion (*ganqing*) but *understanding (liaojie)*. Understanding means accepting a common frame of reference. The same stimulus will call forth the same response … . I mentioned that propinquity and familiarity breed a mutual awareness. Such *feelings of mutuality* and a condition of being emotional are completely at odds with each other. Mutuality rests on a harmony that is continuously reproduced. Mutuality is silent, whereas emotionality needs to be voiced. (1992: 88, italics added)

At first glance, this paragraph seems contradictory with the claim that 'emotional proximity' is the foundation of Chinese association. Nevertheless, if read carefully, Fei actually defines emotion in a narrow way and limits its application to 'personal psychological states'. He contrasts emotion with 'feelings of mutuality' as one can see clearly from the highlights in the paragraph earlier to the term he uses in his original Chinese text: *qinmiganjue*, that is, 'a sense of intimacy or proximity'. Moreover, he argues that his sense of intimacy arises in the process of familiarization, and it is the consequence of 'long-term cooperation to coordinate the interactions of individuals' (89). More importantly, this sense of intimacy guides people's everyday actions and reactions. Therefore, it can be argued that Fei regards 'the feeling of mutuality' – 'emotional proximity' as I call it in this book – and the 'understanding' that arises through it as the basis of Chinese sociality and group formation.

To sum up, in this section, I have pursued a long line of argument. My main point is that if one wants to study the social tension or conviviality between Chinese migrants and their African hosts by looking into how Chinese socialize and how Chinese groups are formed, it would be inadequate to focus solely on the practice of instrumental *guanxi*, as many recent anthropologists have tended to do (a point also made strongly in Yan 1996). One should not overlook the significance of social roles played in everyday mutual perception, the impact of the embedded 'emotion' in roles and situations on everyday mutual comprehension, and, most importantly, the essential position of emotional proximity in the formation of Chinese groups or community. As briefly mentioned earlier, reinterpreting and extending Fei's theory on sociality in aspects of role ethics, situational affect and emotional proximity, in this book, My aim is not only to understand the tension or conviviality between Chinese migrants and their Zambian hosts but also to see how Chinese anthropological theory may contribute to current anthropological theories in general.

Introducing my field sites: Stories of two Chinese farms

As noted earlier, I carried out sixteen months of fieldwork in Lusaka, Zambia, from late 2010 to early 2012. My main field sites were two farms – one private, the other educational with Chinese state sponsorship. I accessed my first field site, the state-sponsored educational farm, through a connection with my father, and stayed there for seven months. While I was with them, I was also introduced to the Confucius Institute in Zambia, where I did a one-month voluntary internship and became acquainted with the Zou family. I spent the rest of my time in Zambia at the Zou family farm.

The educational farm is physically attached to the UNZA farm in an eastern suburb of Lusaka. It was founded under the new Sino-African policy proposed at the 2006 Forum on China-Africa Cooperation Summit. The official name is 'China-Aid Zambia Agriculture Technology Demonstration Centre'. This project is fully sponsored by Chinese central government, classified as an aid project, and its main purpose is to provide training for local agricultural students and farmers. In total, there are fourteen similar projects across Africa. The funding (30 million RMB for each project) is distributed by the Chinese Ministry of Commerce to different Chinese provincial governments. Each province assigns its provincial agricultural university to take charge of the implementation. The project in Zambia was allocated to Jilin Province, which has been regarded as an agriculturally advanced province, then to Jilin Agricultural University. The programme is coordinated with the UNZA. According to its promotion leaflets,

> the construction of agricultural technology demonstration centre will provide new types of agricultural theory and practical agriculture service, and promote economic and social development .... According to the practical condition and development needs of Zambia, we will fully use local resources such as water, electricity and roads, build necessary basic facilities. Provide necessary agricultural goods, experiment instruments and farming machines. Dispatch a certain number of agricultural experts and administrative staff. Focus on training and demonstration of production technologies of corn, soybean and so on.

The China-Aid Zambia Agricultural Technology Demonstration Centre (ATDC or Demonstration Centre hereafter) occupies 120 hectares of farmland rented free from the UNZA under a five-year contract. During the contractual term, a new training centre will be built with essential infrastructure, such as student accommodation and irrigation system. The training programme will last three years. After the contractual term, the project will be handed over to the Zambian government unless a new contract is signed. Nevertheless, the new cooperation will become commercial as Chinese state will no longer provide sponsorship.

The administrative staffs of the project are permanent employees of Jilin Agricultural University. Like other Chinese organizations in Zambia, staffs are assigned with two-year contracts. While working in

Zambia, staff receive the allowance for 'hardship and bitterness' that I mentioned earlier in addition to their usual salaries, which are paid directly into their bank accounts in China. Accommodation and food are provided free. There are five Chinese administrative staff members working at ATDC: one manager, one deputy manager, two farming technicians and one translator. The manager and deputy manager are both professors and are in charge of lectures. Guest teachers are invited on a temporary basis both from the UNZA and from Jilin Agricultural University in China.

There were six, later twelve, security guards employed permanently by the UNZA and most living on the UNZA farm, which is about a thirty-minute walk from ATDC. The other Zambian workers are hired from nearby villages by the Chinese management team at ATDC on a temporary task basis, usually without contracts. Their work mainly involves daily maintenance of the farm and some seasonal tasks. Most farming is done by the Chinese technicians using heavy machinery.

When I arrived in Lusaka, it was towards the end of the project construction so all the staff were staying at a hotel owned by a Chinese businesswoman, Mother Liu, who appeared in the vignette at the start of this chapter. She came to Zambia in the 1990s and currently runs a restaurant and hotel in Lusaka. Because of her close relationship with the Chinese embassy, she has very well-known among Chinese migrants, even earning the nickname 'grassroots ambassador'. I stayed at her hotel with the others for one month at the beginning of my fieldwork.

After the month at Mother Liu's, I moved to the construction compound with the rest of the ATDC staff. We shared accommodation with the construction workers for another month until the new administrative building was ventilated, and the construction team built a new compound for their next project. The ATDC was built by a Chinese construction company from Anhui Province. The company used to be provincial owned but was privatized during the Chinese state-enterprise reform. There were about twenty Chinese workers staying in the ATDC construction compound; the Zambian workers came to the site each morning on two giant trucks.

During my fieldwork at ATDC, I took a role as voluntary translator. My main task was to assist in the daily negotiation of work problems between Chinese staff and Zambian workers and in the frequent meetings between Chinese managers and Zambian officials. This role as a translator provided me with great opportunities to observe how negotiation is carried on, in what aspects misunderstanding arises and in what circumstances communication is broken.

My second field site, as noted, was a small-scale private Chinese family farm owned by the Zous. It was through the translator Xiao Liu that I became acquainted with the Zou family with whom I spent the rest of my fieldwork. Theirs is a small farm, only about two hectares, next door to ATDC. The land was purchased around 2009 from another Chinese migrant. The family grows Chinese vegetables mainly to supply Chinese companies, although every Tuesday they will sell at the local farmers' market. Father Zou was the first of the family to come to Zambia. Born in the 1950s in a rural village in Jiangxi province, Father Zou initially was recruited to Zambia by his provincial company, Jiangxi Construction Cooperative, as a cook for an aid project in 1997. After the project finished, Father Zou chose to stay and worked for a construction company owned by his *laoxiang* (people from the same region) until 2004 when he had a quarrel with the manager and decided to start his own business. It was then that his wife, Mother Zou, joined him in Zambia. They found shared accommodation in West Lusaka and started to grow vegetables on a small piece of land that they rented from the *laoxiang* landlady. Around 2006, their son, Xiao (junior) Zou and daughter-in-law arrived in Zambia. In late 2008 or early 2009, with their savings and money borrowed from friends, the Zou family bought the land and established their family farming business.

Before moving to Africa, Mother Zou and her son, Xiao Zou, tried various businesses in Nanchang, the capital city of Jiangxi province. They sold breakfast on a street stall, opened a clothes shop and sold DVDs, but none of them was profitable. 'It is too difficult to do business in China,' as Mother Zou reasons, too many administrative officials give you trouble. They visit your shop every day. One day the tax man comes and another day it's the city inspector. They are nobody, to be honest, but they have badges. They can always pick up some problems to give you a fine. If you do not know any senior official [*shangmianmeiren*], it costs a lot to run a business. Profits hardly balance the expenses. It is only in Zambia where our business thrives. Finally, our hard work has paid off.

Another reason why Mother Zou migrated to Zambia is that she wants to save some money for her son when she can still work. She does not want her son to continue living an 'unbearable' life.

The son, Xiao Zou, is in his early thirties. He dropped out of school when he was sixteen and started to help in the family business. Later, he opened his own DVD shop with financial support from his family, but after only two years, the shop was forced to shut down due to the government policy to clear pirated DVD shops. Since then, he had worked as a bus driver before joining in his parents in Zambia. Mother Zou once told me:

The bus company did not pay much, only 2300 RMB per month (around £230). What was worse was the manager. He was very strict and fussy. Sometimes, he would intentionally cause trouble [*zhaocha*]. Even if Xiao Zou's uniform was not clean enough, he would cut his payment. At the end of the month, there were only 1500 RMB left. It is not all about the money. It is the work atmosphere, unbearable. They bully you when they know you are nobody! Seeing Xiao Zou suffer, I asked him to quit and join us in Zambia.

I stayed with the Zou family for six months. Since their family farm is next door to ATDC, I chose to keep my room in the centre as accommodation but commute to the Zou family farm every day. I joined the Zou family for breakfast and left their farm after dinner. The weekly routine included helping the family with preparations for Tuesday market sales and Wednesday delivery, the Zou family's main business. The delivery was made to the Sino-Hydro company in Kariba, more than 300 miles away from Lusaka. Sino-Hydro is in charge of maintenance of the Kariba Dam, and they have more than a hundred Chinese workers residing in the base. The Zou family reached an agreement to supply food to Sino-Hydro. Therefore, every Wednesday, Xiao Zou would drive his vehicle filled with tonnes of meat and vegetables for almost five hours to Kariba in the morning and return to Lusaka on the same day.

The division of work was rather clear in the Zou family. Father Zou was in charge of farming in the field, while Mother Zou took control of domestic tasks and social networking. Xiao Zou did all the work related to the 'outside', such as contacting clients and delivering goods. The daughter-in-law helped whoever needed assistance. There were three Zambian workers hired by the Zou family, two boys and one girl, all from nearby residential compounds. The two boys helped Father Zou in the field with planting and harvesting, and the girl assisted Mother Zou with domestic work. The Zambian workers were hired without contracts, and no accommodation was provided for them on the farm.

Work was usually finished by Friday. In the weekends, the Zou family would visit friends around Lusaka or invite friends over for banquets. Manager Deng and his family are the Zou family's closest friends in Zambia. Like Father Zou, Manager Deng is also from Jiangxi province and came to Zambia as a cook with a Chinese state-owned company before opening the first Chinese restaurant in Lusaka. I will describe more about the friendship between the Zou family and Manager Deng in later chapters. Through the Zou family's social networks, I met several Chinese entrepreneurs in Lusaka. Most of them were from Jiangxi and Henan provinces. Participating in their daily social activities allowed me to observe how Chinese migrants in Zambia socialize with each other.

Organization of the book

This book is organized according to two threads. One thread follows the narratives of first encounter between my Chinese and Zambian interlocutors, and focuses on the issue of misunderstanding and disjunction in communication. The other thread traces the formation of groups or even a community among my Chinese interlocutors, especially concentrating on the impact of 'emotion' on their everyday interaction.

Chapter 1 starts with the everyday life of the Zou family in Zambia. It tells the stories of their fear when encountering 'ethnic strangers' and their anxiety in general when living with uncertainty in Zambia. It introduces the tone of encounter and maps out the conditions that trigger and intensify the anxiety of the Zou family. Specifically, their anxiety is due to the political turbulence in Zambia during the general election, the rumours circulated among friends, unfamiliarity with their Zambian hosts, and what they perceive as the lack of protection and support from Chinese officials. It often comes with their self-perceived 'vulnerability'. Nevertheless, this anxiety, as I will describe in the chapter, is also a pan-phenomenon – a shared, everyday psychological state of Chinese migrants in Lusaka. Fundamentally, as I will argue, this anxiety is caused by the shared perception of the 'outsider'. It is this anxious attitude of my Chinese interlocutors towards strangers/outsiders that fuels their practice of exclusivism, discourages them from socializing with their Zambian hosts and breaks down communication from the start.

Chapter 2 focuses on the Zou family's everyday business activities and their networks to trace the relationships and everyday socialization among Chinese private entrepreneurs in Lusaka. The aim is to investigate how groups are formed from scratch among my Chinese interlocutors and how their social relationships become sustainable. While looking at Chinese private entrepreneurs in Zambia as a whole, it is evident that there are widespread factions. In business, fierce competition arises between groups with pervasive mistrust and suspicion in the 'community'. Nonetheless, looking into the group from the bottom up, 'interactional affection' (*jiaoqing*) is stressed and provides the basis for forming relations. Moreover, relationships become sustainable because my Chinese interlocutors consciously protect 'interactional affection' by discouraging actions calculated to deny affection. If Chapter 1 shows how 'emotion' could hinder interaction (i.e. with Zambians), Chapter 2 is intended to show the constructive impact of affection on forming and sustaining social relations in general (i.e. among Chinese).

Chapter 3 shifts attention back to the ATDC. It looks into the misunderstandings at work between 'Chinese bosses' and 'Zambian workers' when interactions are forced to happen. In this chapter, first, both cultural practices on the 'boss–worker' relationship will be documented for comparison. Furthermore, I argue that each party (re)acts according to their accustomed practices. Nevertheless, what is puzzling is that, despite both accustomed practices being based on hierarchical, dependent patron–client relationships, misunderstanding and tension still frequently occur. Therefore, after investigating the affective dimension of the work relations, I argue that it is the mismatching direction of attentiveness bundled in their practices and interactions that cause tensions at work. Contrasting with analysis of labour relations at Chinese workplaces in Africa from the angle of class struggle and exploitation, I will demonstrate how the emotion embedded in 'boss–worker' practices could trigger resentments, which has not attracted sufficient interest from researchers.

Chapter 4 is the point at which my discussion of the interactions between Chinese migrants and Zambian hosts moves onto more general aspects. This chapter is dedicated to the issues arising in everyday ethical interactions. Heavily engaging with debates in the anthropology of morality and ethics, this chapter shows, theoretically as well as ethnographically, the impact of social roles on the everyday ethical decision-making of my Chinese interlocutors. Also, introducing a young Chinese migrant's personal experiences as a worker and then a boss, I will illustrate the function of social role, especially its associated 'ethical qualia' subject to social expectation, on personal transformation. Following the general line of analysis though this book – the importance of 'emotion' to social relation/social group formation and reproduction – I will push my arguments a step further by showing the embeddedness of 'emotion' in the process of moral reasoning and ethical practices among my Chinese interlocutors.

Chapter 5 takes both field sites into account and investigates the problems existing directly in the process of everyday conversational communication. In this chapter, I argue that the miscommunication between Chinese migrants and their Zambian counterparts in terms of linguistic exchanges arises as a result of the accustomed communicative style – indirect speech – that my Chinese interlocutors employ. They highly value the linguistic performance of 'speaking appropriately', and evaluate others based on their communicative skills. 'Speaking appropriately' requires the actor to be sensitive to the context, not only the social positions and intentions of each interlocutor in the situation but also the affective tone of the situation. In everyday practices, both parties, Chinese and Zambians, are learning and modifying conversational styles from each other; nevertheless, the current phase is only the beginning of a long-term process of transformation.

In the Conclusion, I consolidate the theoretical steps of arguments I have taken in each chapter. Based on my observations at the field sites and reflecting in association with the anthropological literature on emotion in China, I will re-exam Potter's general hypothesis (1988) and argue that 'emotion' is the first-order factor to form and reproduce social relations and social groups among Chinese. Further engaging with Chinese epistemology in relation to the discourse of Chinese migrants, the meaning of 'emotion' will be extended to three dimensions. Furthermore, I will point out the dialectical relations between emotion and sociality in Chinese contexts; that is, 'differential mode of association' as the Chinese social matrix nurtures the social significance of emotion in three dimensions while, in turn, emotion is the basis for forming and reproducing social relations.

1

The tone of encounters
Strangers, anxiety and everyday exclusivism

At 1.00 am on 23 September 2011, Father and Mother Zou were lying awake after a late-night phone call from Manager Deng, their best friend in Zambia. Around 3.00 am, unable to get back to sleep, the elderly couple got up and took two chairs outside to the spot on their one-hectare vegetable farm where they would often sit after supper to watch the stars and enjoy the quietness that African nights bring. This time it did not have its usual calming effect; with so many worries and fears, the old Zous had to start seriously reconsidering their future in Zambia. That night was one of triumph for Mr Michael Sata and his party, Patriotic Front,[1] in Zambia's general election; however, it threatened to become the night of another 'failure' in the lives of Father and Mother Zou. The future had suddenly become extremely uncertain, and undoubtedly their anxiety soared. They feared that Chinese migrants would be forced to leave Zambia very soon, as Sata had threatened before the general election. If this were the case, they would lose everything – all they had saved through their continuous hard work over the past six years in Zambia would be wasted. What was worse was that they would be despised as 'losers' once they returned to their village in China. They would have 'no face' to meet their family and friends again.

Nobody really knows what exactly the Zous discussed that night, but two days later, Mother Zou informed me that they were going to sell the farm: 'Very soon, I am going to sell this piece of land, then rent a place to live (in Lusaka). Life feels steady (*tashi*) when we've got cash in our pockets. Once we've cashed in, I would not be so worried even if we have to leave Zambia.'

This indeed came as quite a surprise to me as Mother Zou had always said that the farm was the 'root' (*gen*) for the growth of their family business. At that moment, although acknowledging that it would not be easy to sell their farm quickly, I simply could not question the decision, seeing Mother Zou's intense anxiety, but only tried my best to comfort her. Nevertheless, her son, Xiao Zou, reacted straightforwardly: 'I did not want to buy this farm at the beginning but you two never listened [to my opinion]. Now, you see the consequence. Well, it is not my business as I am merely "working" for you two. I never have a say here!' Mother Zou did not reply immediately, perhaps because she had too much on her mind. She simply asked me to help her write a door poster in English so that neighbours could call in if they were interested in purchasing the farm. Meanwhile, she was making phone calls to Chinese friends and asking them to pass on the information. Despite Mother Zou ignoring her son's comment, Xiao Zou's words did remind me of a rather similar discussion we had had a couple of months before when we drove by some modern shopping malls in Lusaka. I asked him why no Chinese entrepreneurs were interested in investing in commercial properties in Lusaka. Xiao Zou rationalized that

> No single one (Chinese entrepreneur) has the money! And even if one had the money, he would not invest in infrastructure. You know, Africa is very politically unstable. It is not good to fix too much money here. You may lose everything overnight. Zambia is comparatively the safest. This is why more and more Chinese are coming here. But, there is no guarantee, especially this year. Elections always bring political turbulence. If Sata were elected, lots of Chinese would go back to China.

Just as Xiao Zou predicted, quite a few Chinese had already left Zambia for China weeks before the election, and most Chinese businesses in Lusaka stopped running during the election week. It was a case of '*duofengtou*' – 'hide for a while until the storm passes' – as they described it.

The Zou couple's reaction in the ethnographic vignette given here represents well the anxiety that private Chinese businessmen hold every day while surviving and striving in Zambia, although the personal sentiment might have been exaggerated to the peak in the Zou's case following the extreme uncertainty brought by the general election. Their decision to sell the farm provides me with a clear answer to the primary question that I wanted to ask when I arrived at my field site: How do Chinese migrants perceive and respond to the 'unfamiliar' environment in Zambia that they live in every day?

While studying Chinese and African interactions and mutual perceptions, many researchers and journalists presuppose – for obvious reasons – an imbalanced power relationship between Chinese people and their African hosts; namely, China, relying on its increasing economic and political influence, is imposing its will on African counterparts (e.g. Limos and Ribeiro 2007) and local Africans are consequentially the vulnerable partners (for an overview, see, Giese and Thiel 2014; Giese 2013). As I noted in the introduction, this assumption might well be true at the level of international relations. However, the everyday ordinary life of my Chinese interlocutors in Lusaka tells another story – one in which the dynamics operate very differently, even if it is true that in many cases the Chinese are structurally superior, for example, because they are employers rather than employees (as in the case of Thomas the 'bystander' driver I mentioned in the Introduction). In short, many of the Chinese migrants I met live constantly in anxiety and feel that they are in a very vulnerable position. They believe they might literally lose everything they have been working on for years and/or that they might be physically attacked and even killed. This anxiety is not only raised by the temporary political instability of their host countries but also experienced, communicated and spread in mundane daily life among the Chinese migrants. It is very much a shared sentiment and has become a mode of everyday existence. In this chapter, I would like to capture and describe this *everyday* experience of anxiety at the grassroots level through my account of weekly life events that I witnessed during my stay with the Zou family.

Understanding this pervasive anxiety is important, in my view, because it provides a kind of baseline for initial contacts between the Chinese migrants (especially private entrepreneurs and farmers) and their African hosts. Anxiety is the contextual 'tone' of their encountering, to borrow Humphrey's term (2012). Moreover, this anxiety as everyday lived experience has significant effects on the migrants' ongoing interactions and communication. While writing about mutual perceptions between Chinese migrants and their Angolan hosts, Cheryl Mei-Ting Schmitz describes her informants' uncertainty and their daily concerns about security, and claims that 'Angolans and Chinese in Luanda, rather than occupying positions of absolute segregation, inhabit a shared social world – one in which suspicions and concerns with security predominate' (2014: 44). She further suggests that this 'shared suspicion' could even provide sufficient common ground for the achievement of mutual understanding and socialization between Chinese migrants and their Angolan hosts. Based on my Zambian research, however, I do have some doubts about this analysis. By contrast, I argue in this chapter that anxiety – at least in the cases I am familiar with – is one of the main causes of the *reluctance to socialize* between Chinese migrants and their Zambian counterparts.

In light of other sources, I would actually contend that this anxious state is not particular to my Chinese interlocutors in Zambia; rather, it is a pervasive phenomenon in Chinese communities in Africa. As stated earlier, Schmitz (2014) documents that Chinese officials repeatedly warned her of the safety issues in Angola, and the Chinese private traders there constantly worry about potential robbery on the street. Despite our research being carried out in two very different countries, I find Schmitz's ethnographic descriptions strikingly similar to what I saw at my field sites. McNamee also points out a similar shared anxious state among Chinese migrants after a comparative project across five African countries (South Africa, Lesotho, Botswana, Zambian and Angola) to study Sino-African interactions. He points out that, due to rising tide of resentment from the host societies and intensified fear of reprisal among the Chinese traders themselves, 'only a tiny minority intends to make the continent [Africa] their home' (2012: 5). Recently, ethnographic research on doubt and anxiety has mainly framed the analyses in relation to the specific contexts of local politics and the economic status that research informants occupy (e.g. see Shah 2013). Nonetheless, this approach alone cannot explain why Chinese migrants feel anxious in *various* African countries and even in China. These cross-regional resemblances beg further explanations beyond the underlying political-economic conditions, which obviously vary widely across these locations (e.g. Zambia is actually safer and more stable than many other countries where Chinese migrants live). It seems to me that this everyday anxious life shared by many Chinese migrants has a deeper structural reason. It is this *pervasiveness* of anxiety among Chinese migrants that I try to understand in this chapter.

Contrasting the Melanesian case she studied ethnographically with the North American notion of fear and danger, Catherine Lutz has claimed that the sociocultural idea of *metagu* (fear/anxiety) among Ifaluk people involves more than bodily change. It is often experienced as 'intensely meaningful' and 'woven in complex ways into cultural meaning systems and social interaction' (1988: 8). Fear, as a common form of emotion, also serves as an ideological index to locate interpersonal relationships. Therefore, instead of being a mere individual psychological state, it should be interpreted in respect of sociocultural action and be understood in relation to personhood. As Lutz further explains, 'cultural views of emotion help construct people's interpretations of their experiences … . Each emotion concept is … an index of a world of cultural premises and of scenarios for social interaction; each is a system of meaning or cluster of ideas which include both verbal accessible, reflective ideas and implicit practical ones' (210). To echo her arguments, on the one hand, I attempt to interpret the meaning of anxiety held by my Chinese interlocutors, especially in relation to the experience and practice of sociality; on the other hand, I want to explore how anxiety, woven into the cultural concept of the 'stranger', is evoked to help Chinese migrants to perceive and understand their experiences in Zambia.

While capturing personal life histories in Northeast China, Charles Stafford (2007) has presented a story of the anxious life of an old Chinese man. Stafford argues that anxiety rises partly due to the man's particular circumstances but also due to the everlasting contradiction between a universal human will to control and transcend the unpredictability of our natural and social environment, and the very uncertainty of that world. As he suggests with regard to social ties in particular, 'What is often most anxious-making about [human] relationships is precisely their contingent nature. The people around us have their own plans and intentions and understandings, which may or may not correspond to ours … . What we lack, it seems, is control' (2007: 72). Stafford further argues (2007: 59) that, in order to cope with and possibly even solve this contradiction, actors may draw on cultural schemas[8] that provide them with familiar (and thus somewhat comfortable) patterns for their future perceptions and decisions – a process he refers to as 'pattern-recognition exercises'.

To follow this line of reasoning, I claim that, at my field sites, my Chinese interlocutors as newly arrived migrants (and also, some cases, as long-term ones) face great uncertainty and unpredictability. As a result, when encountering people from other ethnic groups, the general Chinese cultural schema of 'stranger' (*shengren*) is triggered for the purpose of recognition and control. As I will elaborate later in this chapter, 'stranger' as an acquired conceptual category in the mind of my Chinese interlocutors is rooted in their enculturated 'mode of association' and their perception of society as whole. More importantly, 'stranger', as a cultural ideal, is often associated with a number of negative cultural sentiments, including anxiety, suspicion and caution. The generally negative Chinese view of strangers has been extensively documented and analysed along with a Chinese tendency towards exclusivism (*paiwai*, literally 'exclude outside[r]'). The general history of Chinese exclusivism is beyond the scope of this chapter (for more, see Duara 1991; Dikötter 1992, 1994; Sautman 1994). Here, the locus of my arguments is the dialectical relation between everyday sociality and the pervasiveness of anxiety, with a specific stress on the ways in which the cultural schema of 'stranger' helps Chinese migrants to 'comprehend' their new social conditions in Zambia. Echoing Feuchtwang's wording, I contend that my Chinese interlocutors in Zambia apply this cultural schema to 'fabricate a sense of control where there is no real control' (2002: 279). It is this wide application of the cultural schema of 'stranger' – a notion bundled with negative sentiments – that causes the occurrence of pervasive anxiety when Chinese migrants are approached by unfamiliar counterparts.

It may seem, however, that there is a contradiction here. Surely one could ask the question: If the cultural schema of 'stranger' is applied to control uncertainty, why do Chinese migrants still feel anxious? To clarify, the class of 'stranger' is used conceptually in order to handle the ambiguity of the new social environment; however, it cannot eliminate the uncertainty and negative sentiments built in to the schema of 'stranger' itself. In other words, the invoked Chinese cultural schema of 'stranger' adds a new layer of anxiety while diminishing the one brought by new social settings. This explains why Chinese migrants would feel more anxious when unfamiliar people approach (e.g. when they are stopped by police for a random check) but less so when driving on roads by themselves.

In general, the Chinese migrants I met, across gender, age, education and political-economic status, feel anxious when surrounded by 'strangers' in Zambia. For most of them, anxiety is their everyday mode of existence. This sentiment in turn has discouraged interaction between them and their Zambian hosts, and also created a great hurdle for mutual understanding in the course of their initial contacts and beyond. This is the beginning of the story of an initial encounter and anxiety is the background tone.

Before turning to my ethnographic descriptions, I should note that there are different Chinese terms for anxiety and that these relate to different linguistic registers. One can use the terms *kepa* (fearful) or *kongbu* (terror) to describe the extreme state of anxiety, or terms such as *bu'an/butashi* (unsettled) or *danxin* (literally, 'burden the heart'; worry) to express more everyday unease. These different registers clearly connote different shades of anxiety, and various meanings of anxiety can occur due to different contexts. Undoubtedly, at my field sites, the nuance of their anxious states between different Chinese migrants is sometimes related to the different positions they held in the host society; for example, Chinese officials in Zambia might fear unrest less than the private Chinese entrepreneurs because they could mobilize more resources and secure more protection in order to deal with it. Nevertheless, as I will show throughout the chapter, behind all of the variables – age, gender, social status and education – there lies anxiety as a general psychological phenomenon among my Chinese interlocutors in Zambia.

Finally, I would like to explain that the narrative in this chapter is going to be organized in chronological order, like a diary. This 'unconventional' arrangement of ethnographic data[2] serves three purposes. First, I hope that this form of presentation will reveal the real *everyday nature* of the anxiety being experienced by my interlocutors. Second, by taking the reader for a vivid mental tour of an ordinary week in the life of my Chinese interlocutors, I attempt to trace serial images (almost like a tour in an art gallery) so as to raise the readers' emotional resonance to appreciate this 'anxiety', instead of using logical persuasion. Third, each section will begin with a vignette followed by reflections. This form of presentation is classified as *sanwen* (prose)[3] in the theory of Chinese literature. It is considered the most popular and effective genre to convince the reader because it works on the emotional (*ganxing*) as well as the rational (*lixing*) side of persuasion. Instead of arguing for the significance of this linguistic style of Chinese communication – a point to which I will return at the end of this book – in this opening chapter, I would like first to employ the structure of this writing style for the purposes of demonstration.

* * *

Noon, 23 September 2011

After drawing up the poster for the sale of their farm, Mother Zou asked me to help her put it up on the front gate. The gate is made of iron, about three metres tall and fully painted in red. It has three locks – two of them are for the gate while the other one is for the side door on the left side of the gate. On the side door, there is a peephole that itself has a small sliding door and is used by the family to identify visitors before they can enter. If visitors are Zambians, the communication would carry on through the peep box, usually for several minutes. Meanwhile, when a Chinese face appears through the peephole, the gate is opened within seconds and quickly locked tight again in case Zambians see what is inside. Sometimes, if the Chinese visitor is accompanied by a Zambian chauffeur, Mother Zou would request the Chinese guest to leave the Zambian chauffeur waiting outside the gate. For the family, the gate is a symbol of protection that reassures them of their control over access between the two parts of the world, inside and outside, artificially separated by the gate and wall.

Apart from the locks on the gate, there are another three locks for the house: one for the main door, one for the kitchen, and one for the living room and bedrooms. Most of the time, the doors remain shut if not used by the family, so that the farm workers will not have a chance to steal anything from the house even though – in fact – no worker is allowed to step into the house at any time. Mother Zou is the only one who holds all the keys. Her daughter-in-law used to hold an extra set, but after their house was robbed – because her daughter-in-law

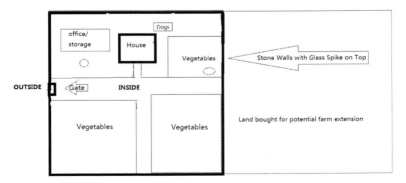

Figure 1 Structure of Zou family farm compound.

left the door open – Mother Zou feels that she cannot rely on anyone but herself. She always complains about the recklessness of the young couple: 'They are too young. They never know the danger. It is always good to be cautious (*xiaoxin*). Being cautious allows one to sail without danger for thousands of years (*xiaoxinshidewannianchuan*).'

This belief certainly cost the Zou family a lot of money when they built the farm. The farm was built on four hectares of land that Father Zou purchased around late 2008 from another Chinese businessman. Before that, for two years the family rented a small piece of land from their Chinese *laoxiang* (people from the same region). The transaction cost the family US$80,000 in total, one-third of which was borrowed from their friends. The family could have purchased land more cheaply from a local Zambian farmer, but they were willing to pay more to keep the business between the Chinese. This is a rather common practice among Chinese private farmers in Zambia, who prefer to buy land from other Chinese. If they cannot find a Chinese seller, their second preference would be to buy from a white farmer. Local custom land (where land belongs to a Zambian chief) attracts very little interest unless it is backed up by the Zambian government. The rationale behind this order of preference is partly due to the degree of familiarity; that is, my Chinese interlocutors like dealing with people they are familiar with because they know the procedure and the rules of the 'interactional game'.

The Zou family farm only occupies one-fourth of the land they purchased; the rest is still left barren. The reason for this, they say, is that they did not have enough money to build a stone wall to surround the full four hectares, so only one hectare was enclosed. Walls are very important for Chinese families in Zambia, since they both exclude strangers from the property and protect the family from the danger outside. They are considered an 'efficient' device of self-protection. The walls Father Zou built for his one-hectare farm cost him about US$30,000, more than one-third of the total budget. Regardless how much he spent, he is certainly very proud of his wall. Every time he has a Chinese friend visiting, Father Zou always comments on how safe his farm compound is and how necessary to have a high wall: 'Walls need to be high so that the local guys won't be able to see what is inside. If they cannot see, they won't want to steal anything.'

Father Zou is not the only one who is proud of his own work on protecting property: his attitude is shared by the general manager of the nearby ATDC. The manager feels that one of the major achievements he has contributed to the project during his service is the highly advanced electronic wall system installed around the farm. Nevertheless, this strong attachment to walls is not shared by local Zambian farmers. When I asked two of my Zambian interviewees why they did not build walls or any defence to protect their farms, they told me that they had nothing to hide and they welcome everyone to visit them. They said that the walls would make people wonder what was going on. The less people could see from the outside, the more they would want to get in – a sharp contrast with what my Chinese interlocutors would have expected.

As well as extra locks and strong walls, dogs are also felt to be good for domestic protection. However, not every kind of dog is good at defence. The 'native dog' (*tugou*) is considered 'incompetent'. Although they are very cheap to purchase on the street, none of my Chinese interlocutors was interested in this breed. On the contrary, a special kind of 'wolf-dog' (*langgou*) is constantly in short supply in Lusaka among the Chinese community. The reason why 'wolf-dogs' are in high demand is based on the explicit view that many Chinese migrants have not only about guard dogs but also against locals; that is, Zambians are 'dangerous', and 'wolf-dogs' bite only Zambians and therefore, the dogs are effective at guarding the house. One has to pre-order the dogs several months in advance by asking for one as a favour (*renqing*). They are never for sale. Xiao Zou was very satisfied after he secured four dogs through his networking skills. He cherished them like babies. High quality *shima* (corn-flour, the staple food for local Zambians) was bought especially for feeding these dogs while farm workers sometimes have to bring their own lunch. After two of his dogs were found dead from snake bites, Xiao Zou was so sad that he always said to himself,

'Two dogs are too few. I would feel steadier (*tashi*) and sleep better if the other two were still here.'

To my Chinese interlocutors, the outside is always perceived as dangerous owing to its characteristics of unfamiliarity and unpredictability. By definition, the outside is less controllable compared with staying inside the farms. This geographic classification, outside versus inside, corresponds with their mental categorization of people in general, stranger versus familiar. The morphemes of the term 'stranger' (*shengren*) in Chinese are a combination of 'raw' (*sheng*) and 'person' (*ren*), whereas 'familiar person' (*shuren*), by contrast, is formed with the morpheme 'cooked' (*shu*). Typically, in the cultural schema of Chinese migrants, 'stranger' is associated with the more general notion of the 'outside' (*wai*). Indeed, in everyday discourse, strangers and outsiders are interchangeable, sometimes referred together as '*wairen*', which can literally be translated as 'outside people', while 'inside people' is normally called *zijinren* (literally, 'self-people'). According to the conceptual correlations, the binary relation among different terms above could be formulated roughly as:

outside : inside :: stranger : familiar :: raw : cooked :: dangerous : safe

This model of categorization related to Chinese sociality was first generalized by Fei Xiaotong (1992 [1948]). As I have discussed in the Introduction, Fei defines this mode of sociality as being based on the 'differential mode of association'. At the end of this chapter, I will come back to analyse the dialectical relations between this 'differential mode of association' and the pervasiveness of anxiety.

For the moment, I would just note that my Chinese interlocutors clearly put this conceptual framework into practice, and the categorization of 'inside and outside' corresponding to 'safe and risky' indeed causes quite a bit of trouble when the Zou family goes out and interacts with the local Zambians. When outside of the farm, Mother Zou always keeps her head down and speeds up her steps when local people try to say hello, sometimes even in Mandarin. For her, it is more like a potential 'threat' than a greeting. She always thinks that those people must want something from her and a 'hello' is just the beginning of a dangerous incident, so it is better to avoid them than to confront them. Avoiding (*duo*) is used as a 'good strategy' by the Zou family to keep themselves out of trouble with locals who are often perceived as 'untrustworthy cheats'.

Not only do the Zou family avoid socializing with locals but they also try to avoid doing business with them. Since they came to Lusaka five years before, the Zou family hardly made any friends among local Zambians. As I mentioned earlier, when it comes to business, they prefer to deal with the Chinese. As they repeatedly told me, 'Chinese are easy to negotiate with (*haoshuohua*). If there is any problem, it is easier to solve it between the Chinese' – an affinity that I interpret as due to familiarity and the controllability of the social interactional rules. Even though worry about being cheated may be quite different from being anxious about troubles knocking at the door, I regard both cases as the consequence of a negative perception of strangers and the unknown. This affinity to familiars and anxiety around strangers is sometimes manifested as explicit racial stereotyping at my fieldsites.

To cite a brief example, I once accompanied Xiao Zou to look for a borehole drill in Lusaka town. Before visiting the supplier, sometimes we had to make a phone call. Because Xiao Zou does not speak good English, I was the one who normally called the supplier. Nevertheless, after the call, Xiao Zou would always ask me to guess the ethnicity of the speaker from the accent. If I said it was a black Zambian, he would simply cross the name out of the list of suppliers – '*Laohei* [the term used by Chinese to refer black Zambians, literally, "the old black"] are not reliable. They cheat whenever they can and cannot do the job properly', Xiao Zou explained.

Nevertheless, sometimes contact with locals would become necessary. In such instances, the Zou family would always take extra caution. They would always take their own set of scales with them when buying vegetables or meat from local markets because they believe that Zambians cheat on the scales. When Father Zou shopped in the markets, Mother Zou would always stay near the car and keep an eye on it just in case it was stolen. Xiao Zou's wife showed more extreme anxiety. She always stayed in the car and tightly locked the doors from inside, even though the hot sun could turn the car into a sauna. Moreover, Mother Zou would ask me to take a tape-recorder when I accompanied Xiao Zou to the immigration office to negotiate the application for permanent residence in Zambia, in case the officers did not keep their promise as had happened once before.

This fear of being cheated might be the result of a series of bad experiences the Zou family had when transacting business with Zambians. Mother Zou repeatedly told me a story of how Zambians had wronged her. At the beginning, when they set up their farm, a local electricity equipment company contacted them offering to connect the electricity for the farm. The Zou family accepted the offer due to the low price quoted. There was no contract. After US$3,000 had been paid, the supplier disappeared without finishing the service. Since then, Mother Zou could no longer trust local suppliers. As she always said, 'Adversity makes a man wise (*chiyiqianzhangyizhi*). It is better to be cautious (*jinshendian*) when one is away from home (*chumenzaiwai*). Better to be safe than sorry.'

Afternoon, 24 September 2011

It was around 2.00 pm when Mother Zou received another phone call from Manager Deng. After a short chat with him, Mother Zou informed her family,

> Deng *Zong* [Manager Deng] just called. Obviously, it is total chaos in town now. There are lots of people on the street, shouting very loudly. Deng Zong has shut the restaurant for the next few days. He said there seemed to be a riot going on in town. It is not safe to go outside at the moment. He suggested that we should remain at home for the next couple of days and wait for his further information.

Then, she told Xiao Zou to let Xiao Xiao (the granddaughter of Mother Zou) have an extra month for summer break and to only send her back to school when outside 'the wind is flat and the swell is peaceful' (*fengpinglangjing*). After she had said all this, Mother Zou turned around and tried to comfort me, saying that 'Xiao Wu, do not go out this week! Just stay at my farm. It is safe here. We got plenty of food; enough to feed you!' Then, Mother Zou picked up her mobile again to notify another friend of hers.

Indeed, among the Chinese migrants, anxiety is like a virus. It is contagious and gets amplified as it passed from mouth to mouth. More importantly, it is transmitted through their enculturated 'mode of association', that is, the existing trust and emotional proximity between familiars provides a reliable foundation for hearsay to spread fast and easily without personal investigation or confrontation. In this section, I describe how rumour, as a linguistic phenomenon, intensifies and sometimes may even create an everyday atmosphere of anxiety for my interlocutors to live in. Through rumour, a negative image of 'the outside' as a dangerous and fearful space is reinforced,[4] whereas group solidarity at the same time is enhanced by this shared sentimental discourse. Just like what happened between Manager Deng, Mother Zou and their friends, anxiety is passed on because people trust each other, and the outside is dangerous only because friends warn them that it is.

Later that afternoon, partly out of concern and partly out of curiosity, I texted my friend living in town to ask how he was getting on and what on earth was happening. 'It is all fine. The PF (Patriotic Front) supporters are just having a street party to celebrate Sata's victory', he replied. Ironically, this social heat (*renao*) displayed by the locals was perceived by the Zou family and their friends as threat and danger.

Similar scenarios occurred regularly during my fieldwork. In the third month after my arrival, a Chinese lady, who used to run a mushroom farming business near Lusaka, was murdered by local Zambians. She was killed after a profitable day at the 'Tuesday Market' just before the Chinese New Year when her husband was away in China. The news was passed on very quickly among the Chinese migrants in Zambia. Every time the story was told, the narrator would add his or her own juicy bits into the storyline as if she or he had witnessed it; and the story was always told with an almost whispering tone as if sharing a secret. Afterwards, the audience would supplement the story with their own 'fearful experiences' with the locals, then discuss them vividly together with the narrator. I never witnessed an audience suspecting the authenticity of the story, but somehow all enjoyed co-telling it.

Among the five different versions I heard during my fieldwork, sometimes the mushroom lady was shot; sometimes, she was beaten to death; sometimes, she was killed because she showed off her money; and sometimes, she was murdered because she had offended others. The story got told again and again for months. After a year, new arrivals from China were still being warned of the dangers of Zambian life with this story as an example. Although no one really knew exactly how and why she was killed, the sentimental essence of the story was indeed passed on – local people can be violent so it is best to be cautious. This view may further provide the baseline for many Chinese migrants to form biased views towards Zambians.

To this day, this murder is still the only such case I heard of. As my Zambian interlocutors always said, Zambia is a safe country as Zambians are Christians and not violent like the people of neighbouring countries (the Congo is normally referred to by way of contrast). Nevertheless, one case is enough to make the Chinese migrants anxious. To me, this anxiety may sometimes have come from their illusory exaggeration, which is registered linguistically as rumour. It is the mutual trust of inner-group members that nurtures the exaggeration; however, this 'illusion' in turn also provides shared experience for them to communicate. My Chinese interlocutors seem to be living together in a 'loop of anxiety' – a loop that they partially create and are constrained by.

Evening, 25 September 2011

The general election passed three days ago, yet the Zou family still have not once stepped out of their walled-up farm. The evening meal was served at 6.00 pm as usual, but Xiao Xiao was not happy as her grandmother did not cook her favourite dish. The process of feeding

Xiao Xiao became more difficult that evening. She ran around the farmyard and refused to eat anything while her mother chased her with a bowl of rice. After a while, her mother became impatient and shouted, 'If you do not finish your dinner now, your father is going to find you a black mother tomorrow. Your new black mother will be very tough and sort you out. I will see what you can do. By then, nobody will care even if you starve to death!' Hearing this, Xiao Xiao stopped running and immediately came back to finish her dish. This trick employed by Xiao Zou's wife is effective every time.

I have described earlier how anxiety is transmitted through rumour among Chinese migrants. This anxiety not only diffuses horizontally among peers but also passes on vertically through generations. In other words, children from my Chinese interlocutors' families in Zambia are taught to be cautious outside. Xiao Xiao, the daughter of Xiao Zou, was born in a Chinese medical clinic in Lusaka a few months after the Zou family migrated to Zambia in 2006. Although she is legally eligible to register as a Zambian national by birth, Xiao Zou and his wife still prefer their daughter to be a Chinese citizen. Specifically for this, they flew back to China one year ago to complete Xiao Xiao's national registration. Like most of the Chinese children born in Zambia, Xiao Xiao attends the Zambia International Chinese School that was founded by six senior successful Chinese businessmen in Lusaka; however, unlike the others, Xiao Zou and his wife are determined to send her back to China for formal schooling rather than allowing her to be educated at the 'white man's school' (*bairenxuexiao*). Sending their daughter to local schools has never even crossed their minds. Since several months ago, Xiao Zou has been seriously considering applying for his daughter to go to a 'private school' in his home city in China. Although this arrangement may be partly due to financial concerns (as I noted in the Introduction, the 'white' school costs more than US$3000 a term), he is convinced that his daughter will get a much better 'fundamental education' (*jichujiaoyu*) back in China. As he told me, 'Chinese schooling is the best. Plus, Xiao Xiao is a Chinese so she needs to be able to speak proper Chinese. She still can come back to

Zambia when she has grown up.' Ironically, even though she was born in Zambia, at the age of five, Xiao Xiao can speak no more than ten English words and no local language at all.

Xiao Xiao is a 'boyish' girl as the family friends would describe her. She likes moving around a lot and cannot sit still for more than one minute. It is at those times when she is naughty and does not obey the adults that 'scary stories' about local Zambians will come into play. When she does not listen to her father but insists on winding up and down the car windows, Xiao Xiao will be warned that black policemen will sort her out and take her to the orphanage. When she does not listen to her mother but refuses to eat supper, she will be warned that her father will marry a black mother soon to discipline her. When she does not listen to her granny but runs around in the city market, she will be warned that black men will take her away and sell her to another black man to do tough work. Gradually, when some local Zambian women in the market try to fondle her because of her cuteness, Xiao Xiao would immediately run away and hide behind her family. After similar warnings day by day, the world indeed starts to sound very 'dangerous' for this little girl.

After the dinner with the Zou family, around 9.00 pm, I was going to walk back to my apartment in the Demonstration Centre but Xiao Zou insisted that he should drive me back although it is only about five minutes' walk, because it was dark outside and the Zou family worried that I might get myself into trouble on the way back. As I usually do every day, after returning to the Demonstration Centre, I decide to chat with the translator, Xiao Fan, to find out what has happened during the day in the Centre.

'It has been a very quiet day today. You know, all the workers are still off work and there are no jobs to be done. Oh, I have not had such a relaxing day for ages!' Xiao Fan answered pleasantly. After a few seconds, he continued but with a cheeky smile on his face, 'Hmmm, I went out to the town centre today!'

'What?! Really? How was it in town? Is it dangerous?' I asked full of surprise. 'No, not at all, on the contrary actually! There were only a few cars running on the street. No traffic jam at all. All the blacks (*laohei*) were singing, drinking and dancing. They look happy.' He paused a few second while checking the news online, then continued.

'I did not see any Chinese on the street today. I did see several white men driving in town though. They seem not afraid at all. Why don't they feel afraid? Why are only the Chinese so afraid of death (*pasi*)?'

As usual, Xiao Fan threw me another big question directly after making his observation. I could not answer him but his 'careless' attitude did attract my interest.

Among my Chinese interlocutors, it seems to me that the younger generation, especially the ones born in and after the 1980s, are less anxious in general than the older generation. In China, this young generation has caused so many new phenomena that the Chinese popular media has created a new term to reference them: *80 hou*, meaning 'post-1980s generation'. They are the 'one child generation' who are raised in the market reform era of China. Xiao Fan is one of the *80 hou*, and he is the friend I texted for confirmation when Manager Deng called Mother Zou. He was in town following the locals and practising to be a 'war journalist' as he joked in his text back to me. The older generation regard the actions of the *80 hou* as recklessness (*bujihouguo*) and the reason is because the younger ones have not entered society deeply enough (*rushishangqian*) so they do not understand how risky it can be. Sometimes, they even criticize the younger ones as being too stubborn and too selfish because they do not take advice easily and do not consider the 'bad consequences' of their own decisions for the people who they closely relate to. 'Do you know how sad and heartbroken your family would be if any harm happened to you?' is a statement usually employed by the older generation to persuade the young not to take dangerous risks. Note here that, interestingly, emotion rather than logical arguments is invoked in reasoning about forbidden acts ('it would cause sadness').

This general perception that society outside is a dangerous and unpredictable space compared with family as insiders is another aspect of anxiety as an everyday mode of existence for my Chinese interlocutors. As Steinmuller and Wu (2011) have pointed out when analysing the infamous cases where Chinese children have been killed at their schools;

> In popular discourse ... 'society' is often a jungle – a space of coldness and indifference. Parents frequently scold their children in order to prepare them to 'enter society' (*zou shang shehui*). 'Enter society' here means to leave the warm space of the family, where people take care of each other, where you can live freely and don't have to worry, for a social space constituted of strangers, where there is much danger and risk. Young people are taught to learn a new set of skills and techniques in order to survive in this wilderness. (2011: 12–13)

Beyond this, the senior Chinese migrants I met also stress the contagious effect of society on personal moral decline. Interestingly, they describe society as 'a giant dyeing pot' (*darangong*) and in order to survive or to be successful, one *has* to be tainted. This negative image of the outside society is co-produced in contrast to the idealized image of the inner self. The self, before stepping into society, is considered pure and innocent. Here, the binary relation given earlier appears again between society and self; namely, self (inside): society (outside):: safe: risky.

Although the different intensities of anxiety between senior and junior Chinese migrants could be due to their variable experiences of interaction with the 'outside world', it is noticeable that there is a distinction of attitude towards strangers – the young Chinese interlocutors often seem relatively relaxed about being in Zambia and about interacting with Zambians. Several weeks after the election, when I met my other two *80 hou* friends for coffee, they mentioned that they were eager to go out on the street and find out what exactly was happening, but their boss would not give them permission. As I will illustrate in later chapters, when encountering others in Zambia, young Chinese are more open-minded, less suspicious and more willing to make friends. Nonetheless, as I will show, this willingness is often constrained by their seniors. Young people are strongly and repeatedly advised not to mingle with black Zambians as they are dangerous and unpredictable. Consequentially, the initial attempt to befriend Zambians is halted and, in the cases I am familiar with, not renewed. Reflectively, the youth are learning from, forced or not, and learning to become similar to their elders. They are learning how to act like 'insiders' by reference to the Zambians as outsiders. Moreover, they are learning to be cautious before stepping into the world outside to face strangers.

26 September 2011

Since the Zou family decided to remain a couple more days in their farm compound, I returned to the Demonstration Centre after lunch. While I walked in, Manager Bao, Translator Xiao Fan and other technicians were joking about what they could do if there was a robbery.

'We could put a bomb in the safe and move it to the middle of the compound and tell the black to take it', Xiao Fan suggested with laughter.

'Lao Xu, make sure you give up the money when the blacks come. If you were killed just for being unwilling to give them little pennies [*xiaoqian*], you would no longer be able to meet your little lover [*xiaoqingren*] in China. It is not worth it [*buhuasuan*]!' Manager Bao teased Technician Xu, as the others all laughed loudly.

Jokes and laughter could temporarily ease the intensity of anxiety at the Demonstration Centre, and the Chinese staff would obtain reassurance from each other through shared intimate knowledge. Nevertheless, from another side, these jokes also reveal some of the racial biases and inner anxieties that they hold.

Very similarly to the Zou family farm, exclusivism is practised at ATDC. Zambian workers are not allowed to step into the main administrative/accommodation building, and the doors are firmly locked every time the staff leave their rooms. As mentioned earlier, when building ATDC, Manager Bao specifically requested two facilities from the construction team – a strong electronic fence surrounding the compound as a whole and a CCTV system installed for the administrative/accommodation building. Both were purchased from

South African companies as he wanted to make sure that they had the most up-to-date technology. Then Manager Bao doubled the number of security guards and bought them military uniforms as he believed that these would scare off the local Zambians. Moreover, through a personal connection, he secured a governmental car plate from the Zambian Ministry of Education so no one could dare to cause him trouble when he was out on the street. When I was in the field, he was still trying his best to obtain guns for the security guards.

By comparison with the Zou family, most of the administrative staff in the Demonstration Centre grew up in cities and are well-educated. Manager Bao himself holds a PhD in agricultural science and was appointed to a professorship for several years. Even though there is a distinction of socioeconomic background, interesting enough, both the Zou family and the administrative staff of ATDC lead an anxious life in Zambia. Notwithstanding, presumably, the anxiety has different degrees of intensity as Manager Bao can mobilize more resources for his protection.

1 October 2011

One week after the Zambian presidential election, all seemed to have passed peacefully; however, no one knew what the future would hold for the Chinese community in Zambia. On the 1 October, as in previous years, the Chinese embassy hosted a celebration for Chinese National Day. In the election year, in particular, people were more willing to attend in order to find out more information from the officials about the updated relationship between the Chinese government and the new Zambian government. In the morning, as usual, Mother Zou received all the details about the evening party from Manager Deng. Immediately after she got the news, Mother Zou invited me to go with the family. I was reluctant as I had not received any official invitation, but neither had the family. Mother Zou said it would not matter as the party is to celebrate Chinese National Day and we are all within the community. However, she suggested several times that I should dress as smartly as

I could in case of losing face. This was the first time I saw Mother Zou put on make-up. The Zou family is always worried that they would be looked down on regarding their social background back in China and the lower hierarchical level they occupy within the Chinese community in Zambia.

Around 6.00 pm, we all dressed formally and set out for the ceremony. When we got to the venue, Mother Zou stopped at the main entrance as she was worried that the usher would refuse her entry since she had not secured an official invitation. She called Manager Deng for help and reassurance. Manager Deng told her just to walk straight in as she normally did. Manager Deng said he did not have any invitation from the embassy either. An embarrassing moment then happened, however: Mother Zou tried to go past the usher into the party hall and she was intercepted and asked to leave. Suddenly, Mother Zou's face burned. She quickly stepped back to the main entrance while murmuring to her son, 'Get me out of here quickly. I cannot bear losing face and being looked down and laughed upon publicly [*diuren xianyan*] here.' Just on the way out, we bumped into Manager Deng and his family. Mother Zou told Manager Deng what had happened and suggested that he should not try to go in without any invitation, but Manager Deng persisted. After Manager Deng made it clear that he is the owner of China Chinese Restaurant – the oldest Chinese restaurant in Zambia – the usher did not even ask for his invitation but welcomed him in with a big smile. The Zou family and I were accepted in as Manager Deng's guests. Once inside, Mother Zou turned around and whispered to me, 'You see, these are the Chinese officials. They are very snobbish [*shili*]: they only like socialising with the rich and powerful. They never cast a glance at us, the little ordinary people [*xiaolaobaixing*].'

This was not the first time I heard such a complaint against the Chinese embassy and Chinese officials in Zambia. For a long time, people were fed up with their bureaucratic style and disappointed with their ignorance of the Chinese grassroots in Zambia, especially when they are in need of help. Perhaps the lack of protection or reassurance from the government is another reason why Chinese migrants in Zambia live anxiously. My interlocutors realize that if they had no personal connection with the top level in any way, they could not expect to rely on anyone officially standing by them. They see that officials are assigned to Zambia just for a short period and that most of the governors only flatter those at the top in order to be promoted quickly; therefore, no one care about the grassroots. To go back to the story about the Chinese mushroom lady being murdered in Lusaka, quite a few of my Chinese acquaintances gave similar evaluations of the actions that the Chinese embassy took regarding to the case – 'Chinese lives are cheap [*mingjian*] after all, especially the ones without "background" [*beijing*]. The government just never cares if we are alive or dead! You see, if this happened to an American, the American Embassy would have already stood out and ask for some action [*jiaodai*].'

Even in business, it seems that the voluntarily organized Chinese Commerce Committee does not fulfil its responsibility either. After a few years of enthusiasm, more and more 'insignificant' Chinese businessmen are quitting the community in disappointment and frustration. Father Zou often complains

> We normally only see them [the Chinese Commerce Committee staff] once a year when they come to collect the membership fee. It is the only moment when they say sweet words [*haotingde*] to us. After they get the money, they just disappear until the next collection. They never ask how our business is running or if we have any difficulty.

I claimed earlier that anxiety as a shared everyday experience enhanced group solidarity in Zambia. Here, it is important to point out that group solidarity is different from community solidarity. On the contrary, there are deep factions and competition within the Chinese community, which I will elaborate more in the next chapter. It is this factionalism, I further argue, that also helps the growth of personal anxiety; that is, the factions diminish mutual reliance and trust between groups within the same community and, as a result, self-reliance is firmly believed, emphasized and practised, which in turn intensifies personal anxiety.

As Father Zou pessimistically put it, 'Nowadays, no one really cares about anyone. One can only rely on oneself. You know that old analogy: husband and wife at first are birds on the same tree; when calamity comes, each flies in a different direction [*fuqibenshitonglinniao, dananlindougezifei*]. If even conjugal ties cannot be reliable, whom else would one rely on?'

Not only does the lack of protection from the Chinese embassy intensify the anxiety of Chinese 'grassroots' emigrants but the embassy also generates another form of anxiety for the officials working in Zambia. Again and again, such officials are reminded that they are representing China and Chinese to the world so they need to take extra caution regarding the image they portray. Officials should endeavour not to damage the Chinese national image because of bad personal behaviour. Since they are evaluated by the top level for promotion, officials are very self-policing and careful about the activities they engage in and even the wording they use in public as no one wants to get into trouble that could ruin future careers. Consequently, unfamiliar people, especially foreigners (researchers or journalists), are mistrusted because they are seen to potentially expose official misconduct. Fear of being reported or disclosed for some misdeed limits officials' socializing with others.

Morning, 2 October 2011

It was the second day of the celebration of Chinese National Day, a Sunday – also the day when the Zambian Chinese Christian Fellowship provides a routine church service. As normal, at 10.30 am, around twenty Chinese got together to listen to a sermon given by a white priest, who the Chinese Fellowship invited as a tutor. The topic of that day – how to face danger – had been specially proposed by Chinese members of the congregation in relation to the political turbulence in Zambia. At the end of the service, a senior member led a prayer. She thanked the Lord for bringing a peaceful presidential election so that the Chinese did not have to suffer political turbulence. Then she requested more protection from God to guide the Chinese to a safe and prosperous life in Zambia.

It was at that moment I suddenly realized that most of the prayers offered were for a safer life and avoidance of tragedy. It was also at that moment when I finally understood what the dialectical relation of that pair of Chinese concepts, *fu* (good fortune) and *huo* (calamity), really means. The meaning of *saiwengshima,* a well-known Chinese allegory,[5] which I learned in my primary school but did not comprehend, was finally revealed itself as well.

Perhaps, in the life of my Chinese interlocutors, calamity (*huo*) is always the norm but good fortune (*fu*) is the true contingency. They assume the badness of things so they can take cautious steps to prevent it happening and prepare for the risk beforehand. They probably have always prepared to live with unpredictable calamity because they believe that the society outside is full of danger all the time and the world is ultimately beyond one's control. That they mistrust strangers by default, avoid socializing with unfamiliar people and take extra caution when dealing with outsiders may be just one facet of how they perceive the world, as they believe that good fortune in life is the luck that one could only 'beg' for (*qifu*) and that could only arrive when one is living with caution and preparation.

* * *

How my Chinese interlocutors, as newly arrived immigrants, perceive their new social settings and how they lead their everyday life in Zambia are the initial questions I want to ask. The daily mundane life and activities of the farming Zou family offered me an answer – they live anxiously. They are anxious that they will be cheated when doing business with the local Zambians; they are anxious that they might be mugged or stabbed when walking on the street; they are anxious that their house would be broken in to at any time and they are anxious that all the things they have saved up after days and nights of hard work would disappear overnight. Anxiety is their everyday mode of existence in Zambia and the tone of their encounters with Zambians.

Along with several episodes from their daily lives, I documented the conditions that may have contributed to and intensified their anxiety. The political turbulence in Zambia, insufficient protection (as they saw it) from the Chinese government and widely spread 'scary' rumours of local people could all count as parts of the contextual reasons for their everyday anxious life.

Nevertheless, not only does the private farming family constantly feel anxious but so also do the Chinese officials working at state-owned projects. The anxiety is pervasive. It is shared by most Chinese migrants – men and women, old and young, educated or less educated. Compared with other communities, it seems that anxiety is a general psychological phenomenon existing in most Chinese communities across Africa and even in China. This pervasiveness begs a deeper structural interpretation.

Earlier, I have referred to a set of binary oppositions – outside : inside :: strangers : familiar :: danger : safe – that that are linked to the Chinese cultural schema of 'stranger'. The categorical equivalence between strangers and danger further triggers anxious reactions when my Chinese interlocutors encounter unfamiliar people in everyday life, I would argue. As previously mentioned, these categorical binaries are related to notions of selfhood and sociality in China and, in association with trust, could be spotted in Fei's original analysis that I elaborated in the previous chapter.

To recap, as Feuchtwang (2009) well puts it, this model of Chinese sociality is not limited only to consanguinity (blood relationships), but encompasses affinity, friendship and expectation of trust that rely greatly on familiarity and affective bonds. First, in Fei's analogy,[6] the circles of association centred around self are not just about different fixed social relations but also about different degrees of *emotional proximity* – the further the circle is from ego, the less there is familiarity, intimacy and trust. At my field sites, according to my Chinese interlocutors' perception, their Zambian counterparts are classified as 'foreigners' (*waiguoren*) who do not share any common ground with the self but fall in the furthest circle in relation to the self. Consequently, they are

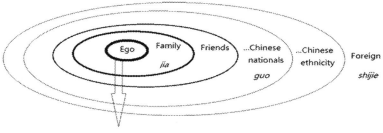

Figure 2 Illustration of Fei's model of 'differentiate mode of association'.

regarded as the least trustworthy, need to be handled with the most caution.

Second, the social categories (such as *wai* and *nei*) are relative, and social expectations are responsive and often come with *positioning*. This relativity from ego's point of view generates responsive sentiment – when the outside circle pushes inside, anxiety rises. Therefore, people approaching from outside are considered to act always *with purpose* and could bring potential threat, but not when the ego actively approaches the outside. This positioning impacts on the interaction between Chinese migrants and their Zambian hosts. The willingness to interact from the Zambian side is often construed by my Chinese interlocutors as approaching unnecessarily; therefore, the actions are perceived as 'dangerous'. Nevertheless, the anxious state would drop when the Chinese migrants actively seek interactions with the Zambians, for instance, helping with immigration issues, as well as when a shared 'outsider' arrives.

Based on the cultural schema of 'strangers' and social category of *nei* and *wai*, a special type of exclusivism is practised in everyday life by Chinese migrants in Zambia. As I have described in this chapter, the exclusivism is demonstrated by physically forbidding Zambian workers from entering Chinese living spaces and by socially avoiding contact with the locals. Discursively, the exclusivism can very often be manifested in racially biased statements against the Zambians. They are linguistic markers of the differences between 'us' and 'them'. As Lan (2016) suggests in her study of racism against African communities in Guangzhou, China, this racial discrimination is produced under specific socio-historical contexts, among which the state and cyber-communication currently take significant roles. She further points out that racism in China is a multilayered process, and skin colour is not the only parameter by any means. In fact, 'personal virtues and socially appropriate behaviours can sometimes outweigh skin color in the construction of group identity' (2016: 308). To the Chinese migrants in Zambia, anxiety constitutes their racially biased opinions of the locals. The unfamiliarity of the new social environment, the self-perceived vulnerability (for more examples, see Sheridon 2019), periodic political campaigns against Chinese migrants and the acquired 'understanding' that 'Africans are dangerous' either from media or from peer influence are all fuelling their anxieties.

As one would expect, exclusivism is also widely practised by Zambians against foreigners, and the case against Chinese migrants sometimes can have a very explicit political underpinning as the Zambian general election, in which migrants were directly criticized, shows. Nevertheless, as I elaborate elsewhere, these two kinds of practices relate to different rationales although they may appear similar on some levels. In a nutshell, for the Zambians, exclusivism is practised along with the idea of economic competition and employment opportunities. In other words, locals would criticize and act against any immigrant who threatened their chances of prosperity (see Van Bracht 2012; Giese and Marfaing 2019). By contrast, exclusivism practised by the Chinese migrants, at least in this context, draws on the cultural schema of 'strangers' and its associated emotion of anxiety.

This constant anxiety does have a significant impact on everyday interaction and communication between my Chinese interlocutors and their Zambian hosts. It hinders their mutual understanding and acceptance from the start. Notwithstanding, this shared sentiment within the Chinese community has not led to any collective action due to intra-community factionalism and competition. This pervasive anxiety also exists in the everyday interactions between my Chinese interlocutors. The mutual suspicion within the community is the topic I will turn to in the next chapter.

2

Interactional affection
Suspicion and sustainability of voluntary cooperation

The Zou family's farming business has not always grown as smoothly as they had hoped or expected. As mentioned in the previous chapter, they started the business with a very small piece of wasteland (approximately one acre) rented from their *laoxiang* (i.e. a person from their native town/province in China). Aiming to save as much as they could, the old Zou couple moved into a wooden shelter on the edge of the land, which had originally been built by the landlady for storage. Mother Zou once told me:

> Life then was very bitter (*ku*). We worked on the farm without knowing day from night. There was no electricity, no well, nothing on the farm. So we had to do all the work by ourselves, just Lao Zou [her husband] and me, two of us. The back pain that I am suffering now was from then. … Our *laoxiang* landlady was not particularly helpful either. At the beginning she was kind, inviting us for meals, contacting business for us etc. but seeing our business become better, she turned very calculating (*suanji*) and even nasty to us. She raised the rent and asked us to pay half of the electricity bills even though we rarely used electricity. What is worse was that she started to secretly cut our vegetables, not the whole lot but just the heart (*caixin'er*). No one is going to buy it with no heart in it! Then she cut our water, blackmailing us to pay the whole water bill and she even said bad things about us to the other Chinese. Why on earth did she do that? I guess she envied us. Chinese people cannot see others being better (*jianbuderenhao*). You can ask Xiao Zou [her son] if you do not believe me.

After four years of renting from their *laoxiang*, pooling their pensions and savings together with some money borrowed from friends, the Zous finally were able to buy their own farm in a suburb to the east of Lusaka. By then, their only son and daughter-in-law joined them to help with the family farming business. As Mother and Father Zou always say, the bitterness they have eaten is for their son to have a better life. The Zou family's business is mainly to grow vegetables targeting the Chinese migrants around Lusaka. Even though they do sell on the local farmer's market, they are forbidden by law from selling any vegetables that Zambian farmers trade in the same market, such as potatoes and tomatoes. Nevertheless, growing Chinese vegetables is a preferable choice for the Zous, not only because the business competition is relatively low (there are only three Chinese farmers stalls on the market) but also because they believe that Chinese are much easier to deal with when it comes to business.

Starting from delivering to a few Chinese restaurants in town, the Zous gradually built up their own personal network. On a friend's recommendation, they secured an offer to supply vegetables and meat to a Chinese tele-technology company with hundreds of employees. Unfortunately, this deal did not last long. About one year later, the company switched to another Chinese supplier simply because the other farmer was able to establish a better personal relationship with one of the top managers in the company. Being squeezed out, the Zous had to start looking for new business opportunities. It was then that the Zou family heard the news that Sino-hydro, a Chinese construction company helping to maintain the water dam in Kariba (which is more than 200 miles away from Lusaka), was looking for a food supplier.

Considering their lack of contacts with anyone from Sino-hydro, Mother Zou decided to take an 'unconventional way'[1] – recommending herself (*maosuizijian*), as she put it. With her son, they directly went to knock on the manager's door. Their 'bold' move paid off. Showing sympathy with the difficulties of running a small business in Zambia without any contacts to rely on (*kaoshan*), the manager accepted their business proposal immediately. Since then, every Wednesday morning around 4.00 am, Xiao Zou has to get up and drive his 3.5 tonne van, preloaded with the meat and vegetables they prepared the day before, four hours to Kariba Dam and then another four hours back on the same day in order to get ready for the business next morning in Lusaka. This routine had been established for three years when I arrived at their farm for fieldwork. In those three years, trip after trip, Xiao Zou came to know the route by heart – where to slow down to avoid a sharp turn and which part of journey is extra bumpy. He even knows in which area baboons could suddenly appear on the road. Xiao Zou never missed a single delivery since the business relationship started as he acknowledges the difficulty of securing a long-term deal, especially when one has no special relationship. When I once asked him if he felt tired and ever thought of stopping this business, Xiao Zou told me:

> Yes, it is tough but this is the only stable business we got so far. People at home always think it is easy to become rich in Africa. It is actually harder. The problem is not that there is no opportunity but that the Chinese here are not united (*butuanjie*) enough. Once someone has earned a little bit of money, others copy them and do the same trade like a swarm of bees (*yiwofeng*). The Chinese only compete with the Chinese and never can run a business together. Although several friends may start something together, nine out of ten times they would break up at the end of the day.

Xiao Zou's reflection on the interplay between the relationships among Chinese migrants and the success of their businesses is shared by many other Chinese private businessmen in Zambia. After I interviewed several 'commonly regarded' successful businessmen within the Chinese migrant community about questions such as the difficulties of business operation, a general response emerged: 'Ten years ago, business was easy but nowadays, especially in the last three years, it has not gone so well. Too many Chinese in Zambia now! It will get worse', to quote Boss Chen's answer as an example. At the beginning, I found this response rather counter-intuitive: surely, as a minority group, the population growth would strengthen the influence of the community and benefit its members. Towards the end of my fieldwork, however, I started to comprehend the implication behind the comments about there being 'too many Chinese'. As in Xiao Zou's statements earlier, when summarizing their personal impressions of the Chinese community in Zambia my Chinese interlocutors most frequently invoke the notion of 'disunity' (*butuanjie*).

This Chinese notion of 'disunity' (*butuanjie*) has had various linguistic registers in different historical periods. During the Republican era, for example, Sun Yat-sen once famously commented that Chinese people were like 'a sheet of sand' (*yipansansha*), while the same analogy was used by the great Chinese literatus Lin Yutang (1935) when writing about Chinese culture. Later during the communist era, a critique of 'petty groupism' (*xiaotuantizhuyi*) was launched by the central government in an attempt to enhance solidarity within the party, which was known to be driven with factionalism (see Sorace, Franceschini and Loubere 2019). One could argue that these patterns of factionalism and unification in China have been the by-product of Chinese political centralization (more see, Qin 1998); nevertheless, in my field sites, *butuanjie* is very much applied knowledge as well as lived experience to be reflected on by my ordinary Chinese interlocutors. To them, *butuanjie* entails two facets: on the one hand, it corresponds to the unsatisfactory reality of unhealthy competitive relationships among Chinese private businessmen and the growing factionalism within the Chinese community; on the other hand, it demonstrates a moral ideal that overseas Chinese, purely due to their ethnic identity, *should* actually share and take care of each other and be united together against outsiders.

I have already explained how the Chinese 'differential mode of association' may promote anxiety when people face strangers and uncertain situations; therefore, it may block everyday communications and interactions between my Chinese interlocutors and their Zambian counterparts. In this chapter, looking at the other side of the same coin, I would like to provide some ethnographic accounts of the anxiety – manifested as mistrust and suspicion of others' motivation in this chapter – among Chinese acquaintances. I contend that pervasive anxiety not only hinders the sociality between Chinese migrants and their Zambian hosts but also nurtures internal factionalism within the Chinese 'community' and further impacts on their everyday business cooperation.

More specifically, I want to document the role of suspicion in the process of daily interaction when my Chinese interlocutors are *approached* by other Chinese migrants. In previous chapters I claimed that *guanxi* (social networking) was the dominant paradigm to conceptualize Chinese sociality and, within its analytical framework, the instrumental characteristics normally overweigh its affective aspect (Yang 1994; Kipnis 1997, 2002; Smart 1999; Strickland 2010). As further illustrated, I contend in this chapter that the ongoing abstraction and conceptualization of '*guanxi*' has objectified the practice and turned '*guanxi*' into a set of special knowledge and social apparatus for people to utilize. This process of ongoing objectification has two consequences. On the one hand, it further pushes '*guanxi*' and its practices towards the instrumental end of the spectrum; on the other hand, it raises people's awareness of situations where social skills of *guanxi* are being employed for personal gains. It is my Chinese interlocutors' rising acute awareness of *guanxi*'s instrumentality that constitutes the social-historical conditions for the occurrence of mistrust and suspicion among Chinese migrants in Zambia.

Moreover, this mistrust prevents the emergence of 'spontaneous sociality' (Fukuyama 1990: 27) between mere acquaintances. In practice, my Chinese interlocutors almost always presuppose action-initiators' instrumental motivation by default unless it can be proved otherwise. This suspicion hinders the formation of business cooperation among Chinese private entrepreneurs; meanwhile, it nurtures factions and encourages competition among Chinese migrants.

I should note, however, that cooperation is of course sometimes also successfully entered into at my field sites. Concentrating on tactics that my Chinese interlocutors apply in everyday business operations, and especially on their descriptions of the interplay between interactional affection (*jiaoqing*) and calculation (*suanji*), I will analyse in the last section how business cooperation beyond family becomes possible and even sustainable for some Chinese migrants.

Structuring my arguments in this order, however, I have no intention to incorporate 'interactional affection' into *guanxi* because I consider that (1) further conceptual incorporation would make the instrumental aspect of reciprocity encompass its affective characteristics and leave no space for *sincere voluntary cooperation* (based on genuine intersubjective sentiment), although some anthropologists endeavour to rectify the imbalance by directly stressing the importance of emotion in Chinese social relationships (see, Yan 2003; Stafford 2000, 2009) and (2) with rising awareness of *guanxi*'s instrumentality, my Chinese interlocutors are more and more inclined to intentionally separate instrumental exchange from affective interaction.

As evidence of the practice of *guanxi,* it is true that, in China as well as in my field sites, there is a tremendous and increasing flow of gift exchanges in everyday life. This is growing not only in terms of quantity but also in respect of price; that is, Chinese gifts have been subject to serious inflation in recent years (Osburg 2013). Consequently, gifts are gradually losing their function to express affection (Yan 1996), and social reciprocity is presumed with players' instrumental intentions. In practice, my Chinese interlocutors are sensitive to the inflation of gifts and aware of the growing utilitarian aspect in social interactions, especially following the rapid process of modernization in China. Therefore, I argue that their acute realization has de facto transformed their practices of socializing; that is, when gifts are widely regarded as instrumental and '*guanxi*' is objectified as social networking skills, either gift or '*guanxi*' has already started losing the function of sustaining social relationships.

As a result of the dysfunction of '*guanxi*' and 'gift', my Chinese interlocutors have to look for alternatives ways to express their sincere affection, form bonds and maintain relations. I claim that, consequently, this awareness of instrumentality and mistrust forces them to emphasize, nurture, cherish and protect interactional affection (*jiaoqing*). They begin employing consistent actions to express their mutual affection. Nevertheless, dialectically, this focus on affective bond and emotional proximity in cooperative groups, to some extent, further segments Chinese migrants at the level of voluntary association and solidifies the factionalism in the 'community'.

In general, if the previous chapter showed how emotion, as contextual tone, influences social perception and blocks the formation of social relations, in this chapter I would like to reveal the other side; namely, how affection constructs relationships and glues people together willingly but at the same time creates factions as a by-product.

Mistrust and suspicion

It was just a normal Sunday afternoon at the Demonstration Centre farm. After lunch, instead of rushing back to their dormitories as they did on weekdays, the administrative staff stayed a little longer in the dining hall to chat. Suddenly, a van drove into the courtyard with a group of five visitors. Recognizing the car, Manager Bao immediately went outside to welcome the guests. 'What wind carries you here today?', Bao greeted the visitors with a big smile on his face.

> Ah, we were visiting some friends earlier on. They live further east down the Great East Road. Since we are passing yours on the way back, I thought we could drop by to see how you are and how the new building is. We have not met since you moved out of my hotel. It has been a long time! I know you are a busy man, so we have to visit without invitation .... Look how magnificent the building is! I am sure this is the biggest building in eastern Lusaka. These are all to your credit (*gonglao*), Director Bao (i.e. Manager Bao)! Without your diligence and wise guidance (*yingminglingdao*), it could not have been built!

With these words, in front of her family and the staff of ATDC, Mother (*dama*) Liu both explained the reason for her 'uninvited' visit and praised Bao for the work done.

'Any time! ATDC is your home. You can come whenever you like!', Manager Bao turned around to the staff: 'We all know how much Mother Liu has helped us. Without Mother Liu, there would be no Demonstration Centre today! We are still using your duvets and sheets! You are not here today to take them away, are you? Otherwise, we would be naked in bed tonight! Haha!' Everyone laughed, and then Bao started to give Mother Liu and her family a tour of ATDC.

As I have already explained, Mother Liu is the most well-known businesswoman in Zambia. Originally from Sichuan province, she arrived in Zambia with only 'one basin and one duvet' as she always says herself. Now settled in Zambia for more than a decade, Mother Liu is currently running two restaurants (one of which is attached to her own motel) in Lusaka and has a branch near Victoria Falls. Even though she cannot be named as the most successful Chinese businesswoman in Zambia, Mother Liu has certainly gained fame due to her sophisticated social networking skills and her close relationship with the Chinese ambassador. Because of her personal experiences in Zambia and her relationship with the Chinese embassy, it has been common for newly arrived Chinese officials or managers of state enterprises to initially seek Mother Liu's help and build up their own networks via her introduction. This is how Manager Bao and Mother Liu became acquainted. As I have explained, the staff of the Demonstration Centre stayed at Mother Liu's hotel for almost a year before they moved into the educational farm compound. When I arrived in the field, it was almost the end of their tenancy; nevertheless, I stayed in Mother Liu's hotel for more than a month, which provided me with a good opportunity to observe her business operational style and her interaction with others.

Mother Liu stayed about an hour before heading back to her restaurant in town: 'We are one family (*yijiaren*). If you need anything, just give me a shout. You must not see yourself as an outsider (*qianwan bie jianwai*)!', Mother Liu told Manager Bao before getting into the car.

'Of course, we all regard you as our mother in Zambia! Now we have our own place. Make sure you come here often so we can treat you to some nice meals and wine', Manager Bao replied.

After we had seen them off, I praised Mother Liu's kindness in visiting the Centre. To my surprise, Manager Bao replied,

> Hehe! People would not visit the Temple of Three Gods if they had no trouble [*wushibudengsanbaodian*]. Mother Liu said she was visiting a friend. Everyone knows she does not have any friends living up this way. She said she came here to see how we are. These are all sweet words said for us to listen to. You know, everything she asked was about farming. A close friend of mine was mentioning that Mother Liu was looking for some land to open a farm. Seeing others earning money from farming, her eyes must have turned red [*yanhong*, envy]. She was here trying to seek more information about how to run a farm! Essentially, Mother Liu is a businesswoman – she wouldn't get up early if there were no benefit [*wulibuqizao*]. Xiao Wu, you are still young. You haven't stepped out in the society long enough. Do not believe what others tell you that easily.

Manager Bao's words left me speechless. The shock was brought mainly by Manager Bao's personal awareness and speculation on other people's 'real' motivation. Given the fact that he is a manager for a large educational farm and Mother Liu is a small entrepreneur, rationally one might suppose that there should be no real business competition between them. Yet the mistrust between them is very easy to detect even though Manager Bao and Mother Liu had interacted for a rather long time before. To unpack the statements of Manager Bao, there are several points that need to be stressed. First, the position of initiator and approached alters the process of personal reasoning and one's corresponding emotional reaction. In this case, it is the approached, Manager Bao, who generates a response of mistrust and suspicion against the initiator of the encounter, Mother Liu.

Second, more importantly, he focuses specifically on the instrumental end of the approaching actor. This is revealed clearly in the Chinese idioms that Manager Bao invoked – *if they had no trouble* or *if there were no benefit*, a person would not initiate the action. This, I argue, is an almost default assumption of my Chinese interlocutors when they are involved in spontaneous association, which I call 'otherwise presumption', namely, encounters or initiators are presumed to approach with instrumental, sometimes malicious end, unless it can be proven otherwise. The saying 'people would not visit the Temple of Three Gods if they had no trouble [*wushibudengsanbaodian*]' expresses this suspicion. Most of my interlocutors have an alternative folk analogy with a similar meaning – 'the weasel goes to pay his New Year's respects to the hen' (*huangshulanggeijibainian*). This implies that the initiator's motives are malicious even when their action appears kind.

Third, there is a strong reliance on the context and other sources of information for this type of personal speculation. In this case, Manager Bao associates his previous experience with Mother Liu, his cultural knowledge and even the hearsay of his trusted close friend to figure out the 'real' intention of Mother Liu's unexpected action (I will elaborate more on this contextual perceptiveness related to the ability for proper speech in Chapter 5).

Fourth, this contextually associated suspicion is considered as a form of social ability or social knowledge in opposition to 'social naivety'. This belief, as stated in the last chapter, is mutually constructed with the folk idea of 'society as a dying pot that contains great danger and necessary sins'. This was the implication behind Manager Bao's advice to me.

To sum up, then, viewing this ethnographic vignette as a whole, there are three obvious aspects: (1) strong personal awareness of the instrumental ends of social actions when they are initiated by others; (2) very explicit mistrust and even sophisticated suspicion associated with such awareness; and (3) a very fragile social association as a consequence of this strong mistrust. Indeed, based on cross-cultural comparison, political historian Fukuyama claims in his monograph *Trust* that 'there is a relatively low degree of trust in Chinese society the moment one steps outside the family circle' (1995: 56). He reasons that this mistrust is owing to strong Chinese familism that itself is the consequence of Confucianism and its dominant position in Chinese ethical education. He further argues that this familism prevents the growth of 'spontaneous sociality', which he believes to be the foundation for voluntary association and professional management.

Although this discussion corresponds well with my observation in the field, I find little agreement with Fukuyama's essentialization of Chinese practices as Confucian. Furthermore, I neither consider that familism or trust heavily invested in family is the fundamental reason for the pervasive existence of mistrust in Chinese society. Not only is Confucianism constantly reinterpreted and even reinvented across history, but also there are of course many reports of domestic conflicts within families. Trust in family should not be deductively assumed merely because one can observe a low level of trust with *non*-family members. Notwithstanding, I find Fukuyama's concept of 'spontaneous sociality' intriguing and useful. I reinterpret 'spontaneous sociality' as a form of willing and ungrounded free association. To say it is 'ungrounded' is to stress that such association is not formed within the frame of family or any pre-existing social organizations and, significantly, the socializing has ends in itself.

Contrasting with Fukuyama's analysis, I argue that this pervasive mistrust between my Chinese interlocutors and the consequential prevention of 'spontaneous sociality' are due to their self-consciousness of the increasing instrumental inclination of '*guanxi*' practices between individuals in everyday interaction, following the expansion of the market and the inflation of gifts. Chinese social interactions and relations, generalized as '*guanxi*', have been associated by sinological anthropologists and others mostly with strong rationality, instrumentality and utilitarian characteristics. Bruce Jacobs defines '*guanxi*' as 'particularistic ties' (1979: 238) that are subject to personal manipulation and strategic plan, especially for the purpose of constructing political alliances. While studying socialist institutions, Andrew Walder sees '*guanxi*' as 'instrumental-personal ties' (1986: 179) informally utilized by workers in socialist factories to secure resources without challenging authority. The most thorough study of '*guanxi*' is perhaps Mayfair Yang's monograph on 'guanxi-ology' (*guanxixue*), in which she treats 'gift economy' and '*guanxi*' as interchangeable (1994: 8).

Aiming to study '*guanxi*' as social fact, instead of mere representation, which constitutes a Chinese 'civil society' against the power of socialist state, Yang tries to understand '*guanxi*' from an emic point of view and stresses its '*art*fulness' that draws on 'the sense of skill, subtlety, and cunning conveyed by the word' (8). Such theoretical treatments, I consider, inevitably leave two negative consequences: first, Chinese social interactions are unnecessarily portrayed as fundamentally instrumental so that Chinese society somehow becomes intrinsically Machiavellian; and second, a focus on the utilitarian characteristics of '*guanxi*' may blind us to the sincerity also found in social relationships, as symbolized in gifts.

Of course, negative views of '*guanxi*' are shared by our Chinese interlocutors. As Yang documented with pages of interviews on the definition and evaluation of '*guanxi*', almost all of the reports contain images of manipulation, self-interest as a driver, deception and symptoms of moral decline (49–74). This awareness could also be demonstrated by Manager Bao's comments on Mother Liu's motivation and his general evaluation of Chinese society, which I presented earlier. This self-consciousness of the instrumentality built in '*guanxi*' practice has soared and been transformed in recent years under the social conditions of continuous marketization, the inflation of material gifts and intense anti-corruption campaign led by Chinese central government. In his recent fascinating ethnography about the social networking among Chinese elites, entrepreneurs and officials in Chengdu, Sichuan, John Osburg has documented the increasing significant role that 'entertainment and leisure' as forms of action are playing in social networking processes because 'the inflation in forms of commodified pleasure has begun to reach its limit' (2013: 39). This transformed version of networking has also triggered a new type of self-awareness. As his informants said, entertaining (*yingchou*) is a job – a statement very similar to what my Chinese interlocutors often mention when talking about relations at work, which I will elaborate more in the next chapter.

All of these various discourses about the instrumentality of Chinese '*guanxi*' are intriguing. Notwithstanding, taking one step back to interpret these opinions, what interests me most is that if everyone is so conscious of the utilitarian characteristics of '*guanxi*' and morally resent its instrumentality, how could '*guanxi*', regarded as an essential device in China to connect the social individuals, be adequately functional? I will explore this question later in the final section, but for now, I would like to argue that this very self-consciousness of the instrumentality of '*guanxi*' practice provides the foundation of mistrust and suspicion between my Chinese interlocutors (as familiars). Furthermore, this pervasive mistrust delays the occurrence of 'spontaneous sociality'; meanwhile, it strengthens existing 'trustworthy' relationships (which I prefer to call 'otherwise-presumptive trust' relationships), often in the shape of blood-tie or region-tie. Consequentially, factions form along with these dynamics of trust and suspicion.

Faction in action: The 'bottleneck effect' of Chinese private business in Lusaka

As argued in the previous section, the pervasive mistrust and suspicion of others' instrumental motivation among the Chinese 'community' feeds the rise of factions. A very obvious effect of this internal factionalism among Chinese in Zambia is that it constrains the sustainability of business partnerships so as to limit the scale of business growth. Relying on previous ethnographical studies by sinologists, Fukuyama speculates that Chinese business would suffer great difficulties in upscaling without the assistance of strong, centralized organizations due to the lack of 'spontaneous sociality'. His speculation corresponds well with the practical 'breaking-up' stories that my Chinese interlocutors experience in business.

In general, the process of 'breaking-up' is that, first of all, several 'friends' unite together and join their capital to form a partnership. Then, following the extension of the business, the profits grow along with the personal authority of each partner. Furthermore, disagreements would appear while the partnership became more unequal or unbalanced.

Then, partners would calculate their personal contribution to the business and the distribution of corresponding profits. Finally, the partnership would be dissolved due to the internal growing hostility and the consequential separation of the partners. Next, some partners would find new 'friends' to start a new partnership. Having heard and seen repeatedly such stories of Chinese business partners breaking up, I propose that there is a 'bottleneck' effect on the growth of Chinese private joint ventures in Zambia. This effect happens not only as a consequence of the dramatic increase of Chinese migrants to Zambia and the intensifying external competitive environment but also, more significantly, as a result of the internal conflicts and factionalism among the business partners.

The first time I heard a breaking-up story was the second month after I arrived in Lusaka. The story was told by the assistant manager of Mother Liu's motel and involves Mother Liu's early business cooperation with others. At the beginning, Mother Liu started a business with two of her friends, both female. They came to Zambia roughly at the same time and because of funding issues, they decided to pool their money together to start a business. As she could not speak a word of English then, Mother Liu was in charge of daily business management while her friends were doing marketing or contacting clients. Once the business started to generate profits, disagreements on accounts and individual contribution also emerged. Finally, the joint business collapsed, and Mother Liu took her initial funds and established her own catering business. The story was told as a legend, and little could be proven as Mother Liu never talked about this piece of personal life history in interviews. Nevertheless, halfway through my fieldwork, it so happened that the story was told to me again when I was helping an institution that was in business with Mother Liu's previous business partner.

Although the legend was unproven, I did witness a conflict that happened in another of Mother Liu's joint businesses when I was with the Zou family. Seeing the money that some white businessmen in Lusaka earned by opening schools, Mother Liu thought it would be a really good business opportunity to found a Chinese school, given that there were none in Zambia. She persuaded six other successful Chinese entrepreneurs to join and run the school together. Nevertheless, the school did not become as popular as Mother Liu planned. It now only survives as a nursery mainly for Chinese private migrants and relies on volunteers who are recruited by Mother Liu every year from Chinese universities. Since there was no profit for several years but significant costs, several partners were thinking of withdrawing their initial investments. The most serious disagreement was between Mother Liu and Boss Mo. Boss Mo criticized Mother Liu's authoritarian managerial style while Mother Liu complained that Boss Mo did not contribute anything to the school's everyday management. Their quarterly board meetings often ended up with quarrels. Fewer and fewer partners actually attended the meetings. I learned all this from Manager Deng, who is one of the seven partners, after the Zou family and I encountered Xiao Zhang, the manager's assistant at the Chinese school, weeping (*kusu*) in the courtyard at Manager Deng's house on a Chinese New Year's Day.

Xiao Zhang got her job due to her close relationship with Mother Liu. She is the daughter of Mother Liu's village friend and presumably under Mother Liu's umbrella of protection. Instead of calling her manager, Xiang Zhang respects Mother Liu as her mother (*gamma*). The reason why Xiao Zhang was weeping in Manager Deng's courtyard was because of a fight she had had with the martial arts teacher at the school. The martial arts teacher had only arrived a month before. Although there were hardly any martial arts students, he was still recruited from China by Boss Mo from his own village. Ever since he arrived at the school, he never stopped causing trouble to Xiao Zhang, as she complained.

The fight started at midnight when Xiao Zhang could not get into the school compound after celebrating the Chinese New Year with several friends in town.

'He locked me out on the New Year's Eve! Can you believe that? Who does that? So lacking in morals (*zhenquede*)', Xiang Zhang said.

After she had knocked at the gate for almost half an hour, the martial arts teacher unlocked the door then accused Xiang Zhang of undignified behaviour.

'You know what he said? He said no good girl goes out drinking until midnight. He said I know nothing about a girl's behavioural discretion (*xingwei bujiandian*). Who does he think he is! My father?'

Then they began to swear at each other and it turned into a fight. Xiang Zhang was beaten and had a cut on her forehead. She then went to a Chinese clinic where she stayed over.

'He is not a man. A real man will never beat a girl! He dared to do that only because he has Boss Mo as the backer (*kaoshan*) – a dog relies on the owner's authority (*gouzhang renshi*). Boss Mo must have sent him to spy on *ganma* (Mother Liu) and me. Ai, I would have no sweet days to live from now on. It is time to go back to China for good.'

Manager Deng advised Xiao Zhang that she should wait till Mother Liu came back from China after Chinese New Year to sort things out.

After Xiao Zhang left, Manager Deng's wife told me that they were rarely involved in the management of school these days although Manager Deng was an initial founding partner. She said that the more people became involved, the more problems would occur.

> We knew from the start that it would not work out well. We never planned to get a penny back. Since Mother Liu asked, she would lose face if we did not contribute something. Two tigers could not live peacefully in the same hill (*yishanburong'erhu*), not to mention there are seven of them. You see what it ends up like. It is better for us not to step into the muddied water. Only harmony could generate fortune. Better not give them more messiness.

About two months later, I overheard from a conversation between Manager Deng and Mother Zou that the martial arts teacher was sent back to China while Boss Mo withdrew his investments from the partnership.

Not only does Chinese private joint venture suffer this bottleneck effect for business growth, but Chinese family business also face the potential challenge of '*fenjia*' (family division). *Fenjia* as an ethnographic phenomenon has long been documented by anthropologists of China (Cohen 1976). Mostly, family division is a result of domestic conflicts among brothers. To some extent, one could argue that family division represents internal factionalism within one family; therefore, to repeat, the analysis provided by Fukuyama (1995), with the presumption that strong familism inherited from Confucian tradition is the reason for the lack of 'spontaneous sociality' in Chinese society, needs to be qualified. In other words, trust does not easily happen without nurturing just because both parties are from the same household – certainly not between mother-in-law and daughter-in-law.

During my fieldwork, there were very few family division cases. The Hu family farm was the only case I heard of. The family farm was established by the senior Hu (in his eighties now) when he came to Zambia more than twenty years ago. After his retirement, his eldest son inherited the farm business, but his younger son and daughter were also given equal portions of the farm land, where they built their own houses as well as shops. Despite the family breaking up, the younger son and daughter still seek financial help from senior Hu when their own business is in trouble. This places an extra burden on the eldest son, who is now taking care of senior Hu, and often causes family quarrels between the eldest son's wife and his siblings, which I overheard several times when Mrs Hu visited Mother Zou to tell 'bitter stories'.

Notwithstanding, the problem of family division arises less and less for my informants because most of them only have one child due to the Chinese policy. Nevertheless, the new problem that successful Chinese private entrepreneurs are facing is that the only child is not willing to inherit the family business. For them, Zambia is too poor and too backward (*luohou*) to be desirable for settlement. Therefore, a common practice is that the family supports the only child to study overseas, mostly in the United States or the United Kingdom, with the plan that the whole family would be able to migrate once the child is settled, despite this meaning that entrepreneurs would have to give up their businesses in Zambia. To place a professional manager in charge of the family business has not crossed the minds of any of my Chinese interlocutors. A simple reason they offer is that one can never trust an outsider to take care of family business, and professional managers are always suspected of manipulating the balance sheet for personal gains. 'One has to manage the business oneself if one wants profits', as Boss Zhang once told Father Zou.

Anti-anti-affection as a way of cooperation

So far in this chapter, I have focused on the negative effect on business operations of the 'differential mode of association', particularly manifested as *'guanxi'* practice here. At least one obvious question has, however, been left unanswered: namely, if everyone is so suspicious and mutual mistrust is so low, how could business cooperation happen or ever be sustained? In this section, I attempt to solve this conundrum by concentrating on the interplay of two cultural ideas, interactional affection (*jiaoqing*) and calculation (*suanji*), which my interlocutors repetitively illustrate and practice every day.

Aiming to balance the overwhelming instrumentality of *'guanxi'*, a popular demonstration of gift exchange in China, a few sinologist anthropologists have begun to incorporate *'renqing'* into their analytical models, a term that so far has literally been translated as 'human feeling' (Yan 1996: 122). As Yan Yunxiang argues in his highly detailed ethnography of gift exchanges in a Northern Chinese village:

> It is clear that in the social life of Xiajia village, sentiment affects villagers' behaviour just as significantly as do moral obligations. The spiritual substances embedded in gifts are both morally and emotionally charged. Villagers exchange gifts are to increase *ganqing* with each other, as well as reinforce *guanxi*. In other words, it is the combination of developing emotional attachments and cultivating personal relations that gives meaning to the practice of gift exchange. … What I am trying to emphasize … is that villagers do not interact

with each other only for utilitarian purpose, and the *renqing* complex is much more than a win-or-lose power game. (1996: 145)

Then he specifies that 'the system of *renqing* ethics has three structural dimensions: rational calculation, moral obligation, and emotional attachment' (146).

This relationship of entailment is also clearly stated in Andrew Kipnis's monograph on '*guanxi*' in China – '*guanxi* involves human feelings and *ganqing* involves material obligation. The terms are often interchangeable .... In *guanxi*, feeling and instrumentality are a totality. Additionally, one should not romanticize *guanxi* ... *guanxi* can be seen as unifying what Western bourgeois relationships separate: material exchange and affectionate feelings' (1997: 23–4).

Despite their original analytical purpose, I argue that such incorporation – subsuming *renqing* under *guanxi* – unnecessarily misleads people to instrumentalize 'human feelings', but certainly not to romanticize *guanxi*. This way of incorporating has positioned affection as a second-order social factor and, potentially, brings the danger of leaving little space for the sincere sentiment to be appreciated in everyday interaction. To avoid such potentiality, I would like to borrow the term '*jiaoqing*' (interactional affection) that my Chinese interlocutors always use when talking about relationships, and propose that affection is the foundation (first-order) of voluntary association, sustainable cooperation and a good '*guanxi*' (relationship). Most importantly, this affection is not presupposed with any existing social relations, but grows with long-term daily inter-*action*. Notwithstanding, this long-term engagement in turn may prevent the occurrence of other 'spontaneous sociality' so to form potential factionalism.

The significance of interaction in forming social relations in China has already been clearly pointed out by Charles Stafford. By contrast with the lineage paradigm, Stafford invokes the local concepts of '*yang*' and '*laiwang*', which are held to produce the relatedness between individuals, and further demonstrates how relations are constituted beyond kin and affinity 'in which kinship and friendship are seen to be hard work, the product of everyday human interactions' (2000: 52). It is the 'cycle of *yang* and *laiwang*' – with the emphasis on the nurturing through daily actions – that connects individuals across time and space.

As quoted earlier, the focus on actions and 'shared experiences' have increasingly been realized by individuals due to the inflation of 'gifts' in China. Although it is under the shadow of business networking skills, Osburg has shown how the relationships are 'forged and maintained through ritualized leisure – experiences of shared pleasure' (2013: 26). And he argues that these experiences serve as the foundation for affective ties between men and their social intimacy, which further offers possibility for networking. In my field sites, the affection that grows through interaction is called '*jiaoqing*' and the importance of nurtured relatedness could be represented by the proverb my Chinese interlocutors use: '*yuanqin buru jinlin*' (remote kin are not reliable as neighbours).

Personally, I find *jiaoqing* (international affection) a more suitable term than *renqing* (human feelings) or *ganqing* (emotion) for the analytical purpose of this chapter. First, semantically, the discourse of *renqing* connotes utilitarian aspects and often comes as the Chinese four-character idiom '*renqing shigu*' in which '*shigu*' stresses the sophistication of one's social networking skills learned in social practices. It already entails manipulative inclination. Second, although my interlocutors often refer to it, I consider that *ganqing* focuses more on the inner psyche so to diminish the effect of intersubjectivity. By contrast, the locus of *jiaoqing* is on the affinity/emotional proximity generated through long-term interaction. It pinpoints temporality to eliminate instrumentality and interactivity to diminish individuality. Furthermore, it takes affection as the basis of social relations.

The difference between '*jiaoqing*' and '*renqing*' could be clearly seen in Mother Zou's discourse. Once, when helping her pack some gifts for another Chinese migrant's son's wedding banquet, I asked Mother Zou how they became friends. She corrected me:

> We are not friends. We do not have any interactional affection (*jiaoqing*). We hardly socialize (*zoudong*) at all. To be honest, I do not

really want to go to the wedding but I do not want others to say that I do not know *renqing* (human emotion). The circle [*quanzi*, i.e. the network of Chinese private entrepreneurs in Lusaka] is small here. I won't stay long. I will come back as soon as I give them the gifts.

From her statements, we can see that Mother Zou distinguishes *jiaoqing* from *renqing*. The latter is used in respect of moral obligation: it is what one should do. The former refers to affection grown through socializing: it is what one chooses to do. Interactional affection has a focus on intimacy/emotional proximity, whereas human emotion stresses the psychological side of morality. Arguably, *jiaoqing* is 'interpersonal' (as in between friends), whereas *renqing* is 'universal' (as in Chinese moral norm).

Since most of the time affection is communicated by actions and expressed indirectly at my field sites, documentation of the observation of explicit affection and its direct impact on cooperation becomes difficult. Nevertheless, my Chinese interlocutors do often give evaluations of the actions that may harm interactional affection – a way, I consider, of protecting established intimacy. Therefore, I call this manifestation of cooperation 'anti-anti-affection'.

One of the most common anti-affection actions is calculation. Such action could appear in various ways. Calculation encapsulates the meaning of '*jisuan*' (computing or counting) as well as '*suanji*' (strategic plotting). In linguistic applications, the former is often followed by things as accusative, while the latter is often applied to a person, namely, calculating (*jisuan*) something and calculating (*suanji*) somebody. It is '*suanji*' that my interlocutors mostly resent, as it takes people as a means to achieve personal ends. This kind of action is the one most commonly subject to suspicion and harmful to the maintenance of mutual affection. *Jisuan* could also sometimes be regarded as actions that potentially harm interactional affection. Nevertheless, the relationship between calculating and affection are more dialectic. As Stafford illustrates, counting could be very much emotionally loaded (2009, 2010). If it is aiming for the good of the other party in a relationship or the good of the group as a whole, which may involve self-sacrifice sometimes, *jisuan* will enhance the emotional ties. But over-calculating (*jisuan*) between inter-actors in a relationship may be considered as too formal and as an implied gesture of unwillingness to form an emotional bond. My Chinese interlocutors term this '*keqi*' (over-polite/ritualized) or '*jianwai*' (seeing oneself as an outsider). Doing this to an extreme, one could face the potential danger of converting '*jisuan*' (counting) into '*suanji*' (plotting).

The resentment of calculation (*suanji*) could be demonstrated in various sets of oppositional concepts referred to and practised in ordinary life by my Chinese interlocutors. At my field sites, people commonly complain about those who overemphasize money and personal gains. Overemphasizing money and personal gains during interaction is a characteristic usually termed '*xiaoqi*' (parsimony) by Chinese migrants. *Xiaoqi* is considered as a consequential action of over-focusing on one's gains and loss so that the mutual affection might be in danger of being overlooked. This kind of action is described as '*jianli wangyi*' (to forget friendship/righteous conduct when one sees money), and the people who regularly commit such action are regarded as '*xiaoren*' (petty men).[2] A general attitude towards '*xiaoren*' is trying one's best to avoid socializing with them. The opposite of '*xiaoqi*' (parsimonious) is '*kangkai*' (generous). Generous people are morally praised as they are willing to sacrifice their wealth to maintain interactional affection, especially if one party is in need of help. My Chinese interlocutors often describe such people as '*zhangyi shucai*' (generous with money in the name of righteousness).

Due to its material nature and ease of calculation, money is often used as a test to judge another person's character and the mutual affection between two people. During my fieldwork, borrowing money sometimes became an inevitable practice despite my Chinese interlocutors endeavouring to avoid it as the involvement of money could potentially harm interactional affection. Normally, prospective borrowers would approach people with whom they had already built emotional bonds. This emotional bond could increase the borrowers' chance of getting the loan; meanwhile, it can also provide lenders with some security against the risk of unreturned money. If the money is not paid back, the emotional bond was in danger of being broken.

Zambian workers often seek to borrow money from Chinese bosses. This often causes unnecessary arguments and resentment. To the Zambian workers, borrowing money from the boss is unquestionable as the boss is the one that workers should go to if there is any difficulty; and the boss will take care of the workers (see Chapter 3). Nevertheless, it is a 'taboo' for the Chinese bosses, for whom the workers should not have put forward such request at all because there is no strong interactional affection between the boss and the worker. By being approached in this way, the boss has been forced into a difficult dilemma. Afraid of never being paid back, the boss is very reluctant to lend the money, but refusing to do so is a potential threat to a good working relationship. Therefore, such action often leaves the Chinese bosses very annoyed, and they criticize the Zambian workers who 'do not know the way to deal with human emotion (*renqing shigu*)'.

This function of money as a test is well demonstrated by the money-lending practices that Xiao Liu became involved in. Xiao Liu is a translator at the educational farm. Like most young Chinese, he is very open to talking with Zambian workers and making friends with them. Gasper is one of the Zambian workers Xiao Liu quickly became acquainted with. When I arrived at the educational farm, Xiao Liu had already formed a certain bond with Gasper. He would ask Gasper to help him with some personal matters and told me that I could trust Gasper. However, one afternoon, Xiao Liu looked very worried when he was seeking advice from Liu Wei on the matter of whether he should lend money to Gasper.

> Liu Wei: What is the money for? They are going to get paid next Thursday!
> Xiao Liu: He told me that he needed to attend a funeral in Livingston this weekend and he is short of money to travel. It might just be an excuse.

Liu Wei: En, sometimes, they (Zambians) can be full of bullshit. Do you think he (Gasper) will pay you back?

Xiao Liu: He seems a trustworthy guy. Normally, my heart is at ease (*fangxin*) when he helps me with tasks. He is not like other blacks. Sometimes he even brings me something he has cooked at home. [He] seems to have the 'sense of human emotion' (*renqingwei'er*). Plus, he did not want to borrow a lot. I do not want him to think me too parsimonious (*xiaoqi*).

Liu Wei: How much?

Xiao Liu: 50000 kwacha (US$10).

Liu Wei: Hmmm, it is not much. If he did not pay you back, you could consider it as a lesson learned and there would be no need to socialize with him in the future.

Xiao Liu lent the money to Gasper, and two weeks later, Xiao Liu came to my room and told me pleasantly, 'Gasper is good. He paid me back. It is worth getting to socialise with him more deeply (*zhide shenjiao*).'

Another common sign of resentment towards calculation is the negative attitude that my Chinese interlocutors hold towards drawing up contracts. Contracts to them seem cold, fixed and formal, which is the opposite of what proper mutual affection should be: fluid and informal. Therefore, drawing contracts between friends is perceived as a gesture of 'alienation', implying mistrust and potentially damaging interactional affection (*jiaoqing*). If such intention is ever raised, a typical response from the counter-party is 'relying on our long-term interactional affection, can't I trust you?' A Chinese phrase could well capture the interplay between contract as a form of law and affection as the fundamental bond in social interaction: '*fa bu waihu renqing*' (law does not lie outside the sphere of human feeling). Note, here again, that human feeling (*renqing*) does not merely refer to the instrumental character of social interaction but also embraces the notion of sympathy and moral sentiment as a whole.

It was halfway through my fieldwork when I started to notice the reluctance of my Chinese interlocutors to draw up contracts. The vegetables on the Zous' farm often suffered the problem of premature growth. For example, the corianders often blossomed before the leaves grew big. After trying several different types of seeds, Father Zou was convinced that the problem could be solved with more advanced agricultural skills. As no one in the family had farming experience before coming to Zambia, Father Zou was eager to get help from agricultural experts. They family treated Technician Xu from ATDC next door to several nice meals and asked some advice; nevertheless, considering their 'unfriendly' relationship with the general manager (i.e. Technician Xu's leader), it became more and more difficult to invite Xu over. Seeing their worries, I suggested that Father Zou could hire the UNZA farm technician as a part-time consultant. At the beginning, he was hesitant, but he decided to give it a try after he realized that getting help from the Chinese technicians next door was a dead-end. Having discussed the matter on the phone a couple of times, the UNZA technician was happy to take the position. When we were meeting for a tea to talk about the details, he mentioned that he needed a formal agreement for reference. To me, it was a very reasonable requirement; however, Father Zou looked concerned. Although he said nothing, the meeting finished a couple of minutes later when Father Zou said he still had other things to attend to. Driving back to the farm, Father Zou told me that it was better to postpone the negotiation, and wait and see if he could contact any other Chinese experts for help. I was very puzzled by his reaction as I could see nothing wrong during the meeting, so I asked him why he did not want to pursue the work. Father Zou told me, 'He does not trust us. What is the contract for? If it is already so problematic (*mafan*) from the start, it will be more trouble in future. So it is better to leave it now.' Clearly, in Father Zou's mind, a contract is for people who do not trust each other. And, what is more interesting is that a contract is designed to prevent problems in future; nevertheless, it is considered problematic already by my Chinese interlocutors.

Overall, the interplay between interactional affection and calculation could be illustrated positively by the Zou family's cooperation with Boss Deng. As introduced at the beginning of this chapter, the Zou farming business hardly survived when they were renting a plot from their *laoxiang* (people from the same region). They were seriously considering returning to China when their several attempts to borrow money failed. It was at that difficult time when Boss Deng was introduced to the Zous. Boss Deng is from the same city as the Zous. Initially coming to Zambia as a cook with his company for a construction project in the early 1990s, Boss Deng decided to stay after his peers returned to China and in the following year, he opened the first Chinese restaurant in Zambia.

> When I first met Boss Deng, I was really scared. You know he has a serious face and hardly smiles … . Then, I found out that he used to work in the building across the road of where the department store I used to work was. No doubt that I felt I have seen him somewhere. He must have bought things from our shop. We had never spoken to each other in China even though we worked building by building. Now we are good friends on this foreign land. What karma (*yuanfen*)!

Mother Zou told me this when I asked her how Boss Deng and the Zou family made their acquaintance. *Yuanfen* here refers to an uncontrollable force governing social relationships. It is similar to the notion of fate and could be loosely translated as karma. Nevertheless, the connotation here is of its 'unplanned' or 'by chance' nature. By landing on *yuanfen*, one is eliminating the instrumental part of the relationship and emphasizing the emotional bond between parties. Knowing how to cherish '*yuanfen*' is a good moral characteristic to my Chinese interlocutors.

Acknowledging that the Zou family needed money to be able to keep their farming business going, Boss Deng lent them US$30,000 without charging any interest. Five years later, the Zou family still owes him US$10,000. Several times, the Zou family suggested paying interest to Boss Deng but he would firmly refuse it. Once, I heard Boss Deng tell Mother Zou while she was offering him money as interest:

> 'If you do this again, you do not need to come to mine any more. Why are you seeing yourself as an outsider (*jianwai*) so much? We have known each other for years. I lent you money out of our long-term interactional affection (*jiaoqing*). Now you give me interest. If someone who does not know our relationship sees this, they would think I am

some kind of parsimonious person. Did I lend you the money just for that interest? You are putting me in an immoral (*buyi*) position!'

Hearing this, Mother Zou left blushing.

Boss Deng's action earns enormous gratitude from the Zou family and praise from every Chinese who hears the story. People compliment Boss Deng as '*youqingyouyi*' (possessing an affectionate and faithful character). Mother Zou often said to me that if there were no help from Boss Deng, they could not survive in Zambia.

> Only adversity reveals the real interactional affection (*huannan jianzhenqing*). He (Boss Deng) is our family's saviour. It is our family's fortune to meet Boss Deng. We will never forget his gratitude-emotion (*enqing*).

This deep emotional bond between the Zou family and Boss Deng makes this business cooperation run rather smoothly. As he runs a successful restaurant, Boss Deng would purchase Chinese vegetables from the Zou family. The Zou family would always give much cheaper prices to him and give him extra for free. When I asked Xiao Zou's wife that if they could actually earn any profits through transactions with Boss Deng, she firstly got very surprised that I could even have asked such question; then she said it was not about gain or loss at all. She told me that the Zou family visited Boss Deng every weekend and usually stayed at his house for dinner, but Boss Deng never calculated the loss. 'If everything is calculated so clearly, there would be no friends,' she said.

Giving extra for free is a common practice the Zou family employed when dealing with long-engaged Chinese customers. It is a gesture to show one's willingness to maintain mutual affection for the longer term. Giving extra for free is an action to demonstrate one's intention to be anti-calculative through actual careful calculation.

Conclusion

The Chinese interlocutors at my field sites in Zambia could be said to be caught up in factions, which they say results from the Chinese community being '*butuanjie*' (not united). These factions are on a small scale, but mostly hinder business cooperation, encouraging internal competition and preventing the business upscaling. Instead of tracing this back to the Confucian ideal of familism, I investigate how the faction is formed and realized through everyday interaction. I propose that it may be the increasing self-awareness of the instrumentality of '*guanxi*' practice in China as a whole that provides the foundation for strong suspicion and mistrust among acquaintances. In turn, the mistrust shifts people's gaze towards long-term interaction and affection, in search for sincere cooperation. This inclination has also been exaggerated as a result of decades of economic boom and corresponding inflation of gifts in China. To some extent, gifts are gradually losing their adequacy to convey mutual affection and to maintain a sustainable and genuine voluntary cooperation.

I want to stress that genuine voluntary cooperation does happen at my field sites. Earlier, I endeavour to show how its occurrence and sustainability are formulated around mutual affection growing in the daily interactions, which I have argued is the first-order condition for formation of social relations. Rather than interpreting '*guanxi*' as a social fact to organize Chinese society, I take it as the second-order social representation that builds on the foundation of 'interactional affection'. I consider this separation is necessary, as an overwhelmingly utilitarian '*guanxi*' leaves little space for social sincerity and voluntary cooperation, either analytically or practically. This separation may be criticized as falling into 'Western bourgeois dualism'; however, the context of China has transformed dramatically after years of modernization and marketization, as have the evolving practices of sociality. At my field sites, voluntary cooperation is nurtured with continuous care, affection and interaction. My Chinese interlocutors consciously cherish the interactional affection, with cultural devices testing and acting against any calculative actions that may potentially harm the relationship – not merely between Chinese migrants but also with Zambians. Notwithstanding, this concentration on interactional affection and its crucial role in forming and maintaining long-term relationships is likely to further intensify the factions that already exist. For my Chinese interlocutors, in the context of hierarchical association, forming an attachment and deep affectionate bond with one may alienate the other.

The segmentation of overseas Chinese communities, particularly during Chinese migration to Southeast Asia, has long been documented by anthropologists. Most famously, Crissman (1967) describes how the traditional Southeast Asian Chinese communities segment based on lineage, common region of origin, dialect and surnames; at the same time, organizations are constituted to represent the segments. Together, Southeast Asian Chinese migrants have 'almost invariably set up a segmentary hierarchy of associations which organize their members into a hierarchy of inclusion' (Benton and Pieke 1998: 12). In this chapter, instead of taking the category 'Chinese community in Zambia' as granted, I focus on how groups are formed through interaction. By no means have I argued that there is a 'Chinese community'; rather, the Chinese migrants in Zambia are living in factions.

Perhaps the difference – between the *segmentation* model based on Southeast Asian communities and *factions* found among Chinese migrants in Zambia – comes with various perspectives of analysis. Still, there are two contextual reasons worthy of note. First, as I have mentioned in the Introduction, most of my private entrepreneur interlocutors moved to Zambia because they did not like the political games or '*guanxi*' games played between businessmen and officials in China. In a way, they emigrate for 'business autonomy'. Therefore, there is a brought-in internal disjunction between Chinese migrants coming to Zambia as private entrepreneurs and those who are short-term government representatives. Second, to survive and strive in Zambia, sometimes connecting with Chinese officials becomes inevitable as the Chinese government has easy access to political and economic resources. Comparatively, the current Chinese migrants to Zambia are under stronger supervision by Chinese government than those moving to Southeast Asia mostly in the era of Republican China.

This centralization of power and inevitable dependence diminishes the growth of self-organized association yet encourages internal competition and faction. To put this differently, it is the competition (between individuals) for 'love' (from the hierarchal top) that reinforces the faction – a point I turn to in the next chapter.

3

Emotional labour

Leadership, dependency and everyday work relations

It was 10.00 pm and the last truck was driving into the farm compound bringing Zambian workers from another construction site as Liu Wei (a young Chinese administrator) and I were chatting in my room. Suddenly, the quietness of the Lusaka suburban night was broken by the heavy steps of workers jumping out of the truck and the high-pitched metal clatter as they put their tools away.

'Good night, Boss!'
'7 hours tomorrow, no late!'

I heard this short exchange through my window. About ten minutes later, someone knocked at my door. It was Lenny – standing outside my door looking absolutely exhausted. Mud and dirt covered most of his red uniform. Lenny was the first Zambian worker whom I became acquainted with after I arrived at the Demonstration Centre. At that time, as noted, the main administrative building of the farm had not been finished so we, ATDC tutors and I, shared accommodation with the Chinese construction team for three months. Then Lenny was recruited as a general worker by the construction team. I consider it inaccurate to label Lenny as a worker due to his different background from other Zambian workers on the site. Lenny was only eighteen years old and had just finished high school in the summer of 2011. Having already applied to the law programme in the UNZA, Lenny thought it would be good to find a summer vacation job and save some money for his future university life so that he would not have to request money from his father, who had retired as a professor from UNZA a couple of years before and was now managing the family farm. Knowing Lenny's age and educational background, the general manager of the construction team took a liking to him and so allocated him only some gardening work and put him under the supervision of Liu Wei. Both being young, Liu Wei and Lenny quickly became close, more friends at work than boss and worker. Their relationship quickly started to annoy the general manager, however, as he thought that this 'inappropriate' relationship provided Lenny with excuses for being lazy at work; more importantly, it had set up a bad example for other Zambian workers to follow. The general manager was concerned that if the close relationship continued, other Zambian workers might be infected with a 'lack of organization and discipline (*wuzuzhi wujilv*)'. After warning them about this twice, one day when he saw Lenny hanging around in Liu Wei's room instead of cutting the grass, the general manager could no longer contain his anger and, on the second day, Lenny was sent to do heavy labour on another construction site in town. It was that night when Lenny knocked at my door.

'Good evening, Dr Di. I heard David (Liu Wei's English name) was in your room?' Lenny sounded huskier than normal.

'Yes, do come in please. Can I get you some water?'

'I am OK, thanks. I came here to see David.'

Liu Wei stopped playing with my laptop and turned around when he heard Lenny was there to see him.

'Oh, how was your first day [working in town]?' Liu Wei asked Lenny.

'Why do you ask? You know it's tough. I do not think I can do it anymore.'

'You shouldn't have argued with the general manager.'

'What do you mean? If the boss is wrong, I shall let the boss know. Right?' Lenny asked.

'No, the boss can never be wrong! Just do whatever the boss tells you to do then you will be fine.'

'Perhaps that is so in China; but in Zambia, if the boss is wrong, everyone can advise him.' Lenny paused for a few seconds. 'So, this [being sent to do heavy labour] is my punishment!' It seemed that Lenny suddenly realized the rationale that Liu Wei was trying to imply. 'What should I do? I do not think I can do another day of this work. It is very hard. Can you ask the big boss to bring me back?'

'No! You can ask him if you want: not me!' Liu Wei firmly refused.

'But you are my boss. A boss should take care of his workers and help them when they are in trouble, just like a family. I cannot ask the big boss [i.e. the general manager] as he is your boss, not mine. I can only ask my boss.'

'Sorry, I cannot do it for you. I do not want to upset the boss. In China, workers try not to cause the boss any trouble and they cannot challenge his authority.'

'This is Zambia. You should learn the Zambian way.'

'But you work for the Chinese! You should learn the Chinese way.'

'What can I do? I cannot do this job. It is too tough.'

'Well, you do not need to. I would quit if I were you. Think about it tonight.'

Liu Wei accompanied Lenny to the main farm gate and saw him off. When he came back, Liu Wei looked rather sad. He sighed and told me.

> Sometimes, I really pity them [i.e. the Zambian workers] and feel bad when I cannot help – but really, there is nothing I can do. Even if I spoke to the leader, he would not listen anyway. Besides, I still want to work here! I do not want to upset our leader and get fired just because of protecting them [i.e. Zambians]. You know, I still have family back in China who rely on me.

Then Liu Wei sighed again. That was the last night when I saw Lenny in the farm compound. He did not come back after work on the second morning. Months after the construction company moved out of the farm, I encountered Lenny at the UNZA campus. In our brief conversation, I found out that he never took another job after that night but went back home to help his father on the family farm.

Introduction

During my fieldwork, complicated situations of the kind outlined earlier often took place between Chinese bosses and Zambian workers. Stepping back from my own ethnographic observations, it is obviously the case that labour issues involving Chinese enterprises in Africa – at a more macro level – have repeatedly come under the spotlight of Western media and scholars (Wang and Flam 2007; Utomi 2008; Baah and Jauch 2009; Lee 2009; Moumouni 2010; Dittgen 2010; Giese 2013, 2014; Arsene 2014; Men 2014). The published media reports about this are overwhelmingly negative in tone – referring to China's extraction of African resources, exploitation of African labour and corruption and violation of African and international law (e.g. see Human Rights Watch 2011). But the generalizations about 'China-in-Africa' are, perhaps, too 'morally right' to be entirely true. As the sociologist Ching Kwan Lee argues, 'the rhetoric of Chinese colonialism … reveals little about the varied capacities, interests and constraints of the foot-soldiers of Chinese projects on the ground' in Africa (2009: 665). Aiming for a more balanced analysis, especially in relation to 'the politics of casualization' in Chinese businesses in Africa, she compares the labour tensions and strikes at a Chinese mining enterprise in Zambia and a Chinese textile company in Tanzania. Then, she reaches the conclusion that the reason why Zambians successfully halt the tendency towards casualization, whereas this does not happen in the Tanzanian case, is mainly due to the local history of socialism and unionism. Then she further claims that labour relations at Chinese businesses in Africa should be understood in relation to the nature of the business and to the 'varied collective histories and power' in different settings (665). Given the thrust of my own project, I obviously support her call for historical specificity and micro-analysis when thinking about China in Africa. Still, her paper on casualization leaves me wanting to know more about the dynamics of everyday negotiations, arguments and compromise at a relatively mundane level. For sure, the structural analysis that Ching Kwan Lee applies can provide convincing rationale of the political-economic reasons behind social behaviours and relationships. Nonetheless, it does not really capture the laughter, tears, genuine affection and anger that I witnessed every day in the workplace, as well as the desires and the motivations of the workers and the bosses. Crude or not, I argue that it is exactly this affective component of relationships at work that causes the misunderstanding and miscommunication that accumulate and intensify into labour conflicts and in turn effect production. In other words, starting out from the level of everyday one-to-one interactions, I intend to supplement the structural analysis with vivid ethnographic stories.

My perspective in this chapter draws mostly on two theoretical sources. One is James Ferguson's article 'Declarations of Dependence' (2013). In this paper, he challenges the value that has been given to 'autonomy' in the liberal tradition – in part because of its association with moral critiques of slavery and 'dependency'. Having reviewed the previous ethnography of Southern Africa, he encourages scholars to think of dependency as a form of membership and as a way of offering people life choices through social inclusion instead of as mere exploitation and absolute inequality. As he writes;

> It seems that for poor South Africans (as for a great many other people in the contemporary world) it is not dependence but its absence that is really terrifying – the severing of the thread, and the fall into the social void (232). ... the sort of employment for black men in South Africa that is nowadays nostalgically longed for was hardly ever a vehicle for independence. On the contrary, it constituted precisely a form of dependence, albeit a highly valued kind of dependence that brought with it a kind of unequal incorporation that I have termed 'work membership'. Men's desire for employment of this kind cannot be figured as a yearning for autonomy; it is on the contrary precisely a desire for attachment (italics added) – for incorporation, even under highly unequal and often dangerous and humiliating terms, into a social body. (235)

This emphasis on workers' desires and interpersonal attachments, which mirrors my own interests, is another reason why I find Ching Kwan Lee's structural analysis a little bit unsatisfactory. Reading across her published papers in recent years, it seems that casualization, which Lee takes as equivalent to informalization (2009: 648), entails negative moral connotations even though she never makes this claim explicit. For Lee, casualization or informalization represents inevitable exploitation and needs to be abolished. Labour relations should be based on equal rights and constrained by formal legal frames. By contrast, in my impression of work relations in Zambia, sometimes informalization is workers' intentional choice as it allows them greater flexibility; moreover, in the Chinese bosses' eyes, rigid rules or contracts leave no room for *jiaoqing* (interactional affection) to be played out and may potentially damage sociality, as I have demonstrated in the previous chapter. For both parties, morality at work that bonds the boss and the worker is more important in the end than rigid labour laws. Therefore, I consider that interpreting merely from the perspective of structure could potentially lose sight of everyday intersubjective and informal interactions at work.

Aiming to investigate the affective dimensions of work relations and production, another theory that I draw upon in this chapter is that surrounding 'emotional labour'. Arlie Hochschild (1983) first proposed this concept to study the service industry. By emotional labour, she means

> the management of feeling to create a publicly observable facial and bodily display; emotional labour is sold for a wage and therefore has exchange value … this labour requires one to induce or suppress feeling in order to sustain the outward countenance that produces the proper state of mind in others – in this case, the sense of being cared for in a convivial and safe place. (7)

Despite the original definition being restricted to emotional performance as part of a wage transaction – for example, flight attendants are paid to show attentiveness to customers regardless of their inner feelings – I consider that 'emotional labour' could be interpreted more broadly and could be applied to any form of work relations especially in the post-industrial era. Arguably, to some extent, any work can contain a certain amount of service (or performance). At my field site, although the emotion is not directly sold for a wage, the affective performance is still required due to highly moralized and often informal relationships at work. Chinese leaders on the farm as well as in the construction company not only require efficient work output but also demand proper affective performance. By contrast, in the Zambian context, farmer workers predominantly expect their Zambian bosses to perform care in exchange for their loyalty and support.

To draw on these two theoretical sources, in this chapter I would like to investigate the hierarchical dependent relationship at Chinese workplaces in Zambia. I suggest that boss–worker relationships depend on a cultural schema, ideal as well as practical, that both Chinese and Zambians use to comprehend, negotiate and practice every day when they encounter each other. As Max Bolt correctly points out in his recent review of Ferguson's article, 'dependencies work differently and mean different things … subordination and protection between a white farmer and a black labourer are not the same as between a black mine foreman and black mineworkers' (2013: 243). The various meanings of dependency cannot be better demonstrated than in the misunderstandings that occurred at work every day at my field sites – Chinese in Zambia have a different notion of boss–worker dependency compared with the one based on Zambian moral ideals and ethical practices. Such difference is manifested in daily negotiation and struggles at work. It can be plausible to argue that this misunderstanding is caused by different forms of dependency across social groups; notwithstanding, in my opinion, the everyday misunderstanding at work is more significantly due to the mismatch of the affective component bundled in the structure.

In the specific case in my field site, this mismatch appears as the conflictive direction of attentiveness between boss and worker. To put it simply: the attentiveness usually goes up from the worker to the leader in Chinese workplaces, while the attentiveness usually goes down from the boss to the worker in the Zambian context. If it is correct to say that dependency is a form of patron–client relationship, a vertical dyadic alliance, this alliance should at least contain two parties and be constituted with the exchange of different kinds of benefits, tangible and intangible, and 'involve the direct personal attachment of two individuals to each other' (Schmidt et al., 1977: 20, italics added). This attachment, I argue, contains a direction of attentiveness required in practice. In this dyadic alliance, attentiveness is, perhaps sometimes in a form of service, subject to exchange for other kinds of benefits. It can function as an offer and demonstrate personal intention and willingness. Therefore, in this way, attentiveness has a timescale and can be asymmetrical. In Chinese workplaces, the vertical patron–client relationship requires an upward attentiveness performed first by the worker in exchange for extra welfare and job promotion in the future, so the focus of dependency lies on the top; whereas, on the Zambian farms, the attentiveness goes down in exchange for mass support, loyalty and authority, and the focus lies at the bottom. It is this mismatch of asymmetrical attentiveness that produces some of the most important misunderstandings within Chinese enterprises in Zambia.

To follow this line of thinking, in this chapter, after introducing more context of my field sites, I will first concentrate on describing how attentiveness is required and performed every day at work based on the comparison of how the leader (in the Chinese case) or boss (in the Zambian case) understands the work relationship. Then, I will further demonstrate the direction of attentiveness in a dependent relationship from two angles: respectively, the independence of workers and task-sharing between leader and worker. In the Conclusion, based on my comparison of the cases presented in this chapter with the ones that I described in the last chapter (i.e. about the relationships between Chinese private entrepreneurs), I would like to put forward an analytical notion, 'the spirit of structure', in order to highlight the significance of emotion in everyday production and work-related interaction. If the previous two chapters are dedicated to understanding the reluctance of Chinese migrants to interact with their Zambian hosts, this chapter goes one step further to document how Chinese-Zambian communication is further hindered by the effect of affection even when interaction becomes inevitable at work.

One educational farm and one construction team

Although I spent the second half of my fieldwork primarily with the Zou family in Zambia, the descriptions of work relations in this chapter will predominately be about ATDC and the Chinese construction company that built this farm. This also enables me to show the significant impact of the *danwei* ('work unit') institution on the practice of attentiveness in Chinese workplaces.

ATDC is a cooperative project between UNZA and Jilin Agricultural University. As I have already discussed the background to this project in the Introduction, here I would like only to point out one distinctive characteristic of this farm. In China, universities are classified as *shiye danwei* (non-production work units). This is a historical residue of the communist planned economy, and has long been subject to reform since China started to liberalize the market (Lu and Perry 1997). Although these organizations are non-profit and are established for public services, such as education, medicine, media, such 'non-production work-units' are very different from normal NGOs in the Western concept because they are directly funded by the Chinese government; yet they are distinctive from Chinese private companies, as they are legally prevented from generating profits despite the practice of many 'non-production work-units' having affiliated companies for business purposes.

As Lu and Perry (1997) have summarized, the *danwei* (work unit), as a rather unique social institution of China, has several distinctive characteristics: (1) It is managed according to a national administrative ranking system; that is, staff are assigned by higher authorities and have governmental titles; they enjoy particular privileges and treatment according to corresponding administrative hierarchies; (2) The employees in the work units are controlled by management of their dossiers (*dang'an*); therefore, the mobility of the workers is limited and top level officials usually have the final say on promotion and job transfer; (3) The more general social function of the *danwei* is to 'lighten the state's burden of social welfare and entitlement provisions' (1997: 9). Medical insurance and public housing are typically provided by the work units. Consequently, 'members become dependent on the unit for both political and economic resources' (11). These characteristics of the *danwei*, I believe, are particular institutional reasons that influence the practice of attentiveness in the Chinese workplaces I describe.

The construction team that built the farm is from a private Chinese construction company; however, it used to be a state-owned (provincial level) company a couple of years ago before Chinese state-enterprise reform. In China, state-owned companies share similar administrative characteristics with non-production work units but aim for financial profits. Even though this construction company had been privatized for decades, during my stay with them, I had a strong impression that there was a continuity of *danwei* (work unit) management style within the company.

At the beginning of my fieldwork, ATDC was towards the end of its construction. Therefore, the tutors had to share accommodation with the staff of the construction company before the main farm building was completed. This offered me a great opportunity to observe and compare two distinctive organizations for three months. Even though one is a non-profitable farm with the focus on agricultural technology demonstration and education and the other is a private enterprise with the purpose to achieve financial gains, the similarity in practical management overtakes the differences. By comparison with other ethnographies of Chinese workplaces after the Cultural Revolution (Walder 1986; Rofel 1999; Fang 2012), I regard this similarity as due to the social continuity of the Chinese *danwei* (work unit) system and to some extent, this continuity is re-triggered and amplified by the contexts of my field sites: that is, strong mistrust of others, resulting in closed communications with strangers, firm control of workers and distribution of welfare by the Chinese companies.

First, the organization/company arranges Chinese workers' overall welfare in Zambia. Accommodation and food are free so workers live in the same compound and eat together every day in the dining hall. Entertainment is provided, which usually includes table tennis and basketball courts for physical exercise, mah-jong and poker for after-work social games, and sometimes karaoke. Salaries are paid directly to workers' bank accounts back in China and taken care of by their families. A small allowance (normally less than US$50) is distributed to workers every month. Now and then, a group day trip is organized on public holidays. Second, as most of their daily needs are provided by work and since the majority of the Chinese workers cannot speak either English or a local language, workers tend to stay in the compound. Even if the younger workers (those who can speak English) like going out, they are subject to the strict control of the leader. If anyone wants to leave the compound, s/he needs permission from the managerial team, and usually the permission is given with a time limit. If s/he needs to stay out longer, the worker has to phone the leader for further permission. By contrast, Chinese managers enjoy no such physical control over such matters as there is no directly superior Chinese official present in Zambia. Third, welfare and priority at work correspond with administrative hierarchy.

The hierarchy is not just on paper or in one's job title but very much a lived daily experience. It can be demonstrated in accommodation arrangements, dining position allocations and work task assignment. A worker relatively high in the hierarchy can have priority to live in an en-suite room facing the sun instead of sharing with other workmates and can sit close to the leader while dining. This hierarchy at work is drawn not only according to formal governmental regulations but also through informal relationships. It is drawn according to mixed criteria of age, locality, education and closeness of personal relationships to the leader. Distribution, awards and promotion are mostly at leaders' discretion. Consequently, both organizations have strong informal social networks within formal work relations. Favouritism is widely exercised at work. Regarding the strict control by the leader, both over daily socialization with the outside and welfare allocation, and the great discretion of the leader, a dependency is reinforced and attentiveness to the top is required and performed by the workers in order to become the leader's 'personal favourite' and so enjoy extra privilege and benefits at work.

Direction of attentiveness I: The Zambian case

Although I was always interested in the criteria of being a 'good boss' during my fieldwork, it was Mr Mbozi who pointed to me the significance of attentiveness in the workplace. This happened halfway through my fieldwork. It was one evening after work when Mr Mbozi came to the farm to see Manager Bao after hearing that the newly recruited Zambian workers (seven in total) had quit their jobs again. A similar thing had happened three times in the past five months. The workers not only complained about the toughness of the tasks, the low pay and the long hours of the job but, more importantly, were also not satisfied with Manager Bao's attitude. The workers told Mr Mbozi that Manager Bao did not care about them at all especially when they needed his help. After acknowledging the reason, Mr Mbozi considered it necessary to share some of his experience as a boss with Manager Bao before the situation became worse. Mr Mbozi was worried that if Manager Bao continued using his Chinese management style, no more local men would be willing to work for the educational farm. It would be very bad because it would not only effect the daily operation of the farm but also damage Manager Bao's reputation and authority. Mr Mbozi told Manager Bao that in Zambia a boss needs to treat the 'boys' (this was how he himself referred to the farm workers) like his own children and to help the boys at work as well as in their lives. Only when the boss helps solve workers' troubles at home and keeps them happy will they can stay without worries and work hard on the farm. Manager Bao listened and smiled, but after Mr Mbozi left, he said to me that Zambians knew nothing about '*zhongguoguoqing*': this literally means 'Chinese circumstances', but note that the last character *qing* also means 'emotions'. This term is normally applied in China when the speaker justifies why the interlocutor's utterance should be ignored based on the simple reason that the interlocutor does not know anything about Chinese culture or the Chinese context, and therefore his comments are irrelevant.

Mr Mbozi is the general manager of the UNZA farm. He was born near Livingston and was sent to Czechoslovakia by the Zambian government for a master's degree in agricultural science. After his graduation, he returned to Zambia and took charge of the UNZA farm. There are roughly three hundred workers on his farm. As the educational farm was built on a piece of wasteland belonging to the UNZA farm, Mr Mbozi was assigned as the Zambian manager for this project. Nevertheless, he has never been called on by Manager Bao other than to deal with some emergency or any issues with local administration. However, in the Zambian workers' eyes, Mr Mbozi is truly a good boss, and his kindness has certainly earned him a very good reputation in the local community in eastern Lusaka. Many workers want to work for him. When I asked thirty-six Zambian workers why they thought Mr Mbozi a good boss, several common traits came up. They said Mr Mbozi was kind and generous and was always willing to help the workers. He loaned money to workers and helped them to build houses. He drove the workers' children to clinics. He bought workers beers after work. Also, he gave good advice to his workers and listened to workers' advice when he made mistakes. They said Mr Mbozi was reliable and like a father to them. These traits corresponded to the answers I obtained from interviews when I asked, 'What is a good boss in general?'

Mr Mbozi's ideas are shared among other bosses I talked with near the educational farm. Lindsey is the owner of a small banana farm less than a kilometre away from the centre. Born in Lusaka and having worked for British Airways as a flight attendant when she was young, Lindsey retired to a small farm with her mother and daughter. Apart from bananas, she also grew flowers and raised chickens for sale to generate extra income. There were around twenty workers on Lindsey's farm. Now and then, I went to her farm to buy bananas as well as to chat. Once, after I saw how she taught a worker to deal with customers and keep sales records, we started to talk about her farm workers. She told me that one of her boys was leaving her farm soon to work in a tobacco farm managed by a white Zimbabwean. Lindsey had recommended this. Even though the worker was a little bit reluctant to leave, Lindsey thought it was necessary. She told me that the worker would benefit more from working for the white farmers. He would not get paid as much but would learn many modern managerial skills that she could not offer. She said it would be good for her boy's future career. As a boss, she needed to be responsible for her workers and help them to achieve things in their lives although sometimes it means that they had to leave her farm.

From these statements, it is not hard to summarize the following: (1) the notion of family is often invoked to describe the relationship between boss and workers rather than formal managerial terminology; (2) to be a good boss is to be responsible for workers – not only at work but also with domestic issues – helping workers with trouble in their lives and advising them on life options; and (3) a good boss takes care of his or her workers and is always attentive to workers' needs. In return, loyalty is repaid and stable working relationships are sustained to the satisfaction of the worker. It is a result of long-term negotiation and reciprocity. By demonstrating one is a good boss through being attentive to the needs of one's followers, one would be able to attract more followers, to build up one's local authority and personal influence, and, more importantly, to prevent potential conflicts and distraction in the production process. Therefore, in this context, the boss and farm workers depend on each other – the former needs the workers' support for fruitful production, while the latter needs the boss for everyday welfare. Notwithstanding, this dependency has a focus at the bottom and the direction of attentiveness goes from the boss to the farm worker.

Similarly, while studying Chinese-Ghanaian employment relationships, Karsten Giese and Alena Thiel also document this moral practice of 'good boss' in the social context of Ghana. They point out that for the Ghanaians, the employer's role is often defined as 'benefactor, guardian and protector', and

> Ghanaian employers are highly appreciated for their availability to employees for personal advice and assistance in cases of financial emergencies. In that sense, employers assume the role of elders, figures of respect and wisdom. Youth employment, in this light, is widely recognized as a way to give a person a chance to progress in life beyond the mere material dimension. (2014: 1106)

Direction of attentiveness II: The Chinese case

The dependency implied within hierarchical relations in China has also been well documented by sinologists (Solinger 1995; Shaw 1996; Rofel

1999; Fang 2012). Among others, while studying leadership and culture of authority in post-revolutionary Chinese *danwei* (work unit), Andrew Walder argues that the reward system under communist regime creates an 'organized dependency' between the leader and the subordinate.

> The politicization of reward system had unintended consequences, however. In making workers' livelihoods highly dependent on the personal political evaluations of their superiors, politicization created strong material incentives for workers to develop calculative strategies for exhibiting the proper loyalty in front of their superiors. ... More importantly, the ability of superiors to reward employees flexibly, according to subjective evaluations, has provided fertile ground for the growth of pervasive networks of informal social tires based on personal loyalties. (1983: 52)

This system, as Walder summarizes, emphasized flexibility, discretion and subjectivity, and was reinforced by the lack of employment alternatives in the post-revolution era. These characteristics of the reward system produce certain behaviours at work. According to Walder, '*Biaoxian*' (performing) is an important tactic developed by Chinese subordinates to secure job promotion in competitive workplaces. *Biaoxian* not only shows one's political thoughts but also 'refers to a realm of individual qualities broader than one's political attitudes' (62). 'In practice, employees who are unfailingly helpful, cooperative, and courteous in dealing with their supervisors make a more favourable impression on them, and tend to receive better evaluations. ... In fact, it is the former [subordinates] who are more helpful to the supervisors on a daily basis, who make their jobs easier' (63). Although Walder never formally made the emotional component of this dependent relationship explicit, I consider that *biaoxian* already connotes a direction of attentiveness; that is, in order to secure individual welfare at the flexible discretion of the leader in competitive workplaces, the subordinate needs to demonstrate loyalty by showing/performing personal affective attachment to the leader. Therefore, this attentiveness has an upwards direction.

Not only in *danwei* (work unit) is this type of dependency constructed, but there is a strong patron–client network formed in the Wenzhou migrants' enclave in Beijing, as Li Zhang has also discovered. Among the migrants, the leader mobilizes extended-kinship networks and invokes fictive kinship relationships to consolidate his or her power. On the other hand, the migrants' leader acts as a middleman to mediate the relation between migrants and local officials. Among the interviews that Zhang carried out with migrants' leaders, one particular paragraph caught my eye:

> He [one of her informants, Boss Jin] believed that a good *guanxi* relationship needed constant cultivation and care, and he did his best to maintain good personal ties with officialdom. He once made an analogy between making *guanxi* with officials and establishing a relationship with a deity: one cannot expect to get help from the Buddha if one does not go to burn incense and show devotion on a regular basis. (2001: 81)

Strikingly, similar idioms are cited by my Chinese interlocutors in Zambia. Here, it is important to point out that by emphasizing the direction of attentiveness in a patron–client relationship, I do not mean it is only a one-way system. On the contrary, I argue that the care, although often appearing in different forms, is exchanged and goes in two directions. Surely, Chinese leaders have great responsibilities to look after the workers; nevertheless, it is the worker who needs to be attentive first and constantly in order to stand out from the workforce and to exchange attention for favourable distribution of welfare and job promotion in the future. Therefore, this attentiveness has a temporal dimension and the long-term accumulative effect (in the Chinese case) is upwards in direction.

Social continuity or not, this kind of dependent relationship did appear at my field sites – a migrants' *danwei* (work unit) enclave – between Chinese leaders and Chinese workers. As I briefly introduced earlier, the workplaces at my field are hierarchical. Workers enjoy welfare but are subject to the discretionary power of the leader. They are also under strict daily control. Obvious favouritism is widely applied, as a matter of routine, and work relations are highly personalized. There is little more to add regarding these shared characteristics; instead, in the following sections, I would like to give some ethnographic accounts from two facets to demonstrate the direction of attentiveness within this dependency. Along each point, I will also insert some relevant descriptions of daily struggles between Chinese boss and Zambian workers. To me, everyday misunderstandings at work provide an ideal case to prove the significance of the direction of attentiveness in dependent relationships.

To serve the leader

'To serve the leader' (*weilingdaofuwu*) is an ironic twist on the old communist slogan, 'to serve the people', which was used in Mao's era. 'To serve the people' is still used as a linguistic ritual in China today, especially on anniversary military parades in Tiananmen Square. At my field sites, the twisted version is often used by the Chinese workers to, first, mock the gap between the communist party slogan and social reality and, second, to express daily frustrations at work – 'unlike in the early days of communist China, when the people were the centre of political gravity, nowadays leaders are the true centre', Barry (a Chinese translator for the construction company) once explained to me.

To serve the leader requires workers being attentive to the leader's needs all the time and endeavouring to keep the leader pleased. It is not just about fulfilling the leader's requirements at work. More importantly, it includes assisting the leader with personal issues at and outside workplaces. These matters may include arranging accommodation and transportation, carrying suitcases, making tea, keeping the leaders company while shopping or banqueting, welcoming and entertaining the leader's family when they are visiting, and assisting the leader to deliver gifts during Chinese festivals. If it could be put more simply, to serve the leader is to look after the leader or to be the leader's 'valet'.

Keeping company, '*pei*' in Chinese, is a crucial means to show a worker's care towards to the leader. Usually workers show their attachment through gifts to the leader. Gifts go upwards and are normally tangible material goods such as clothes, alcohol, jewellery. In return, the workers can obtain intangible 'gifts' from the leader – favours. Gifts can be given at any time of the year, but normally during Chinese festivals or special events such as weddings or funerals. Nevertheless, gift-giving follows one rationale, that is, 'nobody is going to complain of too many gifts' (*liduorenbuguai*). All the same, considering that everyone can buy gifts, presenting gifts is relatively effortless; therefore, it is not sufficient to demonstrate one's 'having heart' (*youxin*: making effort/care) or 'sincerity' (*chengyi*). Consequently, showing one's attachment and affection to the leader in daily action becomes a touchstone since it requires long-term, constant performance. *Pei* becomes a popular strategic choice. As Barry once told me half-jokingly, 'To serve the leader good means three *pei* – *peichi* (keep company for eating), *peihe* (keep company for drinking), *peiliao* (keep company for chatting). Just adding one thing – *peishui* (keep company for sleeping) – I would be their [leaders'] mistress! Thank goodness I am not a girl.'

Pei as an effective service to the leader can also be extended to the leader's personal close contacts, such as friends or family. To be attentive to the leader's close contacts is considered equivalent to showing one's care to the leader himself/herself. This leads to one phenomenon in my field, which is borrowing (*jie*) workers. *Jie* is done through interpersonal relationship between the leaders. Workers normally do not have a say in such matters. Although it is extra work, they do not get paid for it. On the contrary, their routine work has to be delayed but still needs to be finished. As a result, this intertwined formal-informal work relationship makes Chinese workers occupied almost all the time. Indeed, 'busy' (*mang*) is the response I would hear every day when greeting other Chinese workers.

However, not everyone is needed to do these extra tasks. The leader only chooses the workers who s/he considers to be 'competent' and 'promising'. For the worker, carrying on some private matters for the leader may be a fast track to being promoted. Refusing such tasks, particularly without reasonable excuses, is considered as 'not being able to comprehend the leader's great expectation' (*bushitaiju*). To be judged as '*bushitaiju*' has serious consequences. Such worker will fall out of the leader's favourite group and gradually be ignored at work. Workers' attentive services to the leader are linked with the evaluation of workers' performance at work. The criteria of evaluation are very subjective. It is not enough if the worker just finishes the tasks required: the worker also has to make the leader pleased. This subjective evaluation leaves great uncertainty for worker's self-assessment of performance outcomes; meanwhile, this uncertainty renews the worker's desire to be more attentive to please the leader. This circuit could be very well illustrated through Barry's story.

Born in the mid-1980s to a peasant family in Northwestern China, Barry came to Zambia as a translator for the construction company. After having worked at the construction team for a year, Barry finally had a chance to accompany his leader on a week-long trip to South Africa. He was very excited when he was assigned; however, when he was back a week later, he looked rather sad.

'So how was your trip in South Africa? Was it good?', I went to see him in his room immediately when he was back.

'The city (Cape Town) is very good, clean and beautiful; much better than Lusaka. But the trip did not go well.' He replied with a quieter tone than usual. Sensing that he was not in the mood for talking, I left him alone with his unpacking. Only a few days later, I heard that his leaders were not satisfied with his 'work' while in South Africa and even yelled at him several times in public. Out of concern, I decided to pay Barry another visit. This time, he told me the whole story. The reason why his leaders were unhappy with him was that the hotel Barry booked did not successfully register the booking so that they had to change hotel. The leaders blamed Barry for not double-checking beforehand and not being diligent enough. Moreover, during the whole tour, the leaders thought that Barry enjoyed the scene too much himself but did not 'serve' the leaders properly. He only assisted the leaders when asked rather than taking initiative. Several times, his leaders had to ask him to take pictures or book dining tables for them. The leaders criticized him as 'not mature enough and not attentive enough' (*buchengshubuxixin*). Barry commented;

> I still need lots of hardening (*duanlian*: training). Sometimes, I am too careless – not attentive enough and let the leader bother (*caoxin*) too much. 'To accompany the emperor is like accompanying a tiger' (*banjunrubanhu*). These things happen. It [being yelled at] is good. I actually learned a lot from this trip. Next time, I would pay much more attention and perform better.

As Barry's case has shown, a Chinese leader expects the workers to be versatile, multitasking and attentive to take on any matter that the leader needs to get done. This idea of work and working relationships is different from the one Zambian workers hold. This conflict appears in daily negotiations of job descriptions. Being attentive does not mean there is no division among the Chinese workers based on occupation. Nevertheless, when it comes to the work that everyone is able to do (*lisuonengji*), such as cleaning, the division of occupation blurs since Chinese workers are ready to carry out various tasks to keep the leader pleased. By contrast, the Zambian workers place more emphasis on the division of occupation. Therefore, the negotiation between Chinese leaders and Zambian workers over job descriptions is always about what tasks and duties come with a certain type of job. For example, the Zambian workers would refuse to sweep the ground if they were hired as chauffeur. They would refuse to carry tables and chairs for a conference if they were employed as security guards. For the Chinese boss, sweeping the ground or carrying tables are tasks everyone should be able to do (*lisuonengji*) and shall do; for the Zambian workers, these tasks are not within their job description so they have no responsibility for them. Refusal to take on '*lisuonengji*' tasks is regarded by Chinese bosses as challenging authority and very upsetting; and being forced to do a task outside one's job description is considered by Zambian workers as downgrading one's social status and being used as a slave.

Consequently, every day the task allocation is questioned. The general pattern of the arguments is normally as follows:

> Zambian worker: This is not my job. I am a [profession]. If you want this work done, you should hire [profession] to do it. I am not a general worker.
>
> Chinese boss: It is not hard work. Everyone should be able to do it. You are a worker. You should do what the manager asks you to do.

As a result, argument by argument, Chinese bosses have learned a strategy: that is, when employing new workers, everyone is labelled as 'general worker' in the contract. Gradually, there is no gardener, no driver and no cleaner, but only general worker. Ironically, the general worker earns the lowest pay among all occupations. Indeed, in this case, for Chinese bosses, workers earn more rewards because they are attentive and versatile at work, but for Zambian workers, they should earn more rewards because of their occupation.

Don't give the leader extra trouble

If the desire 'to serve the leader' focuses on the active attentiveness that the workers pursue every day at work in order to stand out from the competitive crowd, the advice 'don't give the leader extra trouble' stresses the passive side of worker's behaviour. The first time I witnessed the leader's attitude towards the problem of extra trouble (*luan/mafan*) was when we were welcoming a Chinese delegation at Lusaka International Airport. Members of Chinese delegations are normally from a higher administrative ranking than the Chinese leaders in Zambia, so being attentive suddenly becomes the leaders' main task. It is usually the busiest time for the leader as they need to carefully design the itinerary according to the personal preferences of their leader (the delegation's highest ranking official) and liaise with many Chinese companies in Zambia to arrange accommodation, meals, party venues, transport, day trips, entertainment and so on. Preparation to host a delegation can sometimes take months. During the whole process, other routine work is inevitably delayed. A subtle and smooth welcome can demonstrate the leader's management ability and his attentiveness to his leader. The main principle is to make the whole arrival procedure run as smoothly and quickly as possible to cause less trouble for the delegation.

Manager Bao, as the main leader of the educational farm, took charge of the welcoming. Having chosen his favourite workers, Bao arrived at the airport three hours in advance. He asked the translator Xiao Liu to negotiate with airport security so that they could drive the car into the landing field so the delegation would not have to queue to go through immigration control. The initial negotiation failed due to a recently published airport security control policy. Nevertheless, as they had succeeded before, Bao blamed Xiao Liu for not explaining the situation to the airport security clearly enough and insisted Xiao Liu should try again. 'Tell them, this time big leaders are coming! (*dalindao*)', Bao stressed. After another half hour of negotiation, Bao lost patience and changed his plan. He went to the arrival lobby and attempted to go past the immigration control onto the landing field himself so he could assist the delegation personally when they exited the airport. After another long negotiation, Bao got through this time. By talking with the immigration officers, Bao persuaded them to open the fast track usually reserved for diplomats even though the delegation members were not qualified as diplomats. So far so good.

Once the plane landed, Bao immediately sent Xiao Liu to collect the delegation's luggage. Without waiting in the long queue, the delegation took the diplomatic track and quickly passed the immigration control. By the time they arrived at the luggage zone, Xiao Liu had already collected most of the luggage. While waiting for the rest, Bao explained his initial plan for welcoming the delegation by car in the landing field and asked the delegation for forgiveness that they would have to drag their own luggage about ten metres to the airport exit where the car was already waiting. All went through the checkpoint very fast with no problem until it came to the last member of the delegation, the deputy party secretary of the provincial education ministry.

'Sir, please take your luggage there for a customs check', a young Zambian officer pointed to a luggage checking platform. The deputy party secretary looked confused and I explained to him that it was a random luggage check.

'There is nothing to check', the secretary told the customs officers in Chinese while they were going through his luggage. Then they pointed to some boxes in the luggage and asked, 'What is inside these boxes?'

'Nothing!'

'Sorry, we need to open these boxes and check.' Seeing the officers start to unpack the boxes, the secretary became upset. He turned to me and said,

> 'Tell them, these are the gifts for their national leaders! The Vice-president! If they break anything, can they take responsibility?' Noticing that the officers had not stopped the search, the secretary began to accuse them,

> 'Tell them, I am a leader! I am here to aid Africans. If they keep causing trouble like this, even in such a small matter, who on earth will help them in future!'

I did not translate this sentence in the end partly because I was shocked by such an explicit statement and by the leader's very own awareness of the privileges coming with his title. For the secretary, it seems that being a leader has the right of priority and the priority comes with the leader's own will with smooth conditions of fulfilment created (*chuangzaotiaojian*) by the subordinates. As the secretary commented in the end, rather irritated, 'this thing would have never happened in China!'

'Don't cause trouble for the leader', expressed as *butianluan* in Chinese, is the other side of the same coin of 'care for the leader'. It may contain two aspects: avoid causing unnecessary trouble to the leader and show self-discipline (*zilu*) and independence (*zili*), respectively. The implicit rationale as some workers explained to me is that the leader is already busy enough and should focus on grand matters (*dashi*) at work instead of solving workers' personal problems. Workers therefore are supposed to take care of themselves and to make the leader's work as smooth as possible. The function of the leader is to make crucial decisions and corresponding orders, while the function of the worker is to succeed in reaching their target without bothering the leader too much.

As argued earlier, in work relations, Zambian workers expect the boss to take care of them, at work as well as at home. This understanding is not very compatible with the Chinese emphasis on self-discipline and independence. In practice, the Zambian workers did seek daily help from the Chinese bosses when they were in trouble. They would ask for salt or sugar if they were short for cooking lunch. They would ask for washing liquid and gloves if the boss asked them to clean up. They would ask the Chinese boss to arrange a car to drive them back home if their bicycle was broken. They would ask for a loan from the boss if they needed money for lunch, a bicycle or home renovation. At the beginning, the boss did not mind helping, but, as time went on, he became rather annoyed, and frequently complained about the Zambian workers:

> They are just like spoiled children, so demanding and not independent at all! They ask for everything, even though their wage already covers it. They find you for every little 'sesame trouble' (*zhimadadeshi*). It is very annoying, just like a 'hassle-mother' (*shi'erma*: a female always causing trouble). I have so many important things to deal with. Who has the time and energy to deal with them all the time! Why can't they just take care of themselves?

To be independent and to avoid extra trouble for the leader does not mean that workers can make their own decisions at work. Making decisions is the demonstration of a leader's authority and power at work. It is also a form of control. In general, the Chinese workers are supposed to obey the manager's orders, report frequently on their work progress (*huibao*) to the manager and ask for instruction (*qingshi*) when a decision is needed. Failure to report or to ask for decisions may cause the manager's dissatisfaction and lead to the worker being criticized as '*shanzizuozhu*' (making decisions when one is not the position to). It is considered as bad self-discipline and disrespectful to the leader's authority. This is the criticism that Zambian workers usually suffer.

Thomas (who I introduced at the very start of the Introduction) was the driver for the educational farm. In his mid-thirties, he worked as a taxi driver in Lusaka for several years before being recruited by the farm manager. After having refused to take orders from the manager to clean the car, water the flowers or sweep the ground, Thomas was downgraded from driver to a general worker when the manager renewed his employment contract although driving remains his main task. Most arguments took place between Thomas and the manager when they were in the car. On three very extreme occasions, the manager even forced Thomas to stop while driving in the highway and gave him an angry lecture because Thomas made a decision without the manager's permission. Such decisions sometimes included a sudden detour to the petrol station while the manager was late for a business meeting or taking a new route that the manager was not familiar with when he was in a rush. For Thomas, these decisions may be with good intention, such as saving travelling time or avoiding accidents, but for the manager, they were unpredictable, might potentially ruin the whole plan and were not ones Thomas should have made. When I asked Thomas the reason for such actions, he told me,

> I am just trying to help. I have been a professional driver for twelve years. I know what I am doing. In a car, the driver should be the one in charge. You arrive safely at the place then it is fine. You Chinese are very difficult to communicate with. Always want me to do it the way you want. You never listen to advice. I am not stupid, you know. I think too.

As time went on, gradually the arguments became less and less. On one hand, the translator supplemented the manager's orders by adding extra information. For example, instead of merely translating the destination, the translator would also add extra sentences to make the order very explicit, such as 'no need for extra petrol' or 'use Great East Road'. On the other hand, Thomas was learning how to obey the orders. In my last discussion with Thomas before I finished my fieldwork, I asked him what he had learned from working for the Chinese. One point that he made rather clear was that 'Chinese are good as long as I do what the boss asks me to do'.

This reflection of work relations is not just limited to the Zambian workers. Quite a few Chinese workers, especially the young workers in my field, are very aware of their conditions, especially after observing how the Zambian workers respond to the Chinese leader. Many times I have heard complaints about the working relationship between Chinese leaders and Chinese workers. First of all, workers complain about tiredness. A senior Chinese worker once told me after we played ping-pong together:

> The work just seems endless. When you finish one task, another one comes in. Sometimes, one has to do lots of work at the same time. Plus, leaders are always in a hurry. Everything needs to be done very quickly. It is so frustrating, especially here [Zambia]; they [Zambian workers] work too slow. [Sigh] Nowadays, everyone is a *ye* [literally 'grandpa' or leader]. You can't offend anyone. So tiring!

Furthermore, lack of personal freedom is also a common topic when workers talk about their experiences at work. *Meiziyou* (no autonomy) and the requirement of *tinghua* (obedience) are the terms they frequently use. The workers complain of the strong interference of the leader over their work and life, and also advise me that it is better to be obedient and not to challenge the leader. Once a translator told me,

> Here [Zambia], they [the leaders] control everything and want to know everything. There is no freedom at all. One has to get permission even just to go out with friends for dinner or cinema! They [the leader] always say that this is for our [the workers] good and this is them being responsible. We all know it is just bullshit (*pihua*). But we have to listen. No one wants to upset the leader. As long as the leader is happy, everyone will be happy. Only obeying the leaders' words (*tinglingdaohua*) can keep one out of trouble. Just do whatever the leader asks you to do.

Although I heard many such complaints privately, I saw few Chinese workers speak straightforwardly and confront the leader, perhaps concerning their future career. Ironically, showing great attentiveness first to the leader so to get into his/her personal favourite circle can offer the workers a way out of the 'toughness' at work. Therefore, to some extent, attentiveness from workers to the leader at Chinese workplaces is not just exchange for welfare or job promotion; sometimes, it can simply be a tactic to avoid a heavy workload. To become the leader's personal favourite means one can fall into the leader's authority shadow, turn into a middleman and enjoy certain privileges in the competitive work environment.

Conclusion

Returning to the vignette I presented at the beginning of this chapter, how can one understand the negotiation and the trigger of negotiation between Liu Wei and Lenny? To recapitulate, Lenny was trying to claim his own rights at work by invoking local ethics and practices in boss–worker relations, such as 'a boss shall take care of his workers and help them when they are in trouble, just like a family'. In his defence, Liu Wei was concerned with the Chinese way of dealing with the leader–worker relationship, for example, 'workers shall try not to cause boss trouble and cannot challenge the boss'. From a purely objective point of view, one can easily unveil the exploitative nature of labour relations and argue that the cause of this vignette is the lack of legal protection for local workers at Chinese enterprises in Zambia. Nevertheless, as I have argued in this chapter, this approach would face the danger of losing insight of the impact of intersubjectivity and emotion played and performed in everyday work relations. One point is clear in the vignette – that is, neither Lenny nor Liu Wei was questioning the inequality or the exploitation between boss and worker at work. On the contrary, it is the ethics and informal work relationship that they are both concerned with and it is 'membership' that they desire – a form of membership that relies on mutual dependency filled with care. As a result, for them, the focus of negotiation is the issue of what form of dependency shall be applied on a Chinese farm in Zambia.

By broadly applying the concept of emotional labour, in this chapter, I have argued that it is the affective component bundled in dependency that causes the everyday misunderstanding and arguments between Zambian workers and Chinese bosses. In other words, the Zambians expect the Chinese bosses to take care of the workers (attentiveness goes down) but the Chinese bosses expect the workers to show great attentiveness towards them (attentiveness goes up). These conflictive expectations of affection not only trigger everyday disagreements but also haunt the sociality between Chinese and local Zambians. As I have elaborated earlier, even though young Chinese workers are willing to be friends with Zambian workers, this willingness to bond is inevitably hindered by the Chinese leaders' social expectations, their control and the competition for attentiveness with Zambian workers.

Nevertheless, as I mentioned at the beginning of this chapter, this direction of attentiveness is not exhaustive or exclusive. It is an accumulative inclination after long-term negotiation of work relations and subject to contextual variations. Between Zambian bosses and Zambian farm workers, attentiveness is morally expected to be performed by the boss in exchange for the worker's loyalty and personal reputation as well as stable and non-conflictive production. The attentiveness goes downward, I speculate, due to the political context of long-term unionization in Zambia so that the locus of power resides with workers. Meanwhile, in the case of Chinese leaders and Chinese workers, the context of this accumulative inclination is multifaceted. On one hand the *danwei* (work unit), as a socio-historical institution, provides a solid conceptual foundation for my Chinese interlocutors to practice dependency at work. However, as Yan documents, regarding the political power relations in Xiajia village, there has been a shift in the role of cadres following decollectivization and marketization in the PRC. As he points out,

> The reforms have eroded cadres' previous power and privilege by breaking their monopoly over resources and by creating new income opportunities that make the accumulation of personal wealth more attractive than the political rewards offered by the party state. Their political role in village society has also changed from that of the tyrannical 'local emperor' ruling the village as the agent of the party state to prudent middlemen who negotiate between the state and village society. For villagers, the reforms have ended their dependence on the collectives and the cadres who ran them, and have thereby to a great extent freed them from cadre domination. (2009: 50)

Clearly, Yan reasons that the absolute power of cadres over villagers before reform was fundamentally drawn from the fact that villagers had no alternative but to depend on cadres for the resources under their control. Bearing this change in mind, though, specifically at my field sites, this form of dependency is reinforced under the condition of Chinese leaders' strict control over Chinese workers' activities and welfare in Zambia. As my Chinese interlocutors repeatedly mentioned, they are longing to go back to China immediately after they finish their projects, as in China they enjoy more freedom.

This notwithstanding, although the direction of attentiveness may vary when the context changes, there is indeed a dimension of affection bundled with different forms of dependency. This impact of affection has been clearly demonstrated by John Osburg's ethnography on everyday socialization among elites in Chengdu, China. He describes the important function of courting favour (*goudui* in his informants' term) in gaining officials' trust. He contends that, against the inflation of material gifts and commodified pleasure, affections become crucial to attract the protection of officials. Subordinates need to 'employ techniques of entertaining, flattery, and gift giving to win the favour and affection of his superiors' (2013: 96). Instead of analysing how 'the market' is transforming the social life in China, Osburg intends to 'demonstrate how "marketization" in China is best understood as a process of embedding new economic structures and opportunities into existing and emergent social networks that straddle state and society'(28). Strikingly, there is great similarity between his ethnographic descriptions and my data. Therefore, it seems arguable that even after decades of economic reform in China the significance of affection embedded in any form of social relations (attentiveness at work in this chapter) is strengthened rather than diminishing.

Considering this significant impact of the affective component within dependency not only on everyday production but also on sociality formation, here I would like to propose that when studying social structures and institutions anthropologists should not omit the affective component. Here let me provisionally term this embedded affective component 'the spirit of structure'. By the spirit of structure, to emphasize again, I mean, the affective component bundled in social structures. This bundled affection needs to be performed according to social expectation. Broadly speaking, one could claim that every meaningful social representation includes certain social expectations of affects, and the social performances of these affects, although not necessarily to be capitalized in every case, certainly influence everyday social perception, decision and interaction. I will elaborate more on the embedded affective component in the next chapter in relation to everyday moral interaction and role performance. So far, I hope that in this chapter I have raised enough awareness, in presenting my field sites, of the significant role that affect plays in everyday interaction and production at work. I consider this perspective needs to be specially stressed following the arrival of the post-industrial (especially service-based) era and the boom of cross-cultural contacts and cooperation.

4

Ethical qualia

Role ethics and the moral transformation of young Chinese migrants

In the last three chapters, by introducing everyday interactions as I observed them in my field sites, I have been demonstrating the significant role that emotion plays in forming and sustaining social relations between Chinese migrants in Zambia. Furthermore, I have noted how emotion, specifically anxiety and suspicion, may serve to cut short the initial interactions between Chinese migrants and their Zambian hosts. In the previous chapter, I began to take an analytical turn to stress the embeddedness of emotion in the process of sociality and in the cultural practices of social relationships; more particularly, I examined how communication is hindered at work between Chinese leaders and Zambian workers in spite of their interactions being unavoidable. From this chapter onwards, I would like to zoom out my lens a little to look at general problems in the process of Chinese-Zambian interaction in relation to moral and linguistic communication. Theoretically, instead of merely focusing on *person-to-person* emotion, I will further concentrate on the *embeddedness* of emotion in lexicons, social roles and interactive situations. As I briefly mentioned in the Introduction, 'emotion' not only entails individual inner psychological states (e.g. fear) and empathy between people but may also be extended to a third dimension; that is, 'emotion'(or affect) is built into material and social objects and everyday situations. It constitutes the meaning of the symbol, influences the process of mutual appreciation and interpretation, and directs people's actions. It is also worth noting that this attachment of particular emotion/affect to particular symbol itself is a historical aggregation.

This dimension of emotion further encourages or prevents communication between individuals, and influences the formation and sustainability of social relations. In other words, a smooth communication often requires interlocutors synchronously to recognize and react to the 'emotion' bundled in objects and situations in a similar way. This shared intersubjective response to objects or situations (people-to-things) in turn enhances the emotional proximity and intimacy between individuals.

To trace and demonstrate the impact of 'embedded emotion' on the process of interaction, this chapter will document the everyday life experiences of these young Chinese migrants in Zambia, especially in the aspect of their moral transformation after they take the role of 'boss'/'leader'. Among the handful of ethnographies of 'China-in-Africa' thus far, there is serious lack of attention to the roles played by Chinese youth. Nevertheless, I contend that it is important to tell the story of the China-Africa encounter from their perspective – not only because it can supplement and diversify the existing analyses of China-Africa relations but also, more crucially, because these young people are among the most important players in the process of China-Africa interactions on the ground. 'Young Chinese migrants' refers to those born in the 1980s and the 1990s. They are normally referred to in Chinese as *balinghou* and *jiulinghou*, meaning 'born after 1980' or 'born after 1990'. As shown in the previous chapters, they are raised in the era of Chinese market reform and are the generation after implantation of 'one-child' policy. In contrast with more senior generations, most of them have better educational backgrounds and can manage to communicate with locals in English. Therefore, in practice, the young Chinese are the main workforce who carry out daily tasks as well as act as intermediaries in negotiation between Chinese seniors and local Africans. They are the bridge and the lubricant in the chain of China-Africa communication.

Undoubtedly, the 'young Chinese migrants' in Zambia are not a homogeneous group, and individual experience varies according to their differences in gender, regional origin and family background; however, when reading across their life stories it is not difficult to spot that certain experiences are rather widely shared. This is partly owing to their age and shared understanding of the basic aims of moving to Zambia. In line with what other anthropologists have observed about Chinese youth migration elsewhere (e.g. Fang 2012; Kajanus 2015), many young Chinese in Africa perceive migration as a way of growing up and learning about life. Among the many lessons learned at my field site, ethical learning – and in particular how to deal with ethical dilemmas – is arguably the most salient type.

Indeed, during my fieldwork, young Chinese migrants frequently talked with me and with each other about their ethical frustrations. These frustrations are partly due to their intermediate positions in the hierarchy of China-Zambia interactions. On the one hand, they endeavour to be 'an appropriate worker' in the eyes of their Chinese managers; on the other hand, they also want to become responsible and caring bosses to their Zambian workers. As I will illustrate later, these two ambitions, for the young Chinese migrants, are often irreconcilable. In brief, to be a responsible and caring boss to the Zambians means to disobey orders and to be unfaithful to Chinese managers; whereas, to become an appropriate worker in the eyes of Chinese managers, the young Chinese have to learn how to be cruel to their Zambian subordinates. Being torn between these two roles, many young Chinese experience an inevitable and somewhat uncomfortable transformation of the moral self.

In this chapter, to follow the previous one, I highlight some of the deliberate moral reflections of young Chinese migrants in Zambia. Through their stories, I will seek to illuminate the significance of social role in the process of everyday moral interaction. More specifically, inspired by Munn's theory of 'qualisign of value' (1986), I propose a synthetic concept, *ethical qualia* – a term that I shall explain further – to analyse this significance. Based on Ames' notion of 'role ethics' (2011) in China, I further argue that ethical qualia attached to social roles are critical criteria for moral evaluation, and also a crucial component of ethical self-cultivation among the Chinese migrants I came to know in Zambia. It is the embodiment of ethical qualia that induces the young Chinese migrants' moral reflections and leads to potential moral transformations.

When it comes to studying moral experience in everyday life, the recent anthropology of ethics[1] mainly draws on two intellectual sources (see, Faubion 2001 2011; Laidlaw 2002, 2014; Lambek 2010, 2015; Fassion 2012; Mattingly 2012, 2014; Stafford 2013). One is the theory of virtue ethics, which descends from Aristotle and has been revitalized by Alastair McIntyre (1981). Taken together with the writings of Bernard Williams (1981, 1985) and his general rejection of utilitarianism and deontology, this approach leads anthropologists to shift their gaze from the question of 'what is right' (which is often associated with duty) to the question of 'how one should live' (which is usually related to desire and aspiration). This strategic shift aims not only at separating ethics from Durkheimian social (moral) obligations – so as to grant agents some degree of freedom – but also at shifting morals away from utilitarian explanations – so that ethical actions can be taken as a distinctive space for social analysis.

The second intellectual source is Foucault's notion of subjectivation and self-problematization. In line with his 'techniques of self-formation', the anthropology of ethics has focused on the practices that 'permit individuals to effect, by their own means, a certain number of operations on ... their own bodies, their own souls, their own thoughts, their own conduct – and this in a manner so as to – transform themselves, modify themselves, and to attain a certain stat of perfection, happiness, purity, supernatural power' (Foucault 1997: 177, cited in Laidlaw 2014: 101). Invoking Foucault in this way is not just done in order to map out the genealogy through which Western morality has developed over time but, more importantly, to secure some space for agentive autonomy. Overall, briefly put, the task of the anthropology of ethics is to capture the evaluative side of ordinary life and, by describing the process of ethical actions and moral decisions, to grasp individual freedom (Laidlaw 2014, 2017; Lambek 2010, 2015).

If moral evaluation and self-cultivation are set as two focal points of these studies, I consider that at least two questions need be further addressed for these theories to be practically applicable. First, in terms of describing and analysing moral evaluation, it seems that anthropologists cannot bypass the notorious philosophical 'is-ought problem' – what links 'practice' with the 'ideal' (see, Robbins 2015; Keane 2015)? In other words, how are morals actualized in mundane life? And what is the semiotic mediation (Vygtsky 1978) entailed in the process of making moral evaluations (intrapersonal as well as interpersonal) and moral decisions? Second, self-fashioning and self-cultivation area lifelong project. It is a process of formation as well as a project of art. If so, then anthropologists perhaps need to ask, while documenting ethical practices on the ground, what role body and aesthetics play in this lifelong course of cultivating a virtuous self? I hope that the stories of young Chinese migrants in Zambia could shed some light on these questions. In particular, I hope that their practices and understandings of moral learning – together with my analytical concepts of 'ethical qualia' and 'role ethics' – can further supplement recent theories from the anthropology of ethics.

With these questions in mind, in what follows, I will describe everyday situations first when ethical qualia are applied as the criteria for moral evaluations between Chinese managers and young Chinese migrant workers. Then, I will narrate a story of a young Chinese migrant reflecting on his moral transformation since he was promoted to a managerial role at work. With this story, I aim to demonstrate how my interlocutor's moral reflection and moral transformation is linked with the embodiment of social roles (via ethical qualia). In the Conclusion, based on the analysis of my fieldwork stories, I will present an overview of the potential theoretical contribution that Chinese virtue ethics (role ethics in particular) could bring to the anthropology of ethics.

To possess the managerial aura: The story of Xiao Liu

It was just another quiet summer's night in the suburb of east Lusaka. When I was about to finish writing my field-notes before going to bed, I heard heavy steps across the dormitory courtyard. A moment later, Xiao Liu rushed past my window.

As I briefly mentioned in the previous chapter, Xiao Liu was one of the first friends I made after my arrival in Zambia. He was born in a fishing village on a small island near Shanghai in the mid-1980s. Being the only child of the family, his parents insisted that Xiao Liu should pursue further education and build his own life in big cities instead of inheriting the family seafood business. After graduating with a master's degree in agricultural management, Xiao Liu was hired to join the ATDC project in Zambia. To him, being selected for the ATDC project was an honour, and working in Zambia was an eye-opening (*kaiyanjie*) opportunity, one that he cherished dearly.

Due to his ranking at work and his ability in English, Xiao Liu was allocated lots of jobs. Not only did he have to prepare company documents, negotiate with local officials and people in business and manage the Zambian workers but he also needed to help the chef to do grocery shopping at the local market and accompany the project manager bargaining at gemstone shops. Indeed, Xiao Liu was very busy – too busy to have lunch on time every day. In the last couple of weeks, he had been working until midnight. Since we did not have a chance to talk for a couple of days – even though our rooms were next to each other – I decided to knock on his door for a quick chat.

'Are you all right?', I asked tentatively, seeing that his face was covered with dust and he was looking rather sad.

'I am OK. Just feeling a bit frustrated (*nanguo*)', Xiao Liu murmured, on his way to the bathroom to get a basin of water to clean his face.

'Why frustrated?'

'Ai', he sighed.

'There are lots of things to do everyday. I am working from dawn to dusk (*meirimeiye*). I do not mind doing lots of work. I am young and need to work hard to get experience. It is good for my future. But it seems that no matter how much I do, the manager never shows appreciation. He always criticizes me *buxiangyang'er* [literally, "does not look like any shape"; this complex phrase, which I will analyse further below, could mean "aura-less", "unpresentable" or "not conformed"].'

'What does that even mean?' I asked.

'Only ghosts know [*guizhidao*]! But, like today, he said to me that I was not mature enough and still did not fit my role at work. He suggested I should learn more about how to deal with the world [*chushizhidao*].' Sensing that Xiao Liu was not in the mood to explain more, I left him to relax.

Xiao Liu's frustration is shared by many young Chinese working in Zambia. Like him, the majority of the young Chinese were born as 'only children' during the 1980s and the early 1990s. They were usually employed in China immediately after graduating from university, then come to Zambia with Chinese organizations and enterprises to work mainly as engineers, administrators and translators. As they were brought up and educated in the historical period of economic liberalization in China, many young Chinese migrants regard values of liberalism highly. As I have stated in the previous chapter, democracy, personal autonomy, human rights, privacy and so on are regular topics of conversations among the young Chinese people at my field site. To them, as with Xiao Liu, to go to Zambia means to gain experience, to open one's horizons (*kaiyanjie*), to 'harden' (*duanlian*) oneself, to learn more and to fundamentally to grow up (*chengzhang*). When it comes to interacting with local Zambians and embracing local customs, the young Chinese tend to be a good deal more open and adventurous than their Chinese seniors. Indeed, it is this difference in attitude that triggers quarrels and frustrations in practice.

After that night when Xiao Liu used the phrase '*buxiangyang'er*', I kept searching for the meaning of it. On several occasions, I heard people use it (in slightly varying formulations such as *meigeyangzi* [have no shape], *buchengyangzi* [does not form any shape]) when they rephrased their managers' comments. Nevertheless, when I made further enquiries, no one seemed to know its exact meaning. After a number of interviews, my overall impression was that the term was a very vague and slippery one – people use it to mean many things at the same time, and its connotation varies dramatically according to the situation. With great frustration, I stopped looking for explanations and convinced myself that perhaps the term had no real significance. It was towards the end of my fieldwork at the educational farm, during one casual dinner with the farm manager and technicians, when I suddenly grasped the meaning of '*buxiangyang'er*'.

Xiao Liu took the evening off to meet some of his friends for discussing potential business cooperation. As usual, the farm manager and two other Chinese technicians – all born in the late 1960s – were having a quick dinner in the kitchen. Halfway through, they began to talk about Xiao Liu.

'I heard that Xiao Liu now was contacting people to set up a business together? And, he is thinking of quitting the job?' The farm manager suddenly asked me.

As it came as a shock, I did not know how to answer the question, so I merely replied, 'Hmm, I do not know. He did not say much.'

'How could you not know? You two live next to each other. I know you are friends, but there is no need to hide for him. I know it already. He met one of my friends to seek business opportunities. My friend called me as soon as Xiao Liu left. You see how stupid he is!'

'Indeed, he never knows what is good and what is bad for him [*buzhihaodai*]!', one of the technicians echoed.

The manager commented:

> It is OK. I thought of firing him already. Now, he gives me a good excuse. Look at him – never conforms to whatever he does [*wulunganshenmedoumeigeyangzi*]! He has been working with us for two years and now manages many workers; yet, he still does not look like a manager. Look at what he wears. Always so casual [*suibian*]! He doesn't stand correctly, or sit the right way [*zhanmeizhanyang'er*,

zuomeizuoyang'er]. Not to mention the way he speaks! He is still too young, not mature enough to fit into the role. If he is not suitable, it's better to give it to someone else.

Another technician replied: 'It is not all about age. I do not think that Xiao Liu is that kind of material ["to be a good manager" *bushinakuailiao*]. Xiao Lao, the regional manager of that construction company, is even younger than Xiao Liu but shows more managerial manner (*paitou*). Xiao Liu does not have that feel [*meinaguzijin'er*].'

Through the dinner, I kept quiet. I did not mention this episode to Xiao Liu either. Nonetheless, the conversations between the farm manager and the technicians clarified my confusion about the meaning of '*buxiangyang'er*'. Looking into the dialogue given earlier, it is not difficult to spot that, first, '*buxiangyang'er*' is used as a form of moral evaluation – a way of expressing disapproval of someone's moral character to be more precise. Second, taken as a form of moral evaluation, what one is being judged by is rather a peculiar type of criteria. To unpack the term, as its variations (such as *meigeyangzi*) show, '*yangzi*' (*yang'er* is the informal equivalence) is the key measurement of evaluation. '*Yangzi*' or *yang'er* could mean shape, appearance or form in English. '*Buxiang*' can be translated literally as 'not like'; therefore, '*buxiangyang'er*' semantically denotes 'one is not like a certain form'. Third, despite that 'form' is articulated as the criteria of moral evaluation, I want to stress that 'form' here is a holistic concept (almost Platonian). It is a package of various virtues – perhaps similar to the concept of aura – and it is of one's office or social role. In other words, when making a moral evaluation, my interlocutors measure actions against the ideal form in their minds of the office or role being performed. Moreover, and crucially, they bridge these two poles with analogy and feeling. Just as the technician in the conversation pointed out, it is a kind of feeling (*jing'er*) – which I will term later as 'ethical qualia' – that they seek when judging whether Xiao Liu is suitable for the role or not. Fourth, because moral evaluation is about matching the feeling of the role's form with the aura of the moral agent, in practice, '*buxiangyang'er*' comes across as vague and obscure (at least to an unknowledgeable outsider of the interaction). Nevertheless, I want to stress that it is due to this 'vagueness' that it has the strength of flexibility – *'buxiangyang'er'* is not a rigid moral command, but always needs to be further interpreted in relation to the role in question and the situation of interaction.

Not only was *'buxiangyang'er'* used by senior Chinese leaders at my field site to criticize young Chinese migrants but it was also the applied criteria when the young evaluated their seniors. Before coming to Zambia, the farm manager was a lecturer in agricultural science. When his university was assigned to take charge of the project, the farm manager volunteered as he considered it as an opportunity for promotion. Xiao Liu met the manager several times when he was studying for his master's degree at the same university. After they had some disagreements, Xiao Liu complained to me that the manager was not a good exemplar of a teacher at the university and now he did not show the aura of a suitable manager either. Once, he told me,

> This project won't last long if he is the manager forever. He does not have the aura of a good leader (*meiyoulingdaodeyang'er*) – too indecisive (*buguoduan*) and he does not show the strength of being authoritative (*meiquanwei*). Day and night, he only thinks how to compliment the general manager but never takes responsibility for us (his subordinates). Look at his wretched appearance (*weisuoyang'er*)! His heart is narrow as the hole on a sewing needle. How on earth could he keep followers' hearts?

How should one analyse the mutual evaluations between the farm manager and Xiao Liu? Undoubtedly, their criticism of each other occurred in a hierarchical work relationship, and their comments could be interpreted with the presumptive attitudes of exploitation and resistance (see Lee 2009; Lampert and Mohan 2014). Notwithstanding, if one cross-references the texts of their moral evaluations, it is clear that the invoked criteria are the same despite their differences in age and social positions. As I explained earlier, both the farm manager and Xiao Liu try to match the ideal image of the role in their mind and the moral characters of the person in practice when making moral judgements.

This process of matching is an activity of drawing analogy, and dis/approvals are made based on a feeling – both of the presentation of the moral agent and the performed role.

Analytically, I refer to this feeling as 'ethical qualia'. Inspired by Charles Pierce's pragmatic philosophy and Nancy Munn's notion of 'qualisign', anthropologists use qualia to mean 'experiential instantiations through which abstract potentialities called *qualities* are known' (Hankins 2013: 53). When actualized qualia are associated with certain objects or interpretants, they function as *qualisign* (Peirce 1997[1897]). To clarify further, 'qualisigns are not symbols representing qualities (e.g. the word 'red'), but rather are qualia serving as signs' (Harkness 2013: 14). Under Munn's conceptual apparatus, qualisign is referred to as 'certain embodied qualities that are components of a given intersubjective space-time [the "more comprehensive whole"] whose positive or negative value they signify' (1986: 17). Note, in this definition, qualisign has two crucial characteristics. On the one hand, the embodiment is necessary for the actualization of qualia. As Peirce claims, 'it cannot actually act as a sign until it is embodied; but the embodiment has nothing to do with its character as a sign' (1998 [1903]: 291). On the other hand, qualia (qualisign) are not purely individual mental phenomena. It is embedded in materials – natural as well as social – and can be shared between subjects. Qualia are 'points of culturally regimented, socially realised intersubjective orientation' (Harkness 2013: 15).

Extending this application of qualia to analyse ordinary moral interactions and self-cultivation, I propose 'ethical qualia' as a complex of qualitative experience and affective information registered in the process of instantiating ethical ideals. Following qualia's general characteristics, ethical qualia are encapsulated in moral materials, including virtues, exemplars or social roles at my field site, and represented in moral actions. These processes of encapsulation and representation are the result of institutionalized practices. They are 'frequently conventionalised, and it is their conventionality that makes it possible for social actors to recognise particular people (and particular things) as having particular "qualities"' (Chumley and Harkness 2013:

6). Conventionalized ethical qualia function as indexical signs in the course of moral interaction, which orients recognition, interpretation and reflection when people engage with the moral world. As I have described earlier, my Chinese interlocutors actively seek ethical qualia – which they call 'feeing like the form' (*xiangyang'er*) – when they make moral evaluations in everyday situations. For them, it is ethical qualia that mediate between ideal forms of virtue and actual virtuous performance. In this way, cultivating virtuous self entails the embodiment of the ethical qualia – a point that I will now elaborate.

Learning to be cruel: The story of Eagle

Thus far, I have shown the importance of ethical qualia in the process of moral evaluation in the intersubjective and interactional aspect. In this section, I describe how ethical qualia – especially related to the embodiment of social roles – can generate individual moral reflection and transformation and can further orient the project of ethical self-cultivation. Undoubtedly, ethical qualia can be actualized in practice through various mediums – cassettes in the Muslim community in Cairo (Hirschkind 2009), exemplars among the Urapmin of Papua New Guinea (Robbins 2015; 2017) or food at Moonlight Pond Village in Southern China (Oxfeld 2017); at my field site, it is in the embodiment of social roles and offices. This effect of ethical qualia on moral reflection and transformation could be well demonstrated by the story of Eagle.

Like Xiao Liu, Eagle was also born in the 1980s. Trained as a police officer back in China, Eagle did not pursue his career after college but went to Beijing for an office job. After a couple of months, with the similar aspiration as his peers to see the world when still young, Eagle took a tour in several countries around Africa and visited one of his friends in Zambia in 2010. He had stayed there ever since. When I asked him why he decided to quit his job and move to Zambia, he told me that it was the freedom that he was eager for.

> Life in China is too tiring – not only do I have to work according to the leader's temper (*kanlianse*), but also there is so much social networking among friends. If you want to live well, you have to be cautious all the time and try not to upset anyone. Not to mention the food safety problem: at least in Zambia the milk is safe.

Eagle told me all of this after we had played frisbee together. Then he continued,

> You see everyone in China now only cares about money and is busy to get rich first, even if sometimes it means that they need to do nasty things. It is so shallow. I do not want to become one of those people. The society is a big dyeing pot [*darangang*]. If I stayed, I would have to play the game according to their rules and eventually become just as black as them. That would not make me happy. So, I left.

For people who read ethnographies of China or more specifically of China-to-Africa migration, these sentiments may sound familiar; however, what is interesting about Eagle is that, as far as I know, he is one of only two Chinese in Lusaka choosing to work for non-Chinese companies. He first got a position in a Greek-owned paint company in charge of marketing to Chinese construction companies in Zambia. Then he shifted to a Malaysian-owned wheel company in charge of sales.

> I never thought of working for the Chinese here. I mean, I knew I would not want that as I worked while I was in China before. You know how complicated it is to work for the Chinese – so many hidden rules (*qianguize*). The work is never just about the work itself. The main reason why I left China was that I do not like the way Chinese manage people. Plus, the payment is low, and you never get your own time. Even though you have to work like a donkey 24-7, the boss may still not be satisfied and accuse you. By contrast, working for the foreigners is very straightforward. The work is easier, and everything follows the rules. They pay me well and even provide me with a car. More importantly, I can have holidays, and I can do whatever I want to do.

Even when it comes to his non-work time, Eagle tends to socialize with non-Chinese. He organizes sports event with the 'white guys' in

Lusaka every Sunday, and he is the only Chinese I know who has rented a flat with non-Chinese in one of the Zambian residential buildings in town. More interestingly, Eagle is also one of the organizers of the Lusaka Chinese Christian Fellowship that is attached to the American Baptist Commission in Zambia. He started to show an interest in the Christian church when he was in college. He told me that in the beginning his intention was to practise English. The more he participated in the activities, however, the more he was attracted to the Bible and Christianity. A year after joining the group, Eagle decided to be baptized. After he arrived in Zambia, he became acquainted through business with a Christian family from Hong Kong, and started to organize a Sunday congregation and study group under the guidance of American Baptist Missionaries. Eagle's main role in the fellowship is to translate and assist in organizing social events such as a Christmas party. Although the tasks are small, Eagle showed great enthusiasm. He never missed a service and always tried to rehearse the sermon translation nights before the church services. The pastors appreciate his effort and capability, and intended to train him to preach directly. When I asked him what his experience was like in the fellowship, Eagle told me:

> The Bible guides my life. It is not dry doctrines but actually reveals meaning to people through life. If I have problems, I will look into the Bible, and the answer will come to me one day. At least, I feel happy when I am in the Fellowship. I like the atmosphere. Fellows genuinely help each other no matter who is in trouble. It is rare nowadays when society is full of deceivers, and people use people for some personal gains.

Eagle disapproved of the way that some of the Chinese managers in Zambia treat their Zambian workers; perhaps due to his personal working experience before. He criticized the segregation between Chinese migrants and local people in Zambia and tried his best to rectify it at least through personal practice. He would join in a local street football match and drink shake-shake (a Zambian alcoholic drink) with the guys afterwards. He likes chatting with local Zambian vendors and gets to know his neighbours. And he enjoys sharing food with Zambian workers in his office:

> I prepare some food in the evening and take it to work. I share it with the workers. They seem to like it a lot. Well, they do not like rice that much. They also share their food with me. I do not know why people sometimes say their food is disgusting. It is simple but quite tasty. Here, I know Chinese do not eat food at the same table with Zambian workers. I cannot see why we shouldn't. Aren't we all from a mother's womb (*doushimashengde*)? Nothing different. Actually, Zambians are better than lots of Chinese. They are nice and friendly people, very extroverted, easy to get on with. I certainly have made friends with the guys in my office.

Eagle told me this when we were dining in a Chinese restaurant while some Japanese were eating dinner with Zambians at the table next to ours.

From his descriptions, it seems plausible to claim that Eagle prefers an independent lifestyle. His desire for freedom is strong by contrast with his distrust of Chinese society. He is not very keen on the relational (or 'particularistic') game his Chinese colleagues play, but likes a rule-bound work atmosphere. And he is a believer in universal rights and treats his Zambian colleagues as equal with himself and others. So when personal freedom comes with opportunities opened up (by migration overseas and working for non-Chinese), Eagle chose the lifestyle he approved of and practised the virtue he admired. Unfortunately, Eagle's experience is not as simple as he might like it to be.

All of these perceptions have been seriously challenged and doubted since Eagle was promoted to be a manager who is actually in charge of the workers.

> Sometimes, it got very difficult to carry on the normal job if I was too close with the workers. I mean, I tried to be their friend. I had lunch with them, and I played football with them, but it has messed up our relations at work. Once they saw me as a friend, they didn't listen

to my command anymore. It became very difficult to organise them. You know, the workers can be lazy and full of excuses not to work sometimes. If they knew you treat them as equals and friends, they would 'climb your nose and step on your face' [*dengbizishanglian*; a Chinese expression for disrespect], taking advantage of the friendship and stop taking my orders seriously. Sometimes, it was just outrageous, especially when the work was busy. In the end, I had to stop sharing with them and join the managers for lunch. Now and then, I had to be harsh and shouted at them. Only in this way could they know I am their boss and respect me accordingly.

Whenever Eagle shared his experience with me, his face appeared sad.

It is frustrating. I want to be friends with them and help them, but I cannot show my sympathy. It is right when people say that 'a man who attracts sympathy also has traits for others to hate him' [*helianzhirenziyouhehenzhichu*]. Sometimes, they force you into a position to be cruel to them. I cannot help but discipline them in the name of order. It is a very strange feeling. At that moment when the workers disobey me, it feels like I have been possessed by demons. I cannot think straight except by shouting and accusing them to get things done. Afterwards, when I reflect on it, I feel bad. I think I am changing into another person since I become a manager; well, at least at work.

Eagle – who, as explained, was not working in a Chinese firm – is not the only one who reported such an experience. It is rather a shared dilemma among the newly promoted young Chinese in Zambia. Mr Barry, who I mentioned in the previous chapter, fired the driver at this company, who used to be his best friend among all the Zambian workers, merely because the driver did not obey his orders on route choice. Moreover, Xiao Liu quarrelled with workers many times and fired a dozen after he was placed in charge of them. Like Eagle, they all experienced a transformation after taking different social roles. Nevertheless, what is ironic is that all three of them, after experiencing the dilemma, became sympathetic to their Chinese managers and criticized them less and less. 'Now I understand why he [the farm manager] acted like that.

Sometimes, it is really involuntary [*shenbuyouji* literally, "my body is not controlled by myself"]. Situations push one to do things that have to be done', Xiao Liu once told me.

There are many ways to read Eagle's story – as one of class, of religious conversion (see, Robbins 2004) or of rising Chinese individualism (see, Yan 2009, 2013) – and there are many messages to unpack in his narrative (e.g. the nature of society in China [see, Steinmuller and Wu 2011], the idea of face in China or the story of pursing autonomy through migration [see, Lin 2014]). What my interpretation focuses on are Eagles' moral frustrations and his moral reflections. One of the obvious points revealed in the story is that his frustration and transformation happened in the process of switching roles or status (from being a worker to being a friend, and then to being a boss), to be precise at the moment of embodying his new managerial role. Moreover, Eagle's self-reflection of this struggle is based on his sensitivity, and it is triggered by the conflictive feeling between performing the role (with its embedded qualia) appropriately and the desirable relationship that Eagle would like to achieve at work. Note that Eagle's understanding of 'appropriate role performance' is encultured by his upbringing and education in China. As a newly arrived migrant, his judgement and reaction can be 'automatic' in crisis or urgent events (Kahneman 2012). Furthermore, Eagle's dilemma indeed occurred in the context of the cross-cultural interaction. As I have documented in the previous chapter, Chinese managers and Zambian workers often have an incommensurable understanding of what a 'virtuous leader' entails. These mismatched expectations on the performance of certain roles can lead to disagreements and arguments in the course of interaction. Although cross-cultural interaction could induce moral frustration, it is not a necessary condition. Fundamentally, at least in the case of Eagle, it is the feeling of unease following the actualization of ethical qualia by embodying the role of manager, which makes him aware of his transformation.

Reading Eagle's story as a whole, what is highlighted is the significance of social role, especially the process of embodying roles, in moral transformation. By embodying the role, the moral agent instantiates the ethical qualia embedded in the role. Through instantiation, one feels virtues and cultivates the ethical self. This ethical development associated with roles is conceptualized as 'role ethics'. As Roger Ames cogently argues:

> From the Confucian perspective … in the stead of pre-existing norms we discover a phenomenology of experience that serves as a resource for determining what it would mean to act in such a way as to enhance our relations … . Confucian role ethics takes the substance of morality to be nothing more or less than positive growth in the constitutive relations of any particular situation … . In taking family feeling as the entry point for developing moral competence, role ethics is a programme of personal growth that begins and extends outward from specific partial relations in the direction of the more impartial bonds that secure community more broadly. … The viability of Confucian role ethics relies upon the refinement and exercise of the moral imagination that certainly includes, but is not limited to or dominated by, rational calculation. … Confucian ethics offers a holistic approach to determining proper conduct that includes all of the cognitive, affective, and somatic resources human beings have available to them in shaping their best response. (2011: 259)

Under this system, as I will elaborate further in the Conclusion, morals are predominately interdependent, situated and experiential, and, ethical cultivation is an aesthetical project. In embodying different roles across one's life span, one activates the embedded qualia, learns virtues affectively and assembles a unique self.

Same story, different endings

It is six years since I first collected these stories of young Chinese migrants in Zambia. Many things have changed since. Most of them are now in their mid-thirties, and many got married and had children. Some have been promoted to more senior roles at work, whereas others have left work to pursue other goals in life. However, they face the moral dilemma depended on whether they could afford to make choices.

Xiao Liu resigned from his position not long after I left the field site. His reason was simple – he would never fit the role because it was not his character. Even if he chose to stay and change his manner, he would not feel happy. 'Chinese bureaucratic culture [*guanchangwenhua*] is just not in my genes', Xiao Liu once told me in a phone call. After he left the farm, Xiao Liu went back to his hometown and helped his parents running the seafood factory. As the family business is rather successful and Xiao Liu is the only child, there is no urgency for him to find another job and his parents are happy to keep him at home. After all, it is what they have always wanted Xiao Liu to do – coming back home to run the family business after he gained experience from the outside world. However, to my surprise, last time when we messaged each other about one year ago, Xiao Liu was back in Zambia again. Now, he is running his own company, doing international trade in timber. He told me that he just bought a mansion in the most expensive zone of Lusaka. He was his own boss and no longer had to live the way that other people demanded.

Eagle's way to deal with the moral dilemma is to change jobs constantly. Unlike Xiao Liu, Eagle was born into an ordinary family in Northeast China, an economically disadvantaged region. Both of his parents are workers in a state-owned factory. Although he is also the only child of the family, they could not afford to support him without him working. Eagle realized the difficulty so chose to go to a police college (for which a low fee is charged in China) and worked extra-long hours to learn English. It was due to Eagle's English skills that he was employed to work in Zambia initially. One year after I finished my fieldwork, Eagle resigned from his job. He said that he could not cope with the conflict at work. Then, he moved to Kitwe, a Zambian mining town in the copper-belt. Soon, he found a job as a translator. I have not heard much of him in Kitwe, but the most recent one was when I sent him a greeting text for the Chinese New Year, Eagle told me that he was moving to Australia. When I asked the reason, he did not reply much but just said that Australia was more equal and more suitable for him.

By contrast with Xiao Liu and Eagle, Mr Barry is the only one who still works for the same company. Like most young Chinese, Mr Barry adopted an English name when he was in the university. While at the work site, Zambian workers like to call him Mr Barry. Mr Barry was born in a rural village of a Chinese northwest province during the mid-1980s. He is not the only child but has two sisters. Farming is the main source of income for his parents. Due to the lack of funds for university, Mr Barry went to a 'normal university' (which are free in China) to be trained as an English teacher. During his time at university, Mr Barry took several jobs as a private English tutor to help with daily living expenses. It was also in his undergraduate years when he was introduced to Baptist Christians and converted to Christianity. Soon after he finished his degree, he went to Beijing for a short-term contractual job. Six months later, he joined the construction team in Zambia. Mr Barry cherished the job more than anyone I have met, partly because of the relatively high salary compared with peers working in China for a similar position. Also, Mr Barry is the first in his village to go outside of China for work, which increases his parents' reputation. Mr Barry was very careful with money. He sent three-quarter of his monthly income to his parents so that his sisters could go to better universities. It is no exaggeration to say that this job in Zambia is Mr Barry's lifeline.

Like most of the young Chinese migrants, Mr Barry struggled with fulfilling his manager's demands and his desire (especially based on the teachings that he received from the church) to be a caring, fair and kind boss to the Zambian workers. When we were sharing the same construction compound, Mr Barry was the one who was most afraid of Chinese managers. Mr Barry liked to chat with Zambian workers and was curious to know the local culture; however, whenever the manager appeared, he would immediately stop talking to the workers because his manager had warned him that he should keep distance from the Zambian workers to maintain order and gain respect. Mr Barry even stopped going to the Lusaka Chinese Christian Fellowship because his manager did not like it. I have lost personal contact with Mr Barry, but I heard about him from Xiao Liu, who told me that Mr Barry has been promoted to be a project manager and has entirely changed his style. 'He looks like a proper leader now – firm, authoritative, decisive and he is not afraid of making public speeches anymore. He is not the soft scholar [*wenruoshusheng*] who we knew anymore.'

Conclusion: Alternative virtue

Through the stories of young Chinese migrants in Zambia, thus far, I have shown the importance of social roles and attached ethical qualia on everyday moral interaction. I argue that it is ethical qualia that people actively seek when doing moral evaluations; it is the embodiment of social roles that actualizes moral ideals and induces moral transformation. In the way of conclusion, I want to briefly scale up my analysis to a more abstract and philosophical level. By reinterpreting writings on Confucian moral philosophy,[2] I illustrate how Chinese virtue theory could conceptually supplement developments in the anthropology of ethics.

As I have summarized earlier, current theoretical analyses in anthropology of ethics are predominately drawn from two philosophical sources: virtue ethics in the Anglo-American tradition descending from Aristotle and the theory of subjectivation put forward by Foucault. Moreover, moral evaluation and self-cultivation are set as two focal points for study. I consider that grounded on virtue ethics and self-problematization, the anthropology of ethics might face limitations in its practical analysis and its future development if any of these theories were misconstrued. Note, I am not claiming that scholars have already made mistakes when studying ethics anthropologically. What I am suggesting is that anthropologists need to be alert to possible inadequacies entailed in the borrowed moral theories. I consider that these inadequacies may include three major points.

First, while analysing moral evaluations and actions, following Williams' default position, anthropologists may incline to take the internalist view for granted; that is, moral actions are the necessary results of desire. Internalism may well be the case in some circumstances; however, in other societies, moral action can precede desire as a precondition to realize the worthiness of virtue. To oppose internalism with a different take, Webb Keane (2014, 2015) has urged anthropologists to take that 'second person's view' seriously and to unpack complicated moral actions at the interactional level.

Moreover, if documenting moral judgements and choices are two main tasks for ethnographers, anthropologists may incline to omit the non-representational side of ethics. The non-representational side (Thrift 2007) not only refers to the moral evaluation beyond linguistic performances but also denotes the non-cognitive process of making moral decisions. Only through equal attribution of research attention to the 'fast motion' and 'slow motion' of moral reasoning (Kahneman 2012) and to the verbal and bodily dimension of moral interaction, would anthropologists paint a balanced picture of moral practices.

Last, but not least, the anthropology of ethics has, until now, been proposed and developed mainly based on theories of Western moral philosophy. Moral philosophy in the West – especially virtue theory – has progressed under its own socio-historical context (one of which, for instance, is the influence of Christianity). Merely relying on Western philosophy to write ethnography on the ethics of other parts of the world may run the risk of theoretical partiality. To make an adequate anthropology of ethics, I suggest that anthropologists need to embrace other moral, philosophical systems and may even embark on a speculative project – to imagine what moral anthropology would be like with an alternative virtue.

Chinese virtue ethics could potentially make a great contribution if anthropologists of morality take the speculation seriously. Despite the fact that many have questioned the existence of substantial debates on metaphysics in Chinese philosophical tradition, it is widely recognized that moral philosophy, especially virtue theory, is the cornerstone of

Chinese philosophy (Tu 1985; Feng 2000; Haidt 2012). For thousands of years, Chinese scholars have been developing, systemizing and revitalizing virtue theories and trying to implement the principles through governmental policies and state education. So how could Chinese virtue ethics supplement the anthropology of ethics in general? In what follows, I can only attempt to sketch three points briefly, corresponding with my analysis of the theoretical inadequacy earlier, as I consider that only monographs could do justice to the sophistication of Chinese virtue ethics.

'Virtue' in Chinese is termed '*de*'; whereas morality, if one were to treat them differently, could be called '*lunli*'. In practice, *de* is often combined with *dao* (the Way/pattern) or *mei* (beauty) as in *daode* and *meide* for daily usage. *De*, as Ivanhoe points out, is a kind of power. '*De* of a given thing is its inherent power or tendency and in particular its natural effect on other people and things … . Across the different meanings this character has, *de* retains the sense of an inherent, spontaneously functioning power to *affect* others' (2000: x; italic added). To define virtue as a form of influence, from the beginning, Chinese moral theorists focus on the acquisition and cultivation of such power. 'Western philosophers have been much more concerned with trying to define what the good is and worrying about how, if at all, one can come to know the good. Chinese thinkers have focused instead on the problem of how to become good' (Ivanhoe 2000: ix).

Indeed, self-cultivation is one of the main approaches to becoming virtuous. For Confucius, acquiring virtue is not instant via epiphany (Ivanhoe 2002), but a lifelong learning process. It is about accumulation, stresses moral growth and focuses on *becoming*. '[Becoming consummately human (*ren*)] is not "being whole", but the process of "becoming whole" within the multilateral relations that constitute one's natural, social, and cultural environments' (Yu 2007). The ultimate aim of self-cultivation is not to possess certain virtue. The end of this learning process is rather open. It is to achieve an understanding of the uniqueness of self and to become responsive, active, reflexive and sensitive. As Ames summarizes:

This process of person-making is first and foremost a striving and a 'doing' that expresses its life and growth, and that in the production of enhanced meaning, bring with it aspiration, frustration, and hopefully sometimes, satisfaction. Such an understanding of person is wholly naturalistic in that it makes no appeal to a metaphysics of self or to any unifying substratum such as soul or mind, and thus is more of a centred, concentrated vitality than a bounded unity. This process of becoming a person is always embodied and embodying as a porous membrane that strives to achieve meaning and coherence in the changing configuration of its relations. It is hylozoistic – that is, at once psychic and physical. It offers a revisionist and emergent understanding of person that is animated and projective, and that, having developed its own inflected and reflexive sense of itself out of its intersubjective relations with others, becomes increasing enculturated through the semiotic processes and symbolic competencies that come to shape it in these associations. (2011: 132)

Keeping this notion of self-cultivation in mind and looking back at the stories of young Chinese migrates in Zambia, it is not difficult to understand why many of them consider migration as a life-learning opportunity and a way of growing up.

In this process of self-cultivation, social roles and rituals are the two main mediums of learning virtue. Ritual (*li*) here is not limited to a formal and religious aspect. In Confucianism, ritual pervades in every moment of life – the ritual of hosting guests (*binli*), of greeting (*jianmianzhili*), of dining (*yinshizhili*) and so on. It constitutes the social and is the essential part of daily routine. More importantly, ritual and body (*ti*) are treated as a mutually constitutive pair (Zhang 2007). '*Li* have a profoundly affective aspect wherein feelings suffuse and fortify the relational activities, providing the communal fabric with a tensile strength that resists rupture … . *Li* is a process of personal articulation – the cultivation and expression of an elegant disposition, an attitude, a posture, a signature style, an identity' (Ames 2011: 174). Fundamentally, what ritual does is to nurture sensitivity to virtue through bodily activities – to form '*qingcao*' as a Chinese moral philosopher would say.

This function of ritual is often fulfilled with practices of social roles. The significance of roles in Chinese moral tradition lies in the fact that formation of the self is the co-creative process between one and his/her environment. Self is the result of aggregating relations. This aggregation is through role taking.

> Family roles and the extended relations we associate with a community that designate a specific configuration of activity – the roles of father, mother, son daughter, teacher, friend, and neighbour, for example – are themselves a normative vocabulary more compelling than abstract injunctions. Such roles recommend in the most concrete of terms an existentially informed disposition and the search for a course of conduct that is the ground of family and community life. (Ames 2011: 168)

By embodying the roles and living ritually, one feels the virtue, cultivates sensibility to virtue and then acts freely and virtuously corresponding with particular situations in life.

Learning virtue responsively, affectively and aesthetically, through roles and rituals, is perhaps the potential contribution that Chinese moral theory could add to the development of anthropology of ethics. To end, I would like to cite a brilliant summary that Philip Ivanhoe gives to Confucian moral tradition:

> There was much more to the moral life than merely fulfilling certain obligations and following certain practices and norms. Each of one's actions had to be performed with the genuine and appropriate affective attitude for each occasion and an active engagement and concern with adjusting one's performance to the precise demands of each particular occasion. In order to do this, one needed to cultivate oneself by developing a particular set of virtuous sensibilities and dispositions. One was not simply to take up and perform a given role or set of roles. The goal was to become the kind of person – one who was among other things benevolent, righteous, and courageous – who could fulfil the roles and obligations one happened to have in the most humane and harmonious fashion. (2002: 2)

5

Speaking with affect

Speech capital, situational affect and daily (mis)communication

It was a normal Sunday midday during October in the eastern suburb of Lusaka city – dry, hot and quiet. After a quick lunch, instead of having a nap as usual, the Zou family immediately started to get busy again to prepare the evening banquet that they were going to host for a small group of their friends – three families with their associated friends, roughly twelve guests this time. It had become a routine for the Zous and their friends to get together every weekend for socializing. Families took care of the banquets in turns, and it was the Zou family's turn that weekend.

> Lao De [Father Zou], stop being lazy! Go to the field and cut some cabbages, chives and leeks. I need them for stir-fries later. Zou Hua [the son, Xiao Zou], go to the supermarket and buy two tilapia, four if they are small. Ah, if you pass Lao Hu's shop [a small Chinese supermarket], buy some Chinese five-star spices and cumin. It is running low. I am afraid it won't be enough.

Mother Zou began to organize the preparation while sharpening the knife, boiling water and getting ready to butcher the rooster and duck that Xiao Zou bought from the local market on Friday. Although without being *verbally* assigned to any particular task, the daughter-in-law could not just rest but took the beef out of the fridge and began to chop it.[1]

'Can I do anything?' I asked the Mother Zou out of courtesy.

'No, really no need. It is very simple. We will finish this very quickly. If you are tired, you can have a nap. Or, you can watch TV. *Baijiajiangtan* (Lecture Room) is on. It is a very good programme.'

I assumed that Mother Zou answered me this way due to politeness; therefore I chose to stay in the courtyard near the kitchen looking after the granddaughter Xiao Xiao as well as chatting with Mother Zou when she was cooking. We talked about her childhood and her life experience in Zambia in general. We also gossiped about other Chinese businesswomen in Lusaka and discussed the reasons behind their business success. Although it was a conversation, Mother Zou seemed to have dominated the whole discussion. Compared with Father Zou, she is indeed more articulate, which she considered as an advantage, for her and for the household. To her, being able to speak appropriately is a crucial element to business success. 'We cannot all be mute!' she said, 'At least one needs to be articulate in a family. Otherwise, there is no way to do business! I cannot rely on Lao De as you can see. So I have to speak!'

A couple of hours later, our conversation was interrupted by the rather loud sound of a car horn: 'Beep – Beep – Beep.' Hearing the noise, Mother Zou quickly took the keys from the shelf and ran to the farm gate to welcome the arrival of the first group of guests. It was Manager Deng and his family, the most important guests for the evening banquet. To claim that they are the most important guests is due to their long-term personal relationships with the Zou family. As introduced in Chapter 2, both families are from the same city back in China. It was Manager Deng who helped the Zou family to settle in Lusaka and, most significantly, he was the only one who was willing to loan money to the Zou family without conditions when the Zou family almost went bankrupt two years ago.

'Xiao Xiao, come and see who is here!' Mother Zou waved to her granddaughter while Manager Deng was parking his SUV. Having heard the call, Xiao Xiao jumped out of the chair and ran to the car.

'Say hello to Grandpa Deng.' As usual, Mother Zou tried to teach Xiao Xiao good manners.

'Grandpa Deng, hello.' Xiao Xiao raised her voice and loudly greeted Manager Deng.

'Oh, see how lovely and polite our Xiao Xiao is!' Manager Deng touched her hair.

'Xiao Xiao, will you say Grandma Deng is extra beautiful today?' Mother Zou continued.

'Beautiful! Grandma Deng is beautiful! Sister Niu Niu [Manager Deng's granddaughter] is beautiful too!' Xiao Xiao followed Mother Zou's instruction at the same time hugging Grandma Deng without being told by her grandmother. At this moment, a big smile appeared on Grandma Deng's face and she said, 'Wait till Xiao Xiao grows up. She is definitely promising [*chuxi*].'

This episode of encounter and greeting seems very normal. Nevertheless, for Mother Zou, it has great significance. It was days after the banquet when Mother Zou praised Xiao Xiao's performance:

> Xiao is going to achieve much better than us. She is only five but already not afraid of speaking. Sometimes, she can even speak the compliment loudly which I would never dare to say. She certainly is going to live much better life than her parents. Look at them, never learned how to speak appropriately. Now, they ended up unemployable. They have to live with us and carry on being farmers. Xiao Xiao is going to be different. She knows how to speak appropriately [*huishuohua*]. For a girl, being pretty and having a sweet mouth (*zuitian*) is the key to success. Our Xiao Xiao has both. She is much more promising than us.

From Mother Zou's words, it is not difficult to spot how she correlates personal prosperity with one's ability to *speak appropriately* – to use technical terms, as Bourdieu (1991) might have put it, she makes a correlation between 'linguistic capital' and 'social mobility'.

At my field sites in Zambia, people make and are being asked to make speeches, formally and informally, all the time – at banquets, at work conferences, at school, at business meetings, among friends, among colleagues and even among strangers. For them, the way in which one speaks is part of oneself. Speech is one's 'gate and face' (*menmian*), and demonstrates one's capability in association with ideas of quality (*suzhi*), self-cultivation (*xiuyang*) and charisma (*meili*). Furthermore, being able to 'speak appropriately' is a component of 'being a proper human' (*huizuoren*). It is deeply embedded in everyday moral interaction and communication. Most importantly, appropriate speech, especially speaking with affection, has the power to draw people together and enhance the emotional proximity; therefore, if seen from the instrumental point of view, speech has great impact on the accumulation of 'social capital' in practice.

The popular interest in speech and increasing awareness of its significance has generated a market for 'rhetorical training' in China. Since 1983, *Speech and Eloquence* (*yanjiangyukoucai*) has become a widely read magazine in China. In 1988, subscriptions had already reached 1.13 million. This is a magazine especially issued to teach speaking skills. Since 2001, the founder of the magazine, Shao Shouyi, was also invited to be one of the regular speakers on a very popular TV programme, Lecture Room (*Baijiajiangtan*), broadcast on China Central Television (CCTV), which was the only channel my Chinese interlocutors watched at my field sites. Following the popularity of speech skills training, seminars have opened up in universities, and bookshops dedicate special sections to the flood of publications on related topics. To some extent, this exaggeration of speech following its commercialization has objectified speech and turned it into a form of art; and, being able to 'speak appropriately' has been inserted into everyday social expectation. To stand back and reflect on it as a Chinese myself, this obsession with speech is a truly fascinating cultural phenomenon.

Even though it receives broad attention from the public, the cultural significance of speech in China has rarely been studied by anthropologists. Among the few contributions, Hans Steinmuller has documented how irony is employed as a main communicative strategy by villagers in Hubei province. Borrowing the analytical concept of 'cultural intimacy' from Herzfeld, Steinmuller argues that irony as a linguistic style plays a role in forming a 'community of complicity' among rural Chinese (2010, 2013). He claims that this 'community' arises where

> a 'coded tension' exists between official representations, generally linked to nation and state, and vernacular forms in face-to-face communities; this tension expresses itself locally in embarrassment, cynicism, or irony. Such are the reactions when 'cultural intimacy' is exposed, and they can both confirm the official representation *and* satirize it. Inasmuch as these expressions are shared and common, they bind people together in intimate spaces of self-knowledge. (2010: 540)

Despite some questions about how irony as a linguistic style actually constitutes communities in China, I do find Steinmuller's analysis of the relations between intimacy (arising from the communication process) and sociality very helpful. In this chapter, I would like to follow his line of analysis but with two supplements. First, I consider that linguistic interaction and community formation are in a dialectical relationship. On the one hand, as philosopher John Searle has claimed, in order for communication to occur, interlocutors need to have an intense 'shared background' (2010) to hand. In other words, people need to be in a community already to comprehend each other's communicative strategies and intentions. Note, although Searle never makes this point explicit, the 'shared background' here, as I understand, entails history. On the other hand, shared linguistic styles, such as irony or indirect speech, do enhance intersubjective intimacy. Second, I suggest that the notion of 'cultural intimacy' needs to take effect more fully into account. Arguably, it is the resonance for affect (especially the ones historically bundled with communicative situations, which I will term as 'situational affect' later on), mediated by shared speech styles, that exposes or enhances the intimacy between people, and it is the resonance for affect that provides the foundation of group formation.

It is this intertwined relationship of speech, affect and sociality that I aim to describe in this chapter. By unpacking the meaning of 'speaking appropriately' from two aspects of my Chinese interlocutors' everyday practices – indirect speech and contextualization – I intend to analyse their constitutive impacts. In what follows, I will firstly use banquet speech and 'soft command' at work as examples to describe what 'speaking appropriately' connotes to my Chinese interlocutors. Based on Steven Pinker's hypothesis on linguistic implicature (2007), I attempt to propose that the stress on Chinese 'harmonious' sociality, as moral ideal as well as practical interest, provides the condition for specific speech styles, such as emotional speech and contextualized communication. Furthermore, with their realization of the impact of speech on social networking, I will document how my Chinese interlocutors utilize speech at work and in business to achieve personal prosperity.

As in previous chapters, the study is mainly micro-sociological with a focus on everyday mundane conversational exchanges. The main aim is to show the intertwined constitutive relationships among speech, affect and sociality appearing in practices; therefore, this chapter will be predominately descriptive. This perspective for investigation may seem ahistorical and apolitical; however, I have no intention to deny that the linguistic style my interlocutors engage with is subject to Chinese historical and political conditions. Surely, the class struggle during the Cultural Revolution and the state involution before and after communist China and so on, all contribute to the formation of communicative techniques, and any form of linguistic styles could be the demonstration of 'symbolic power' and 'symbolic violence' (Bourdieu 1991). Such perspectives need more detailed future studies and are beyond the discussion of this chapter.

Indirect speech as a communicative preference

Back to the party the Zou family was hosting: Mother Zou immediately sent Xiao Zou to the Demonstration Centre inviting Manager Bao and the administrative staff to join as soon as he came back from the grocery. 'Ask nicely! If Manager Bao does not want to come, make sure you invite Teacher Feng [the mechanic] and Xiao Liu', Mother Zou instructed before Xiao Zou left home.

This instruction was specially stressed regarding the relationship between the Zou family and Manager Bao – they did not get on very well. For Manager Bao, the Zou family were uneducated peasants who came to Zambia to look for windfalls because of their 'failure' in China, so he looked down on their quality (*suzhi*) and peasant's lifestyle; whereas, for the Zou family, Manager Bao was just another pretentious official who fell out of the leader's favourite circle so was assigned to Zambia. Although the Zous acknowledged that Manager Bao despised them, considering ATDC and the family farm were neighbours and both were from China, Mother Zou still made every effort she could to socialize with the staff and to maintain a 'harmonious' (*heqi*) relationship.

About half an hour later, Xiao Zou came back with Teacher Feng. Just as Mother Zou predicted, Manager Bao did not come. After settling Teacher Feng in the lounge, Mother Zou found Xiao Zou in the courtyard and questioned him.

'What did he (Manager Bao) say?' Mother Zou asked in a rather weak voice.

> What else could he say? Just *daguanqiang* [talking in an official style]. He said the farm work was very busy and he needed to keep an eye on it. Also, the central government had specifically issued documents recently stressing that officials overseas should be aware of their image [*xingxiang*] and try to reduce unnecessary entertainment after work. Full of bullshit, as usual! He was playing QQ games in the bed when I knocked at his door! Why did you send me there anyway? You know he does not like us.

Xiao Zou replied with a loud and upset tone.

'Shh, lower your voice', Mother Zou gave Xiao Zou a hint by rolling her eyes in the direction of the lounge and continued, 'You see how busy I am. If not, I would go and invite him myself. Anyway, why did Xiao Liu not come with you?'

'What a question! How could he if Lao Bao [nickname of Manager Bao] didn't!', Xiao Zou started to get annoyed and left his mother to join his friends for poker.

Mother Zou turned to me and complained, 'He is just like his father – stubborn and never knows how to request well. Sometimes you need to throw your face away and say some cheeky words to get things done, right? Nowadays, how much money is face worth! *Siyaolianpihuoshouzui* [willing to suffer but not to give up the face].'

Let me pause for a while to analyse some points of the dialogue in this episode. First, the notion of *guanqiang*: literally, it can be translated as 'official tone'. Nevertheless, the connotation normally contains a negative evaluation. It belongs to a certain type of speech style that usually is used by government officials (see Hansen 2017). When it is used, this style emphasizes the form of speech and the hierarchical relationship between speaker and audience; it has the power to transform the communicative context from informal into formal so to create a sudden social disjunction between the addresser and addressee. It often conveys the intention to de-socialize; namely, using formal speech or official excuses to refuse dealing with informal and practical requests. The negative evaluation of *guanqiang* comes from its patronizing character of the speech form and its emptiness of the speech content.

Second, the intention towards bystanders during the communication has two aspects; one is to avoid overhearing and the other one is to aim to be overheard. The former is associated with the Chinese communicative notion of '*geqianyou'er*' ('it has an ear on the other side of the wall') and the latter is linked with '*zhisangmahuai*' ('reviling/abusing the locust tree while pointing to the mulberry'). Both terms are abstracted from Chinese classics and were cited frequently by my Chinese interlocutors when commenting on communication. I will provide more related ethnographic examples later in this chapter; but Mother Zou's body language of 'eye-rolling' during the dialogue with her son belongs to the former practice of such speech skill. By redirecting Xiao Zou's intention to the lounge, where Teacher Feng was, using body language, Mother

Zou was warning her son about the possibility of their conversation being overheard by Teacher Feng who worked under Manager Bao and presumably was allies with him. From Mother Zou's concern, it is not difficult to see that the group identity of the addressee and bystanders constitutes an important part of the situational context and influences greatly the speech styles that addressors employ.

Third, regarding the relationship between speech and notion of face, it is true to say that speech is subject to the pre-existing power relations among the interlocutors, but it can form new power relations as well, if conversations are perceived as a form of exchange (for examples of power relations of gift exchange in China, see Yan 1996). This character of speech often clashes with moral practice on equality and mutual respect, which in Chinese practice is often bundled with the notion of face (*mianzi*). Face is associated with dignity. During my fieldwork, I often heard my Chinese interlocutors complaining that someone's words did not leave any space for his/her face (*buliumianzi*) and brought shame in public. As a result, social ties were cut off. Since words could damage social relations, my interlocutors are very conscious and careful when talking to each other. As they always say, 'misfortune can come out of a careless mouth' (*huocongkouchu*); therefore, one needs to pay extra attention to whom one is speaking to and what one is speaking of. Note, the content of speech always corresponds with the projected social relations of interlocutors. In turn, this cautious attitude to speech also impacts on people's speech style – the wide application of indirect speech every day.

In general, the brief conversation between Mother Zou and her son above reveals the significant role that situational sociality plays in daily communicative exchange. Not only are interlocutors aware of each other's positional role during the conversation, but also they are cautious about the group identity of the bystander. Moreover, they acknowledge the interplay between speech and sociality. For them, the choice of speech style conveys the intention to socialize and carries the implication of each other's relationship. Careless wording may bring the potential danger of breaking 'harmonious' relations. Two slang phrases that my Chinese interlocutors often refer to nicely capture this interplay between speech and sociality – '*jianrenshuorenhua, jianguishuoguihua*' and '*shuozhewuxin, tingzheyouyi*'. The former can be literally translated as 'to speak human language when meeting a human and talk in ghost words when encountering a ghost'. The connotation indicates that people shall be able to shift conversational content and communicative style according to the status of the addressee, instead of sticking to the truth. The latter means that 'speaker does not have the intention but the wording actually used could be over-interpreted by the listener according to his/her own projection'. In an extreme version, one's words could be misinterpreted against one's self.

In Chapter 2, I argued that my interlocutors are self-conscious about '*guanxi*' (social networking) and cherish interactional affection (*jiaoqing*). Here, I contend that it is this acute awareness of social relationships accompanied by the acknowledgement of the social function of speech that generates and nurtures an everyday communicative style of indirectness. Steven Pinker has proposed that sociality is the reason why human use implicature (2007). I would qualify his hypothesis by adding that the sociality he refers to is mainly spontaneous socialization that often comes with uncertainty and risk. Nevertheless, I consider his hypothesis could very well explain the phenomenon at my field sites. Because my Chinese interlocutors regard social networking as playing an important role in one's personal success yet are never certain of the intention of the conversational other, they choose to use an indirect communicative style.

This perceived cultural value of indirect speech could be demonstrated by misunderstandings that occurred during cross-cultural requests between Zambian workers and Chinese managers at work. When the construction work for the administrative building finished, there were lots of extra materials left, such as paint, bricks and unwanted steel. For the Chinese managers, these materials had no use, but the Zambian workers could well use them to re-decorate their houses. So, suddenly, the manager's room was full of Zambian workers requesting the free materials and it was up to the manager to decide who would get the resources. This discretion gave the manager a chance for favouritism. Thomas considered himself the first who should be granted materials because among all the workers he had been working at ATDC for the longest time. Nonetheless, after several attempts, he could not get any. By contrast, the newly joined security guard Gasper had secured quite a few. Seeing Gasper carrying the materials back home by his bike every evening, Thomas was a little bit upset. So he decided to talk with the manager. As a result, not only did he not get anything but the Chinese manager also used the chance to discipline him verbally. So Thomas was very disappointed.

Among the Zambian workers, Gasper was always the favourite. The manager thought him clever, capable of reading the manager's mind (*youyanglijian*) and knowing how to put forward a request appropriately. On the contrary, Thomas was not particularly liked by the manager. For him, Thomas was too stubborn and often did not know who was the boss and who was the worker. He was always the one who liked to bluntly give advice to the manager and make decisions without asking for permission. Moreover, Thomas did not even know how to speak. When I tried to find out the reason why Thomas did not secure any material, the manager told me;

'You see, he is too arrogant (*kuang*). Every time he asked me, it seemed that I was obliged to give it to him. It felt like I owed him (*qiantade*). If he asked nicely, I would have given him something. Sometimes, I do pity him but the way he speaks really put me off.'

After hearing the manager's judgement, I decided to observe how Thomas made requests. Several times, I followed him when he went to see the manager for the materials. In general, Thomas's requests were rather straightforward. If he wanted something, he would directly ask for it by saying things like 'Can I have …?' For the manager, such expression sounded too blunt and could be interpreted very much with a force of an order rather than a request. It put the manager in an uncomfortable spot – if he gave in, he would feel that Thomas would think he was giving him the material due to his obligation as a boss and Thomas would not be grateful; if he did not give it to him, he could not avoid sounding bad or rude as the way to reply to Thomas' direct request was to use direct confirmative or negative sentences.

By contrast, Gasper's strategy for making requests was very different. If he aimed for something, he would attend to the manager's needs more in the morning. Then he found a chance to make a request, almost like a spontaneous conversation. Instead of directly asking for things, he would firstly chat about some problem at home. Then he would comment on how expensive it was to buy such things in the market. Afterwards, he would mention that he saw some materials he needed in the garage or in the field then ask the manager what he was going to use it for. At the point, the manager would have already understood his intention and tell him that the material had no use anymore so he was happy to offer them to him if he could use them. In the end, Gasper would say lots of sweet words to show his gratitude. Despite knowing Gasper's real intention every time he approached, the manager still liked the way in which Gasper's request was made and was pleased that he could help Gasper to better his living conditions. This does not mean that Gasper would get what he requested every time, but he did make the manager comfortable even when refusing him.

Seeing Thomas disappointed every time, as a friend, Xiao Liu decided to share some communicative techniques with him. One hot afternoon, when driving back to the Demonstration Centre from the city market, Xiao Liu bought some chilled soft drinks. Seeing there were some extra bottles in the bag, Thomas asked to have one.

> T: Can I have one?
> XL: Hmmm, no!
> T: Why not? I thought we were friends!
> XL: Because you should not have asked like that! I do not have to give you any, you know.
> T: How should I ask?
> XL: Hmmm, you should say it is very hot today and you are thirsty. And wait for me to offer you one.
> T: But it is not a question. How can I know you will offer me one?

XL: Well, I will. I am not mean and I am not stupid! Like you said, we are friends. Of course I am going to offer you one. You know, you need to change the way you ask for things. Otherwise you will get nothing. You know Lao Bao [Manager Bao] does not like you.
T: Yes, I know. Is that why he does not give me things?
XL: Maybe
Xiao Liu passed Thomas a bottle of Coke.
T: Hmm, we like Coke. So nice! Thanks boss!

Since that afternoon, Thomas started to pay attention to his style of making requests and began to try more and more implications. Gradually, the manager began to offer him things and expressed pleasure that he had changed and encouraged him to work harder.

This misunderstanding at work raised due to the mismatch of linguistic forms could disclose the dynamic interplay between everyday socialization and communicative styles – indirect speech in this case. For the Zambian workers, precisely transmitted messages weigh heavily in conversation; whereas, for the Chinese managers, the communicative style and revealed mutual perception of each other's social relation and social roles associated with it are valued more. As shown earlier, the pre-existing social positions brought into conversation – manager and worker – provide a social expectation of certain forms of speech performance. It is the form of speech that draws my Chinese interlocutors' attention. For them, the form of speech conveys information that is implicit but nevertheless crucial, such as speaker's intention, perception of the power relation between interlocutors and speaker's social status. It is the choice of form that reveals personal capacity of communication. To some extent, the form becomes part of the content of communication.

To further interpret the previous statements of Chinese managers, indirect speech leaves a communicative gap for interlocutors to fill in – a gap for choice and a gap for both to escape the responsibility for causing embarrassment. By doing so, the interlocutors could avoid potential damage to sociality. The addressee could always claim that s/he has not fully comprehended the real intention of the addresser; while the addresser could avoid being accused of forcing the response.

Perceptive readers may question: By contrasting the indirect speech (as a form of communicative skills) preferred by my Chinese interlocutors with the direct style of communication used by my Zambian interlocutors, am I denying the ability of Zambians to produce indirect speech and also potentially committing ethnocentricism, that is, taking Chinese practice as the standard for analysis? This is not my intention at all. Here, I think that it is worth to point out, first, that this clash of communicative styles is situational. It occurs in a highly controlled Chinese workplace with a strong work unit (*danwei*) type of management, as I have documented in Chapter 3, and the communication usually happens in a hierarchical and coercive power structure. Out of this context, indirect speech could be widely used by Zambians and direct speech can also be appreciated by the Chinese migrants as a sign of sincerity. Second, as I have shown earlier, the clash is one part of the mutual learning and accustoming process not only between Chinese and Zambians but also between Chinese migrants. My purpose in invoking Chinese notions here is merely descriptive instead of prescriptive, that is, to show how Chinese migrants perceive and reason the miscommunication. These notions themselves are subject of analysis but not for analysis.

Situational affect as a contextualization cue

Placing indirect speech as a crucial communicative technique brings an intrinsic dilemma; that is, how could the addresser accurately transmit his or her message to the addressee? Indeed, this is often the question that Zambian workers ask their Chinese peers. To solve this problem, my Chinese interlocutors have further emphasized another set of communicative skills, contextualization, in practice to supplement indirect speech.

In order to succeed in mutual understanding, pragmaticians have argued that interlocutors constantly engage in a set of *contextualization cues*;

> Speakers signal and listeners interpret what the activity is, how semantic content is to be understood and how each sentence relates to what precedes or follows ... these features are ... *habitually used and perceived but rarely consciously noted and almost never talked about directly*. Therefore they must be studied in context rather than in the abstract. (Gumperz 1982a: 131, cited in Duranti 1997: 212, italics added)

When the cues are missed, the message will fail in transmission. At my field sites, to prevent such miscommunication, instead of focusing on precise coding by the addresser, my Chinese interlocutors incline to put the burden of communicative cooperation on the addressee. In other words, in conversational exchange, the addressee often takes the active role to construe and interpret the addresser's intention – which, by definition, may not be very obvious. In this process, the addressee is required to observe as much information as possible in order to achieve accurate understanding, and this often includes acutely sensing the intensity of the 'conversational atmosphere'. This intensity is manifest not only in an interlocutor's tone and movements but also, more significantly, in connection with the participants' relationships within a given situation.

This communicative demand to the addressees is neatly summed up in the northern Chinese colloquial expression '*yanlijian'er*', literally translated as 'having the eye strength to observe'. In practice, it generally refers to the ability to act appropriately in a situation without being explicitly requested to do so. When used in this way, the term often carries a moral evaluation with it. To say that a person 'has the eye strength to observe' is to praise him or her for being clever, industrious and having high emotional intelligence (*qingshang*); people without such a 'capacity' are criticized as socially inept. Speakers consider this communicative technique to function as a means of soft command between Chinese leaders and Chinese workers in the workplace. I call it 'soft' because the commands are always implicit. Nevertheless, they can still be regarded as commands because subordinates will fall out of a leader's favour and potentially lose the chance of future promotion if they cannot perform according to the leader's wishes. The next ethnographic example demonstrates how this communicative technique is negotiated and transmitted between Chinese managers and Zambian workers.

Ever since he was 'downgraded' from chauffeur to general worker, Thomas had been criticized more and more by the general manager of ATDC. Thomas, born in Chirundu (a southeastern region of Zambia) in the 1970s, was a cab driver before he was hired as a chauffeur. Since Thomas started working as a chauffeur, he and Manager Bao had argued on a number of occasions. Manager Bao criticized Thomas as 'lacking a sense of organization and discipline' (*wuzuzhijiluxing*) and as 'making decisions without authorization' (*shanzizuozhu*), among other things, whereas Thomas, for his part, felt that Manager Bao 'never listens to the workers' advice' and 'treats [him] like a slave'. After several rounds of quarrels and threats of being fired, Thomas' position was downgraded to that of a general worker, which was a considerable drop in prestige. However, the criticism didn't stop there. Manager Bao concluded that Thomas, as a general worker, was very lazy and had a very passive attitude towards work, because he would not do any work until specifically ordered to. The manager got this impression from several incidents at work. For example, when he saw Thomas chatting with the security guards, he would pick up a broom to sweep the courtyard in front of the security booth. In taking this action, the manager was implying that he was unhappy about Thomas chitchatting with other workers during work hours. He expected Thomas to observe the situation and understand his intention, and stop chatting, take the broom from him and continue sweeping. In Manager Bao's experience, no junior worker would witness the leader working alone and not join in. Nevertheless, very often, Thomas would just ignore him or sometimes stand beside the manager and watch him finish the task. Needless to say, his response irritated the manager. Manager Bao interpreted Thomas' behaviour as challenging his authority. But this was not Thomas' intention as far as I could tell; several times, Thomas asked the translators why the manager was always angry with him, and sought their advice on how to improve his relationship with him. Manager Bao would criticize Thomas fiercely and command him to re-do work he had just finished. On more than one occasion, I heard the manager sharing his opinions with managers from other Chinese companies. Once I overheard him speaking to the manager of the Confucius Institute in Lusaka when she was seeking some recruitment advice:

> They [Zambian workers] don't have any *yanlijian'er* at all! You have to order them to do work and they only do what you ask them to do, not a tiny little bit more. Even worse, they sometimes just stand there like a piece of wood watching you do their job! This would never happen in China! Make sure you choose some smart ones otherwise there will be tons of trouble ahead for you.

After more and more accusations Thomas became very frustrated. He believed that he had finished what the boss had asked him to do, but that somehow it was not enough to satisfy him. So, Thomas decided to ask translator Xiao Liu for some advice. Xiao Liu told Thomas that he should be more observant of what the manager wanted and preferred. He mentioned that Thomas should actively undertake tasks before the manager asked him to do anything, sharing his personal insights:

> It does not mean you have to work all the time. You just need to be more observant when Manager Bao is around. When you see him walking near the flowers, you can pick up the bucket and start watering. Then he will be pleased. Oh, and when he is doing some work, don't stand there. You should help him. Just do what he wants.

Thomas learned from Xiao Liu and put his advice into practice. This effectively eased the tension between him and Manager Bao for a while. Not only did the criticism decrease, but the manager sometimes even praised Thomas in front of other Zambian workers. Having already planned to fire him, Thomas's change made the manager put his initial thoughts on hold and 'keep [him] for further observation' (*youdaiguancha*). However, his efforts notwithstanding, Thomas's newly acquired communicative skill put him in another awkward spot when a delegation from China was visiting the educational farm.

Hosting a Chinese delegation is a rather common task for all Chinese state-owned enterprises in Zambia. Although a team can be sent by various different institutes, members of Chinese delegations are normally from a higher administrative ranking than the Chinese managers in Zambia. This means that the managers must endeavour to put on a good performance in front of the delegates, so that once their Zambian work is finished and they are called back to China, they can have more chances of promotion. As I have described in Chapter 3, a subtle and smooth hosting can demonstrate the manager's ability and personal attentiveness to his/her superiors. Therefore, it is usually the busiest time for the manager as s/he needs to carefully design the itinerary according to the personal preferences of the leader (the delegation's highest-ranking official) and liaise with many Chinese companies in Zambia to arrange accommodation, meals, party venues, transport, day trips, entertainment and so on. Preparations to host a delegation can sometimes take months. During the whole process, other routine work is inevitably delayed.

In this case, the awkward moment happened when Manager Bao was giving the delegation a tour of some newly built administrative buildings. After being shown around the first floor, they were passing the lobby to go to the east wing. Seeing that the manager was coming, Thomas picked up the broom and started sweeping the floor. When he saw what Thomas was doing from the end of the corridor, the manager immediately whispered to Technician Xu at his side; Xu quickly ran to the lobby, shouted at Thomas, grabbed his broom and pushed him out. That evening after the delegation team left, the manager fiercely scolded Thomas. The recently salvaged relationship sank to a new low.

What had happened? By sweeping the floor without being ordered to do so, Thomas's intention had been to please the manager just as he had before. However, in this case his action caused the manager extreme embarrassment. According to the manager's practices, the building needed

Speaking with affect 177

to be thoroughly cleaned *before* the visit. That was why all of the staff in the Demonstration Centre postponed their routine work and spent almost a fortnight cleaning and preparing the whole farm for the delegation's visit. Cleaning while the delegation was present meant that the job had not been done properly. As a result, Thomas' well-intended action was interpreted as a reflection of the manager's incompetence, thus provoking his anger.

To understand this event, the notion of '*yanlijian'er*' needs to be further explained. Although he told Thomas how to be observant, Xiao Liu did not fully explain the whole gamut of the meaning of '*yanlijian'er*'. Crucially, being observant does not just mean paying attention to the communicative other, but extends to understanding the nature of the situation and the social relationships between every player in that situation, and then acting accordingly. In the episode discussed earlier, the locus of social relations had shifted to that between the manager and his leaders, and the gravity of the situation lay in the intention of the manager to please his leaders. The whole ambience of the situation had transformed. So according to the new relational context, the workers should assist the manager in satisfying his leaders. Any communicative action against this would be construed as non-cooperative, and would carry the danger of damaging the relationship. This would lead to workers falling out of their Chinese leader's circle of favourites and damaging their careers or future prosperity. Hence, we can see that the application of '*yanlijian'er*' entails flexibility. It requires the subject to draw a great deal of information, not only tangible but also intangible, from the situational context and respond to it appropriately.

Fang I-Chieh, in her doctoral dissertation, documents similar communicative phenomena in a factory at Guangdong Province, southern China. Her informants refer to this capability of contextualization as *kanrenlianse*. She explains that this term means literally 'watching other people's facial expressions but means seeing what others feel/want'. She further elaborates:

> What truly marks a 'smart', ideal worker is that they should be voluntarily paying attention to their leaders' *emotions* in order to understand the

leaders' desires and intentions. Then they should react quickly ... . If workers cannot understand leaders' unspoken wishes, or know who might react to things that happened, they will be punished, sometimes without the matter ever being mentioned. (2012: 99, italics added)

What she points out is that emotion is a crucial clue for her informants to construe their leaders' intention. Her findings correspond well with the phenomena at my field site in Zambia. Nevertheless, what I would further add is that this attention to emotion is directed not only at other people but also at the whole context, which I have termed *situational affect*. In other words, the interlocutor's emotion and the effect of conversational situation are equally important 'contextualization cues' for my Chinese interlocutors in the process of reading each other's minds.

The significance of situational affect in communication could be seen in etymology. The English term 'situation' can be translated into Chinese as '*qingkuang*' or '*qingshi*'. Morphologically, '*qingkuang*' is the combination of '*qing*' (emotion) and '*kuang*' (shape/status). When translated back to English, '*qingkuang*' can also be rendered as circumstances, condition and state of affairs. In pragmatics, it is arguable that this term can be interpreted as meaning that one can only comprehend a fact by taking its 'affective dimension' into account. In other words, 'situation' as a Chinese expression already – and always – entails affect. As Roger Ames writes, '*Qing* then is both the facticity of and the feeling that pervades any particular situation. Any perceived fact/value distinction between "circumstances" on the one hand, and "feelings that are responsive to circumstances" on the other, collapses' (2011: 74). When it comes to communication, arguably, meanings are transmitted by affective resonance rather than logical persuasion. This style of communication requires intense shared experiences as a precondition.

Talking with affection

Back to the banquet the Zou family was hosting that evening described before: there is a set of etiquette rules at banquets and the procedure is highly ritualized. At the banquet table, the seating arrangement follows a strict order; banquets are explicitly hierarchical and routinely involve people of significantly different social status. Indeed, the whole banqueting process is partly about turning everybody present – temporarily – into notionally equal partners, before the hierarchy is reaffirmed. During the banquet, attendees are expected to take turns giving speeches. The order of speeches normally follows the seating arrangement. The host gives an opening speech, then each guest follows in the prearranged hierarchical order. Everyone needs to address a semi-formal speech to the whole table with a toast for the first round, after which informal toasting continues between individuals. The first round of speeches can be presented on behalf of households as well. Speeches are meant to be spontaneous and are not usually prepared beforehand, since their content needs to correspond with the event and with the other speeches. Hence, they are a good way of demonstrating speakers' communication skills. Often, the opening speech of the host includes the purpose of the banquet; the special relationship between the host and the guest of honour, who normally sits next to the host on the right-hand side; welcomes to any new acquaintances; and general good wishes for all the guests.

Father Zou, as the head of the family, was requested by the guests to give the opening speech, although he was not especially willing. Despite the rules I have just outlined, he simply said, 'Thanks for coming here for dinner. The dishes are simple but please enjoy yourselves.' Then he emptied his Chinese whisky shot-glass. Seeing this, Mother Zou immediately stood up, holding her glass and made a supplementary speech.

> Our Lao De is very down-to-earth (*shizai*) as you all know. He is not very good at speaking (*bushan yantan*) but a very reliable man in business. All of you sitting here are our close friends. This meal is the first meal we have together since our family farm is fully built. This is to thank all of you sitting here. Without your generous help, we would not be able to build this farm or even stay in Zambia. Our family especially feel grateful to Manager Deng and his family. You are our benefactor [*enren*].

At this moment, Mother Zou turned around and faced Manager Deng directly as she continued speaking with a slightly shaky voice and tears in her eyes.

> Many people turned away when our family was in big trouble. It was you who helped us but did not ask for anything in return. We would never forget your goodness. If it were not for your help, we would not be here today, not to mention this meal. I represent my whole family to make this toast. We wish you and your family health and that your business grows bigger day by day! Also, to all the friends sitting here, good fortune! I am going to empty my glass first to show my respect [*xiangan weijing*].

While Mother Zou was still drinking, some guests already started praising her speech and her ability.

'Enjoy the dishes. Enjoy the dishes', Mother Zou served some meat onto the guests' plates.

Moments later, Manager Deng raised his glass and suddenly all the people at the banquet stopped chatting.

> First of all, we need to appreciate the Zous' heart [*xinyi*] to invite us here today and offer us an opportunity to get together. Nowadays, everyone is busy with business and earning money. So little time left for friends and family. Without *zoudong* [visiting each other], people inevitably become disacquainted [*shengfen*]. It is not worth sacrificing each other's affection [*qingyi*] for money. Everybody sitting here knows that it is not easy to survive here (in Zambia) long away from home [*beijinglixiang*]. We have all experienced the bitterness [*ku*, difficulty] at the beginning. Helping each other is what we should do, not to mention that we are from the same region. The old saying puts it well: 'People need to rely on friends when stepping out of home' [*chuwenkaopengyou*]. We are all good brothers and sisters [*xiongdijiemei*] united through suffering the same together [*gonghuannan*]. I propose a toast to our long-lasting brotherly affection [*xiongdiqingyi*]!

Manager Deng emptied his glass, then everyone followed. By then, a very warm and convivial affect had been created at the banquet.

Of course, the idea that commensality produces and enhances relationships has been extensively discussed by anthropologists. But here I would like to say a little more about the particular ways in which convivial affect is produced at Chinese banquets. First, taking the role of her husband to toast after his rather short, seemingly cold, speech, Mother Zou explicitly set up the emotional theme of the banquet – gratitude to friends. Standing up while speaking not only showed her respect to the guests but also gave the impression of intensifying her sincerity; she now must have really meant what she said. This atmosphere was further enhanced through Mother Zou's bodily performance – watering eyes, a shaky voice, the turning of her body as she engaged with individual participants. Her slightly exaggerated way of saying things, relatively loud voice, and embellished body movements (including the dramatic drinking of a shot) at the end of her speech noticeably boosted the energy of the banquet. Second, Manager Deng's speech echoed Mother Zou's tone. It aimed to increase emotional resonance by pinpointing shared identity and experiences, for instance being 'away from home' and 'suffering bitterness'. Again, like Mother Zou, Manager Deng used a loud voice and bodily movements to amplify the emotional state of the event. Third, standing back to interpret the event as a whole, the function of the audience was important as well. They provided a rhythm at the table through individual speech (which was relatively quiet but ongoing), followed by collective praise (which tended to be noisy), then more individual conversation (quiet again), and standing up together (noisy). Affect was reinforced and intensified by this rhythm of contrasts.

After Manager Deng gave his speech, people at the table started to get up and toast each other. Now and then, several toast conversations would overlap. Suddenly, it was getting very 'hot and noisy' (*renao*) around the table, and the sound, mixed with chairs moving, glasses clinking and people shouting 'bottoms-up' to each other, became louder and louder. Sometimes at these events, when people get a bit drunk, guests are asked to sing songs to further 'boost the atmosphere' (*zhuxing*). Rather crude adult jokes are sometimes told, at which attendees will burst into loud laughter. Men often play drinking games involving many hand gestures and other bodily movements. If this is all taking place in a restaurant with karaoke facilities, instead of in a private home as with the Zou banquet, people sometimes dance to loud music towards the end of their excessive drinking and eating.

During my fieldwork, I attended thirty-two banquets, informal and formal, official and familial. I tape-recorded twenty-one banquet speeches. From what I gathered from my Chinese interlocutors, in general, a good banquet speech needs to show the speaker's courtesy, good intention and sincerity. Nevertheless, all of these need to be expressed to a precise degree. Too much courtesy may become 'polite' or empty speech (*ketaohua*), and sound superficial, alienating the addressee. By contrast, if the speech is too straightforward, it may be criticized for lacking elegance. More importantly, a good banquet speech should correspond well with both the emotional proximity of interlocutors and the context of the banquet. A good banquet speech needs to be emotionally loaded and affectively provocative. It is explicitly intended to produce and maintain an *affective situation*. Such affect is produced by emotional resonance and is often triggered by shared experiences, as shown in the earlier case. Both the speaker and the audience are co-creators of this resonance. They cooperate to create situational affect in order to generate or strengthen their social bonds.

In his study of Chinese religion, Adam Yuet Chau calls this process 'the sensorial production of the social' (2008). He not only highlights the significance of the sense of 'social heat' (*honghuo*) in Chinese social perception but also argues that individual actors are actively (re)producing this sense for the purposes of sociality. He writes that

> the heat in *honghuo* [red-fiery] and *re'nao* [hot-noisy] is thought to reside in the social gathering and is not necessarily a physical/physiological sensation felt by the people in the gathering. What is felt by the people, however, [is] a diffuse psychosomatic sense of satisfaction and fulfilment resulting from having partaken in, and co-produced, red-hot sociality. (2008: 488)

Following him, I further argue that emotional speech is one mechanism for my Chinese interlocutors to (re)produce sensory and affective situations for the purposes of everyday sociality. In other words, as shown earlier, through emotional speech, they create an affective setting in which to resonate, understand and bond with each other. In turn, this attachment pushes them to produce further emotional speech.

Speech, work and favouritism

Earlier, I have described the intertwined relationships of speech, affect and sociality. As I have demonstrated through this book, the sociality of my Chinese interlocutors is based on 'differential mode of association', which is particularistic, affective and responsive. This kind of sociality provides the foundation for wide application of indirect speech and emotional talk in practice; and also encourages the individual to extensively draw information from the context in order to achieve communication. This focus on communication nurtures certain types of habits in speaking, and they reflect back to act upon everyday socializing. In a simpler version, my Chinese interlocutors would be reluctant to socialize with someone who does not use similar communicative mechanisms. In their words, it is because such people 'do not know what to talk about' (*buzhidaoshuoshenmehao*). Meanwhile, shared speech style would strengthen the proximity among interlocutors.

The latter aspect of the intertwined relationship – the function of speech on sociality – has been gradually acknowledged by my Chinese interlocutors. In everyday interaction, my Chinese interlocutors are consciously utilizing speech for social networking to achieve personal desires. In other words, they are using speech to access 'social capital' (Bourdieu 1977). Since 'speaking appropriately' is considered as a form of 'social capability' by my interlocutors and needs to be learned in long-term social practices (note, as I will demonstrate further, not all Chinese migrants master these complex sets of communicative skills), here,

I venture to term the skill in speaking 'speech capital'. Speech capital has subtle differences from Bourdieu's notion of 'linguistic capital'. For Bourdieu, linguistic capital is a form of cultural capital that emphasizes how different social statuses are manifested and reproduced (1991). By contrast, speech capital focuses on how class differences are diluted and how individual social mobility is strategically achieved. Nevertheless, the utilitarian characteristic of analysis is shared. In the rest of this chapter, I will describe how speech is utilized as capital in everyday practices at work and in business. I want to propose that this tendency of commercializing speech will enhance and amplify the power of existing communicative style to the extent of self-regeneration.

If speech is not just a way for the speaker to express himself/herself but also for the audience to perceive and evaluate, it could be argued that speech is a performance – a kind of self-impression management (Goffman 1971). It is enacted for the audience's awareness. Good performance will attract an audience's interest and appreciation while a bad performance will potentially dislodge the audience. Good performance requires certain abilities of the actor, which need to be acquired through a long process of cultivating and practising. Ultimately, it is possible that the speech would change the character of the speaker; that is, metaphorically, the actor is trapped in the play and lives in it forever. The play becomes the reality and reality becomes the play. It is indeed this performative character of speech that most of my post-1980s Chinese interlocutors struggled with, causing frustrations and unsatisfactory complaints at work. The frustration comes from the association between the performance of speech and work evaluation, and the struggle comes from their realization of the fakery of such play. They acknowledged the importance of speaking appropriately at work – speaking well will make them become the favourite so to be promoted quickly by the leader – but sometimes they will feel unease at putting up a show. As Mr Barry always said:

> Nowadays, the one who works hard cannot compete with the one who speaks well [*nenggandeburuhuishuode*]. Leaders prefer the one with

the sweet mouth. Look at them. Doing nothing every day but they still get a bonus. Look at me. Work my shit out every day but our leader still criticises me. What a society [*shidao*]! So unfair!

Barry's feeling of unfairness largely drew from the comparison between his everyday work life and Liu Wei's. Liu Wei shared a room with Barry. As a document filer, indeed, Liu Wei did not have as heavy a workload as Barry. Nonetheless, for me, Liu Wei had another kind of tiresome work. Because he made good banquet speeches, Liu Wei was always asked to keep the leader's company at business dinners, which he did not particularly find enjoyable.

> To be honest, I do not really like that business dinner-entertainment [*yingchou*]. It is so tiring. Full of fakery. People have to say the words they do not want to say in order to please each other. Also, you are forced to drink a lot; otherwise people would think you are not groupy [*hequn*] and insincere [*jia*]. Why bother [*heku*] if people cannot enjoy and be true to themselves?

Liu Wei's negative sentiment and reluctance to business dinner-entertainment, owing to the performance of fake speech, were widely shared among most of my young Chinese interlocutors. Despite the discontent, they do acknowledge its significance for sociality and admire the one who has the ability to speak and perform well in business banquets.

As mentioned earlier, one regular task at ATDC is to welcome the investigation team from China for project examinations. During their stay, putting up official banquets in local Chinese restaurants every day was inevitable. As the general manager, Bao was always in charge of organizing the banquets. Even though there were several Chinese workers at ATDC, Bao still prefers to invite Grace to help during the banquets. As he reasoned, 'It is always easy to speak as a girl' (*nuhai'erhaoshuohua*). The unspoken reason was that Grace was good at supplementing Bao's speech and saving his face when he lost track due to drunkenness. Grace was originally from the same city as Bao was, and she did her undergraduate study in Bao's university before she went to the United States for her master's degree. After her graduation, she immediately secured a position in a Chinese mining company. Because of her overseas experience, she was soon relocated to Zambia to establish a business branch. It was in Zambia where Bao and Grace became acquainted through the *laoxiang* (people from same region) network.

Grace was well regarded and often admired as a girl who can speak appropriately (*huishuohua*). Once after a business banquet, Xiao Liu started to gossip with Liu Wei about the performance of Bao and Grace:

> That girl is tough [*lihai*]. Very good at speaking! [*zhennengshuo*]. There's no doubt why her boss likes her so much and is not willing to let her quit. You can tell how much money she can get just for that mouth. See how happy she made our leaders. Everyone on the table was praising her. I wish I could speak as well as she can. It was funny to see how many times she had saved Lao Bao's [Manager Bao] arse. I mean, what a professor is he? What level [*shuiping*] is he? – does not even know how to speak! No ability [*nengli*] at all! No doubt why he has waited fifteen years to be promoted only as a junior manager.

'Shh, lower your voice. Be aware that there is an ear on the other side of the wall [*geqiang you'er*]!' Liu Wei warned him

'Yes, you are right. I am too inobservant sometimes', Xiao Liu began to whisper.

> You know, if it was not because there was no one wanting to come to Zambia, Lao Bao would still not get the chance to be promoted. He asked for a promotion in exchange for being sent here. You know what the leaders say about him? They say that he does not know how to control his mouth [*guanbuzhuzui*] and speaks everything directly out of his head. No one liked him so they sent him here.

It could be claimed that a good banquet speech can form or enhance the social networks at the table so to bring potential benefits for the speaker. Notwithstanding, Barry's comment that 'the one who works hard cannot compete with the one who speaks well [*nenggande buru huishuode*]' has another layer of meaning. Mastering sophisticated speaking skills does not just bring possible capital around dining tables; more crucially, it is effective in everyday sentence-to-sentence communication in the workplace. Through this informal everyday communication, the leader evaluates the worker's capabilities, such as social intelligence, loyalty and respect to the senior, for future references. Therefore, speech at work is a performance for the leader's perception – one cannot always speak straightforwardly what one thinks, but should speak according to the leader's preferences, as argued earlier. It involves speaking out loud what the leader is willing to say but does not dare to say regarding possible responsibility; or, speaking it indirectly and humbly when the leader cannot make a decision but needs advice or obviously the leader has made a mistake; or, speaking passionately when the leader fishes for compliments.

Speech, network and profits

As described earlier, speech transforms into capital at work by means of favouritism. In other words, a worker who masters the skill to 'speak appropriately' according to the shifting situation is considered by the leader as a promising worker; in turn, the worker would have more chances to be promoted and gain associated benefits. By contrast, the transformation from speech to capital in business is more direct; nonetheless, it is through social networking and social capital that such transformation is fulfilled.

As Mother Zou acknowledged and emphasized in the episode earlier, in order to grow the family business, there has to be at least one person in a family who knows how to speak properly even though sometimes it means losing face. This could be well illustrated in Mother Liu's case. One of the crucial background reasons for Mother Liu's business success in Zambia is her capability in speaking. As Mother Zou observed,

> Sometimes, I wish I could have the guts to speak as Mother Liu does. Most of the time, I think I am just too embarrassed [*fangbukai*]. I suppose

my face is too thin. Do you know that Mother Liu even knelt once to save her business? It was in the early years when she arrived here. She was not as famous as she is now in Zambia and her business could hardly survive. Like us, she was borrowing money to keep her restaurant going. In the end, there were just not enough customers. She almost closed down, she had to 'beg' [*bajie*] the officials. That was where the money was. At the beginning, the officials were not interested. Mother Liu said lots of sweet words and gave them lots of gifts and, once, even knelt in front of their car, crying for help. She was very persistent. I could not have done that. So embarrassing. Well, in the end, she got well-connected with the ambassador and now owns one hotel and two restaurants and is looking for a farm to buy. Ah, nowadays, business is easy – just throw away the face and say some sweet words [*haotingde*], money will come in! Look at our Lao De, he only knows how to work hard in the field. Honesty these days is not worth a penny! When could we be rich?

I never heard this story directly from Mother Liu; however, I did witness how skilful she was when the staff of ATDC interacted with her. Before the farm was built, the administrative staff all stayed in Mother Liu's hotel. After the compound was finished, the managers still liked going to her restaurant for business banquets even though the food was not particularly good. As Manager Lu explained, 'We know her and she is one of us. She is friendly. Everything is easy to talk and deal with here.' 'Easy to talk' (*haoshuohua*) means someone is flexible and up for negotiation. It is true that flexibility is one of Mother Liu's qualities and 'everything is easy to negotiate (*fanshihaoshangliang*)' is a term she often used. Her speaking skills could be shown through the speech she gave. It was a business banquet held by ATDC in Mother Liu (ML)'s restaurant to treat the Chinese provincial investigation team for the aid project.

> Leader: Mother Liu, a toast to respect you. Thank you very much for your warm and subtle hospitality. Although we are in a foreign country, we do feel just like at home.
> ML: Ah, Secretary really has over-complimented [*taiju*] me. I only did what I should do. I was worried that I have not done enough, really. As long as everyone feels pleased, then I will feel pleased. This is your

home, our home. The reason why I set up this business is just for the convenience of the Chinese.

MB: Mother Liu acts as a real mother here. She helps us a lot. Whenever we had a trouble, as long as we called Mother Liu, she would help us without a second question [*erhuabushuo*].

ML: A really old mother! Hehe!

[Everyone was laughing]

MB: Well, you still look very young and glamorous!

Leader: We have given you more trouble when we are here for sure.

ML: Aiya, you are too courteous, my Secretary. Please do not see yourself as an outsider [*jianwai*]. If there was no trouble, I would be bored to death! Haha! We are all friends [*zijiren*, literally 'self-people']. No need to mention trouble or no trouble. See, for fifty odd years in China, we have never met but we all come to this remote country, thousands of miles away from China, and befriended each other here. Isn't this our karma [*yuanfen*]? I cherish karma. So please feel free to let me know if you have any problem here. I will try my best. I am sure that Secretary will do the same if I have any trouble in your province.

Leader: Certainly! Let us raise our glasses for Mother Liu's hospitality!

Here, by starting with a humble reply – 'over-complimented' – to the leader's appreciation and further affirming her duty to serve the leader, Mother Liu was using an indirect way to demonstrate her comprehension of the hierarchical relationships between the leader and Mother Liu in that situation. Then, to draw their relationship closer, she began to informalize the situation by stressing mutual affective reaction (i.e. feeling pleased), group identity (i.e. Chinese, self-people) and shared cultural idea (i.e. karma); furthermore, by the relaxing situational affect created in the exchange of jokes between Manager Bao and Mother Liu. In the end, by pointing out the potentiality in need of support from the leader in future, Mother Liu established a reciprocal tie and messages were communicated – she is showing great hospitality when the leader is in Zambia, so the leader is supposed to take care of her if she has trouble in China.

Note the role of Manager Bao in this situation. He acted as a broker in the conversation. Working under his leader, Bao is considered to be a member of the official group, but he also had interacted with Mother Liu before. Acute awareness of his role in this web of relations at the banquet table, Bao was pinpointing the care that Mother Liu had offered when he was in need. This explicit appreciation of Mother Liu made this debt of care implicitly transmitted to the leader because Bao's loyalty presumably lies with his leader; namely, to care Bao is to give his leader's face. In other words, what Bao was doing by splitting out personal appreciation is to bridge the relationship between his leader and Mother Liu by taking advantage of his role in between. Helping Mother Liu in the conversation also works as a form of personal favour (*renqing*) (because Bao could have chosen not to speak in this way) and enhances the social bonds between Bao and Mother Liu. All of this could be possible because of everyone's awareness of each other's relational position in that situation.

Speech can be transformed into capital through social networking; everyday bargaining is a more direct route for such transformation. Through bargaining, the value of speech capacity is demonstrated and enjoyed by bargainers. Xiao Zou especially liked bargaining even when the benefit negotiated was extremely small. Every Monday, Xiao Zou needs to purchase some vegetables and meat from different Chinese farms around Lusaka for the delivery on Wednesday to a Chinese construction team near Kariba. By shadowing him, I had a good opportunity to observe his bargaining speech. Chitchat before real purchase began was necessary as it enhanced the social ties between buyer and seller in order to decrease the tension of bargaining later on. When the negotiation was underway, sound excuses, such as shared locality, long-term business relationship or potential for more purchases, were needed in order to ask for a discount, but being flexible and easy to talk with is crucial. Next is one of the bargains Xiao Zou (XZ) performed when he was purchasing half a pig from a Chinese farm.

Lao Wang: You are here [*laile*]?
XZ: Eh, busy today?

LW: OK, not much, just building a new pigpen.
XZ: Your business is growing bigger and bigger. I am afraid after you become the biggest boss, you would not care to look at me anymore [laugh]
LW: Impossible [*nakeneng*]!
[While talking, they walked to the butchery house]
LW: How much do you need?
XZ: Less than half … how much per kg
LW: 11500 Kwacha
XZ: More expensive?
LW: No, it has always been the same price. Look at the quality. It is not expensive at all!
XZ: Hmmm, this pig looks quite fatty. I have to cut the extra fat off when getting back home. Make it 9000 Kwacha.
LW: No, no, it cannot be. 9000 is too low. 11000 is OK.
XZ: Aiya, You are the big boss. See your pigpen is growing bigger and bigger. Why do you care about so little money! Plus, we are both from Jiangxi. 'People from the same village weep when they meet outside of their village' [*laoxiangjianlaoxiang, liangyanleiwangwang*]. We shall look after each other. I will come back more often, then you will earn more. We both are happy.
LW: But 9000 is really too low.
XZ: OK. Make it 10000. Easy to calculate.
LW: OK. OK. 10000 it is.
XZ: Hmmm, cut me the lean. This one is too fat.

While we loaded the pig into the truck and drove to the next farm, Xiao Zou looked satisfied and said to me, 'It is a lot cheaper than last week. Lao Wang is a good man, very easy-going and easy to talk to.'

Conclusion

While criticizing John Searle's theory on intentionality in speech act, Rosaldo argues that what is important for Ilongots is the attention to social relations in the process of communication. Therefore, he claims that speech act inevitably reflects and also reproduces Western ideas about sincerity, intentionality and human agency if there is not enough attention given to the variable cultural practices on personhood.

> I want to argue here that ways of thinking about language and about human agency and personhood are intimately linked: our theoretical attempts to understand how language works are like the far less explicated linguistic thoughts of people elsewhere in the world, in that both inevitably tend to reflect locally prevalent views about the given nature of those human persons by whom language is used. (1982: 203)

Bearing his caution in mind, in this chapter, I have described the intertwined relationships of speech, affect and sociality. On the one hand, the mode of association between my Chinese interlocutors – particularistic, role-responsive, situational and emotional – nurtures certain linguistic practices. I argue that their special attention to maintaining a 'harmonious relationship' encourages them to use an indirect communicative mechanism. Due to the indirectness, in order to achieve communication, they are required to contextualize to a great extent, especially being empathic to the affect embedded in the conversational situation. On the other hand, as these nurtured linguistic styles are moralized and made subject to social expectation and evaluation, the performance of 'appropriate speech' according to the Chinese migrants' folk understanding is impacting on the (trans) formation of sociality. What is more important of 'appropriate speech' or any form of communicative action is that it is used to (re)produce sensory affect in which social relation is realized and practised by my Chinese interlocutors. Based on the observations of this intertwined relationship, I suggest that it is these moralized communicative styles and their values in the formation of social relations that causes misunderstanding between Chinese migrants and their Zambian hosts. Nevertheless, as I have also shown through the chapter, both parties are aware of the everyday communicative problems and are learning from each other in order to achieve mutual understanding.

Conclusion

Having started my project with the idea of studying communication and interactions between Chinese migrants and their Zambian hosts, soon after I arrived at my field sites in Lusaka, I realized the deep segregation between these two ethnic groups – which sometimes happens even when they work in close proximity. This 'cut-off' in communication, either intentionally created or inevitably occurring, forced me to reconsider my initial research questions. As noted in the Introduction, much of the existing literature on 'China in Africa' has been written from African points of view; thanks to my own identity giving me a practical advantage (i.e. being a Chinese myself made it relatively easier to pass the gatekeeper of Chinese groups in Zambia), I began to shift my research focus to examine how Chinese migrants actually socialize and communicate with each other in everyday life, and how they form and sustain social bonds and groups – processes that are far more complicated than one might expect. As I see it, however, this shift is really about pursuing the same theoretical agenda with an alternative approach. I consider that in order to understand cross-cultural (mis)communication the researcher first of all has to give 'thick descriptions' of both cultural reference systems and then has to find the points of disjunction. Undeniably, to study China-in-Africa, as a phenomenon of 'cultural contact' and 'cross-cultural communication', is a huge project that requires collaborations of researchers not only from both sides of the interaction but also from different academic disciplines. Against this background, this book is written with the aim of contributing to the understanding of Chinese-Zambian cross-cultural (mis)communication from the perspective of one side of the 'game': the Chinese side.

Obviously, many perceptive readers might feel that, by narrating the story from the 'Chinese side', I am at risk of committing ethnocentrism. That is, having been born and raised in China (although my anthropological training is entirely gained in the UK), I am now describing stories of China-in-Africa from the perspective of Chinese migrants and, at many places, referring to theoretical models of sociality and morality developed by Chinese theorists and sinologists. For reasons that I have explained several times in the book, I do not agree with this criticism. I consider it worth here to emphasize my intention again. First of all, as stated earlier, I always consider my research as one part of a whole; that is to say, to systematically study the China-Africa interaction demands either teamwork or the lifelong efforts of an individual researcher. I consider that neither China nor Africa should be taken for granted. Both deserve 'thick description' before comparison. Nevertheless, with how the stories of China-Africa are told thus far, the voices of Chinese migrants are relatively weak. Moreover, documenting the everyday life of Chinese migrants in Zambia through ethnography is the main purpose of this book. The representations here are descriptive rather than prescriptive. 'From the Chinese side' does not mean that I am using the discourse of Chinese migrants as the referencing point for academic analysis. On the contrary, my intention is to unpack and to deconstruct their discourses with the background of cross-cultural miscommunication. Admittedly, many of their judgements can be racially biased just like how Zambians would judge Chinese migrants; however, reporting these discourses does not mean subscribing to them. In reality, from the very first vignette in this book – where Thomas, the Zambian driver, is basically treated as someone who can be ignored – I presume my own discomfort about the ethics of the Chinese-Zambian interactions will have been communicated. Through the book, I endeavour to contextualize the biases that undoubtedly exist by analysing anxiety, power play (in relation to social roles) and linguistic performances. Finally, borrowing theories from Chinese anthropologists and sinologists is to compare them with models generated under Western epistemology, then to supplement and to develop more comprehensive theories together.

So far, in the book, I have described and interpreted in each chapter how the interaction between Chinese and Africans was intentionally cut off, and how miscommunication is inevitably created. Following a story line of 'first encounters' across chapters in the book, first, I argue that at the initial stage of socializing, it is the uncertainty and anxiety of my Chinese interlocutors – which automatically arise when encountering ethnic 'strangers' – that makes them reluctant to interact with their Zambian counterparts, to the extent that they may avoid interaction altogether (Chapter 1). It is the mistrust nurtured by intra-community competition and factionalism of Chinese migrants that provides them with the psychological foundation of suspicion of their Zambian hosts' instrumental (often projected as malicious) intention, and further prevents the formation of cross-cultural bonds (Chapter 2). Then, in Chapter 3, to take the story a step further, I illustrated how miscommunication can inevitably occur, even when interactions become necessary and unavoidable in workplaces, because of the mismatching practices on boss–worker relations. The misunderstanding sometimes turns into quarrels and arguments. In the final two chapters, I end the story with more general points of 'cultural encounters'. Chapter 4, in respect of moral interaction, explains that the social bond of Chinese migrants and their Zambian hosts is interrupted overall by realization of ethical qualia while embodying various social roles. Chapter 5 shows, straightforwardly, that the communication is deeply hindered by the linguistic styles that my Chinese interlocutors employ and appreciate. Therefore, to read their story of 'first encounters' in this way, it appears that the perceived differences in everyday sociality, morality and language provide the foundation for Chinese migrants to disengage with their Zambian hosts.

Nevertheless, these reasons on the surface cannot answer a puzzle that I constantly faced during my fieldwork; that is, even when my Chinese interlocutors, especially the young ones (born since the 1980s), make efforts to communicate and endeavour to form bonds with the Zambians, their interaction and relationships could not last long. Relationships often drift and are sometimes even torn apart with intense frustration and dissatisfaction. Afterwards, the Chinese migrants usually rationalize it with a general expression: 'They are very difficult to communicate/talk with' (*hetamenjiaoliuhenkunnan*). What do they refer to and what exactly does it mean when they say it is 'difficult to communicate' [*buhaojiaoliu*]? As I have shown in Chapter 5, this evaluation cannot simply be due to the insufficiency of Chinese migrants' English skills since the Chinese translators give similar reports and also 'home-sign' (Enfield and Levinson 2006)[1] starts emerging among Chinese and Zambian co-workers. This question forces me to look beyond superficial reasons and look into the foundation of Chinese sociality.

What sustains the social relationships of Chinese migrants is the second narrative line running through this book. Inspired by Fei's model of Chinese sociality, I have attempted to demonstrate the essential role that emotion plays in producing and maintaining social relationships and groups among Chinese. The presentations and arguments develop theoretically chapter by chapter according to the three dimensions of emotion. At the beginning, the focus is on inner psychological states, anxiety and suspicion, and their impact on initiating social ties and positioning mutual relationships. Then, I highlight the function of 'interactional affection' – a form of intersubjective emotion – on sustaining long-term friendships and cooperation. In Chapter 3, I discussed how intersubjective emotion (attentiveness in this case) is demanded at work and how it is bundled with the structure of 'work relations'. Chapter 4 furthers the argument of the previous chapter and shows how affect is deeply embedded in social roles and transforms the disposition of the post-1980s generation of Chinese. In the end, I argue that emotion is built into the situation as 'situational affect'. The shared affective resonance in the situation (or materials) provides a potential for sociability and encourages proximity. To complete this line of theoretical argument, in this chapter, I want to consolidate these three dimensions of emotion, to explain how my ethnography can offer an alternative view on the issue of the social significance that emotion plays in Chinese society and to point out how the Chinese cases can contribute to anthropological studies of emotion in general.

The hypothesis of emotion in China and its critiques

When studying emotions in China, Sulamith Heins Potter has claimed (in a much criticized formulation) that emotion is irrelevant to the construction of the social.

> Chinese believe that experienced emotion is irrelevant either to the creation or to the perpetuation of social institutions of any kind. ... An emotion is never the legitimizing rationale for any socially significant action, and there is no cultural theory that social structure rests on emotional ties. Thus social relationships persist legitimately without an emotional basis, either real or fictive. (1988: 185)

To support this argument, Potter relies on three premises. First, emotion is about individual experiences and personal inner life (184). In China, there is a lack of individuality and personhood has a socio-centric character: 'A person's socially relevant characteristics are believed to be socially derived rather than individually generated or purely personal.' The social meanings are primarily drawn from social contexts and 'the important aspects of social continuity are external to the self' (186).

Second, as a legitimizing basis for social action, emotion has to be sincerely expressed. 'Relationships are derived from and affirmed by feelings, and feelings are direct expressions of the self. The expression of feeling is the medium of communication between the self and the social order' (183). In China, 'expressiveness is independent of, and implies nothing about, relationship ... the Chinese are not required by convention to provide their interlocutors with a continuing symbolic pattern of emotionally expressive response' (193).

Third, a contrast is made with American society, where

> personal emotion is a critical component of experience. ... Emotional experience is taken as legitimizing basis for social action. ... Every relationship must be enacted on the basis of a continuing emotional validation from within the enacting self that confirms the social and external by reference to the emotional and internal; otherwise the relationships is vitiated and robbed of meaning.

In other words, emotion is crucial in constructing and maintaining the social order.

Consequently, Potter concludes that, because the emotion in China by definition is incompatible with the American one, 'for the Chinese ... the emotions are concomitant phenomena in social life, not fundamental ones. They are *logically secondary*. The Chinese do not locate significance in the connection between the emotions, the self, and the social order' (187, italics added).

Following her declaration of the insignificance of emotion in Chinese society and in search for the foundation constructing the Chinese social order, Potter further contends that it is primarily 'work', as a form of action, that 'is the symbolic medium for the expression of social connection, and work affirms relationship in the most fundamental terms the villagers know [in her field site]' (1990: 195).

I consider that Potter's arguments suffer several serious inadequacies after being deconstructed as earlier. First of all, her first premise concerning the Chinese 'socio-centric' personhood needs further qualifications in relation to both the remodelling of Chinese sociality and the historical change of Chinese individuality. It is correct to claim that 'the social' constitutes the self to a great deal in China; nevertheless, it does not necessarily lead to the fact that Chinese do not possess individuality. As I have explained in the Introduction, 'social egoism' (Feuchtwang 2009) entails the idea that social relations in China exist with reference to the self. Furthermore, as Yan (2010) has argued, China's steps towards modernity across different historical periods have often been accompanied by the rise of individual and consequential individualization of the Chinese society. Writing in the late 1980s, Potter's analysis is a reflection of the historical contexts of China then. Considering the data from my field sites, especially the post-1980s Chinese migrants, it seems that there is an increasing inclination to individualism.

Moreover, as in premise two, Potter limits the communication of emotion only to expressive forms. As a result, the symbolic significance of emotion has been totally mistaken. Even if it were correct to claim that Chinese do not express emotion directly out loud, it would not necessarily mean that emotion has no role to play in forming social ties. As Bernstein (1986) claims, in face-to-face community, the code system of communication is often not elaborated. Due to the great familiarity among social actors, the affection is transmitted predominately with 'implicature', but with no necessity for direct expression. As Yan writes when studying love and romance in a village in northeastern China, 'it does not much matter whether the expression is verbal or nonverbal; what counts is whether the two individuals involved have found a way to express their affection to each other' (2003: 82). Furthermore, being over-expressive in a face-to-face society when there is no need for it may appear as cunning, untrustworthy and against ethical practices. Nevertheless, as I have mentioned in Chapter 5, the rapid urbanization in China in recent decades is capitalizing speech skills as well as estranging people, and it forces Chinese people to articulate more. As a result, emotion nowadays, especially love, is expressed loudly (Yan 2003).

Most importantly, reading the third premise together with her conclusion, in spite of the good initial attempt to search for the distinctive characteristics of emotion in China, Potter unnecessarily falls into an ethnocentric trap while comparing the Chinese emotion to the Western one. In other words, she tries to understand Chinese emotion within the Western reference system and to measure the Chinese practices according to a Western standard. In a nutshell, since Potter does not find American emotion (i.e. the sincere expression of inner psychological states of the self) at her Chinese field sites, the 'emotion' in China logically cannot have the same social significance as it does in American society.

Since its publication, Potter's approach has been heavily criticized by sinological anthropologists. Andrew Kipnis takes Potter's point on the emotional expressivity and argues that *ganqing* ('sentiment' as he refers to it in the book) is central to Chinese social relationships because 'feelings are means of communication that can be used to manipulate *guanxi*' (1997: 111). Dissatisfied with other scholars dismissing the sincerity and ability of expressing emotion in China, Yan Yunxiang uses detailed ethnography to demonstrate the transaction of private and romantic life in Xiajia village. He describes the rising youth autonomy and the increasing conjugal independence. He documents how the notion of romantic love has been popularized and explicitly expressed under the influence of American youth culture (2003: 83). Yan argues that the Chinese family has been dramatically privatized. It is no longer just a system of cooperation but more crucially 'a private haven where the private lives of individuals thrive, and individual identity and subjectivity have emerged as well' (9).

Undoubtedly, Yan has, using rich ethnographic data, convincingly argued against Potter's general claim of the irrelevance of emotion in Chinese social life. Notwithstanding, Yan's arguments are built on an essential precondition, although implicit in his book; that is, the rise of emotion is due to the emergence of individuality after the collapse of collectivization in China. Arguably, this way of reasoning perhaps has left a categorical gap. In other words, it could be logically construed that, before the reform, emotion did not play an important role in everyday interaction or constructing social relations. It is in this way – by pinning the significance of emotions down to the rise of individuality – that I consider Yan might have reaffirmed Potter's conceptual framework by measuring Chinese emotion according to a Western conceptual system and not providing sufficient critiques to avoid Potter's Eurocentric trap, although the necessity of expressivity is eliminated. In the following, I attempt to push Yan's counterarguments further. By summarizing the meaning of emotion used by my Chinese interlocutors, I want to provide a potential perspective to close the gap.

Redefining emotion

This book has been written to investigate the interaction and communication between Chinese migrants and Zambians. While starting the investigation from the perspective of Chinese sociality (i.e. how do Chinese migrants socialize and relate to each other?), the significance of emotion emerged out of complications that arose in the field. Nevertheless, the concept of emotion here has much broader connotation than the one used in the American context. The core conclusion of the book is that emotion is constitutive to Chinese sociality and the social foundation of Chinese society. Its essential role is not only from its impact on the process of everyday interactions, communications and mutual understandings in Chinese community but also from its importance on forming and sustaining social relations and social groups in general. Moreover, the social significance of emotion is further secured by the fact that it is the deeply embedded basis of Chinese epistemology and applies to everyday perception, appreciation and comprehension.

Addressed as earlier, in a way, my conclusion is to turn Potter's claim upside down and my book is a demonstration of the social significance of emotion yet in relation to the Chinese reference system. Theoretically speaking, emotion is the crucial component of the Chinese mode of association (Fei 1992) and sociality is considered as the social matrix of actions (Moore and Long 2014); therefore, it is arguable that emotion is logically the first in constructing Chinese social order instead of 'logically secondary' (Potter 1988). Nonetheless, to argue that emotion is the first-order factor in forming and sustaining Chinese social relations, one needs to redefine emotion. Here, I need to point out that, to some extent, this book is about the study of *emotion in meaning* but not the meaning of certain emotion. However, in order to argue the social significance of emotion in sociality and meanwhile to avoid the ethnocentric trap, I consider that it is crucial to re-examine the social ontology of 'emotion' in a Chinese community according to a Chinese referential system. In this section, I would like to extend 'emotion' into three dimensions (i.e. inner psychological state, intersubjective proximity and affect) according to its characteristics, which I observed in everyday interactions at my field sites and presented in previous chapters, and briefly summarize how each dimension is constructing social ties among my Chinese interlocutors, then compare it with the Western counterpart for distinction as well as similarity.

First, I take it for granted that emotion can be experienced as inner psychological state by my Chinese interlocutors. Any form of denial is to question basic biological science. No matter to what extent emotion may be constructed by the sociocultural matrix, it is undeniable that the existence of emotion must rely on the biological foundation. In what way the self genuinely experiences certain emotion is another question since it is also true that emotions are often socially defined as a form of discourse and function as a form of action (Lutz and Abu-Lughod 1990). As I have described at the beginning of this book, anxiety and even fear are constantly experienced by Chinese migrants and they exist because my interlocutors are able to feel them.

Moreover, emotion is intersubjective. At my field sites, it is manifested as 'interactional affection' (*jiaoqing*). It is required in achieving proximity and sustaining social bonds. Here, I need to point out that, to my Chinese interlocutors, 'interactional affection' and emotion in general are often 'unrepresentable'. 'Unrepresentable' is different from Kipnis' notion of 'nonrepresentational', which he mostly uses to mean concealment and insincerity. 'Unrepresentable' does not mean that my interlocutors are not willing to convey real feeling; by contrast, it emphasizes that (1) there is no necessity to explicitly communicate emotion, and (2) flexibility and subtlety of emotion make any form of direct description insufficient. As shown previously, on one hand, my Chinese interlocutors regard that indirectness not only is functional in maintaining 'harmonious' sociality, but also contains great aesthetic value. Therefore, emotion, when being communicated, shall not be conveyed directly but embedded in actions. On the other hand, to my Chinese interlocutors, words have become cheap following commercialization; and emotion expressed too verbally would only obscure the efficiency of communication by the risk of being perceived as 'fake' (*jiaxingxing*) once people become familiar. Therefore, intersubjective emotion is practically 'invisible' due to its 'unrepresentable' characteristic and embeddedness in action.

Nevertheless, the mere 'invisibility' cannot rebut the significance of 'interactional affection' in forming and maintaining the social bonds of Chinese migrants. As they tell me, the greatest proximity between friends or lovers is '*xinyoulingxi*',[2] and it needs to be appreciated through the heart and not through words (*zhiheyihui buheyanchuan*).

Lastly, emotion to my Chinese interlocutors has a third dimension; that is, emotion is embedded in the material world, and it regulates the subject-object relation directly and intersubjective relations indirectly. As I have explained in various chapters, emotion is not only bundled in actions (e.g. showing attentiveness) but also built into social roles and their associative ethics. More importantly, emotion is attached to situations that I call 'situational affect' in Chapter 5. Situational affect is similar to the notion of 'affect' promoted by many scholars in recent years in the affective turn in anthropology. It is seen as intensity, vitality and energy of the world for individual recognition and embodiment (Massumi 2002; Berlant 2006; Stewart 2007). Contrary to what Massumi has claimed that 'there is no cultural theoretical vocabulary specific to affect' (2002: 27), situational affect has various linguistic and philosophical registers in China. As mentioned before, my Chinese interlocutors often call it '*shen*' (deity) or '*lingxing*' (spiritual) when describing the affect in objects, or '*qichang*' (aura) or '*shi*' (force) when talking about situations. According to Francis Jullien (1999), '*shi*', which he translates as 'propensity of things', insinuates itself into reality as a force of ordering and conditioning; and, Chinese aesthetics and wisdom are grounded on the exploitation of this particular configuration of reality.

In the book, I have explained many linguistic terms that entail emotion (*qing*) as morpheme, such as *qingxu* (emotion), *xinqing* (mood) – both of which designate the first dimension of emotion – *ganqing* (feeling), *jiaoqing* (interactional affection) and *renqing* (human emotion), which refer to the second dimension. Here, in relation to the third dimension of emotion, it is worthwhile to repeat what I have noted in the book; that is, 'situation' in Chinese is *qingkuang* (literally, emotion-condition) or *qingshi* (literally, emotion-propensity). Semantically, one can argue that 'situation' in China entails affect as its component. Furthermore, *qing* is also packed in role ethics as qualia. In everyday language, *qingcao* (sentiment) is used in combination with morality as in *daodeqingcao*. Despite being often translated as 'sentiment', *qingcao* stresses more the affect attached to the social roles/positions and their associative ethics. As Roger Ames (2011) points out, being ethical according to Confucius is to grow into the social roles and to embody the bundled sentiment.

What is crucial to the sociability among Chinese migrants in this third dimension of emotion is that it provides the foundational 'background' (Searle 2010) or 'common ground' (Hanks 2006) for communication to occur and enhances the emotional proximity or 'feelings of mutuality' (Fei 1992). In other words, situational affect offers the potentiality of commonality. Through shared emotional resonance with the affect, subjects form a sense of proximity (*qinjingan*) and find the common ground to interact. It is worthwhile to mention that emotional resonance stresses both the release of inner state and commonality between subjects. It is private as well as public. Resonating with the situational affect in a similar way (*gongming*), to my Chinese interlocutors, secures communication and mutual understanding. In practice, Chinese migrants often tell me that the reason why there is little interaction between Chinese and Zambians is not that they do not like to talk with Zambians, but because there is no commonality (*meigongtongdian*) or sense of proximity (*qinjingan*) when communicating with them, which I interpret as the commonality built upon shared emotional resonance with the situational affect. In the Introduction, I quoted Moore in her recent work of revitalizing sociality in anthropological studies. As she correctly points out, the studies of sociality should not omit the impact of vitality and affectivity of matter, and 'its capacity to have formative influences on human lives and relations' (Moor and Long 2012: 42). I consider that the ethnographic data of the significant role that situational affect plays in Chinese sociality and relationship formation may potentially make contributions to the project of 'revitalizing sociality'.

To further supplement my argument that emotion is the first-order factor constructing the social in China, finally, I would like to note that, because it is embedded and requires resonance to achieve mutual understanding, emotion to my Chinese interlocutors is very much embodied knowledge. It is sensory and also rational. It guides people's perception and appreciation. Emotion is a crucial part of Chinese epistemology. In the Confucian philosophical system, '*ren*' (benevolence), as the essential notion, entails 'not only intellectual and spiritual, but physical as well. ... For Confucius, it is the hard-won culmination of an aesthetic project' (Ames 2011: 177). Also, '*yue*' (music) has always been regarded by Confucius as the unalienable part of 'empathetic education' (*jiaohua*) and necessary to reach social harmony (Liang 2006 [1919]), although its companion concept '*li*' (rites) has received greater attention from sinological anthropologists. In practice, the significance of emotion in epistemology can be captured by the term that Chinese migrants use when evaluating their Zambian counterparts. Considering the embeddedness of emotion puts more weight on the message receiver, which I have explain in Chapter 5, the receiver needs to have relevant social experiences to produce a similar, corresponding, inner emotional state for resonance in order to construe the meaning. In everyday terms, my Chinese interlocutors call this ability '*wuxing*'. This term denotes that one has the ability to understand with a sensitive heart. '*Wuxing*' as the mechanism of knowledge transmission stresses more the impact of sense and emotion produced in personal practices and experiences.

To briefly sum up, earlier I have extended the concept of emotion with its characteristics into three aspects – individual inner psychological state, intersubjective proximity and situational affect. I also endeavoured to demonstrate the crucial role that each dimension of emotion plays in forming and sustaining social relations. To my Chinese interlocutors, emotion is unrepresentable. It is embedded in action and situations. It is embodied as a form of knowledge (sensory as well as rational) impacting on perception, appreciation and communication. It is interactional affection that maintains long-term cooperation, and it is shared resonance to situational affect that encourages proximity and provides the potentiality for communication and achievement in mutual understanding.

A Chinese contribution to the anthropology of emotion

What may this extensive notion of emotion used by my Chinese interlocutors offer to anthropological studies in general? While unpacking the Western conceptual presumptions of emotion, Catherine Lutz points out that emotion in America has always been associated with concepts such as 'impulsivity', 'vulnerability', 'chaos' and 'female' (1986). She claims that emotion in the Western referential system is the 'residual category used to talk about that which deviates from the dominant definition of the sensible or intelligible' (1988: 62). Emotion entails danger, pre-culture and individuality, and, more importantly, emotion before the 1980s in the discipline of anthropology was predominately used to designate 'psychobiological processes that respond to cross-cultural environmental differences but retain a robust essence untouched by the social or cultural' (Lutz and Abu-Lughod 1990: 2). To eliminate this ethnocentric view, Lutz encourages anthropologists to search beyond by extending the range of emotion as judgement and as public discourse (1990: 11), and to concentrate on questions such as how emotion is socially constructed and how emotion is applied as communicative actions. In other words, her main approach was more about constructing different cultural meanings of emotion, rather than investigating the emotions embedded in meaning.

Later on, Margot Lyon categorized Lutz as a cultural constructionist and warned that 'the inchoateness of the concept of culture acts to maintain and leave unquestioned the conventional distinction between emotion and cognition' (1995: 254), and that such approach will reinforce the distinction between material and immaterial. She claims that 'what must be considered are the processes by which collective symbols or anything else acquire power, not merely as they emerge from individual histories (within any given culture) but as they emerge from *social* ones' (254). Then, Lyon proposes that

> This expanded understanding of emotion must take account of the body *qua* body not simply as it is mediated by 'mind' but as part of the conception of emotion itself. ... Emotion has a central role in bodily agency, for by its very nature it links the somatic and the communicative aspects of being and thus encompasses bodily as well as social and cultural domains. The body is the means by which we experience and actively apprehend the world (Merleau-Ponty 1962); through its agency we know the world and act within it. This 'being-in-the-world', this grounding in reality, is fundamentally linked to the material aspects of our bodies . ... An understanding of the agency of the body in society thus comes through its intercommunicative and active functions. Human emotional capacities are closely linked to sociality and thus have an important place in this agency. ... (But while) the phenomenological position, for example, gives emphasis to the sensory interface between body and the world that is experienced through it, the affective component in this process, the *felt* sense, the 'guts', are not fully represented. ... The phenomenological perspective requires further extension through the consideration of emotion and its bodily and social dimensions. (256)

Echoing this debate, I consider that the characteristics of Chinese emotion could make a great contribution to preventing anthropologists from falling into a Eurocentric trap while searching for the significance of emotion. Arguably, the biggest difference is that Chinese emotion is developed through Chinese philosophical tradition that makes no distinction between the mind and the body. In Chinese, heart (*xin*) is the gravity of humanity, which is the ground for emotion as well as rationality. 'The term "*xin*" refers indifferently to activities we [Westerners] would classify as thinking, judging and feeling' (Hall and Ames 1998: 29). Moreover, as Ellen Oxfeld argues, *xin* is also the location of Chinese moral goodness (2010: 52). Regarding the notion of person in China, the physical self only achieves wholeness by the exchange of 'heart' with others (Sun 1991).

Note that 'emotion', in morphemes, is the combination of sense (*gan*) and emotion (*qing*). Both characters, *gan* (感) and *qing* (情), contain the 'heart' radical (忄 or 心), which is rather pervasive in Chinese characters (e.g. in '*wu*' [悟, understand] and '*yi*' [意, meaning] mentioned earlier). This unification of the sensory, the emotional and the rational in 'heart' makes the material have a touch of subjectivity, and subjectivity could be objectified for appreciation, transmission and utilization as knowledge. As stated earlier, knowledge is believed to be gained through experiences and practices, through a sensitive heart interacting with its surroundings: material as well as other hearts. If common knowledge provides the foundation for sustainable interaction, it can be said that, to my Chinese interlocutors, great social proximity is achieved in the unison of hearts. Emotion as embodied knowledge residing in 'heart', I consider, can potentially provide a way out of the dualism and take anthropological studies of emotion a step further forward.

The embedded significance of 'emotion' in Chinese sociality

For many years, the study of emotion in China, partially due to Potter's hypothesis, has been devalued and marginalized (Yan 2003; Zhang 2010). To investigate the relations between Chinese migrants and Zambians, during my fieldwork, I realized the crucial role that 'emotion' plays in Chinese sociality. The significance of 'emotion' in China is that it directly ties people together and indirectly assigns meanings to the social for the people to recognize and to reproduce. Once produced, 'emotion' and sociality reinforce each other in circuit.

Adam Chau explains this circuit well in his studies of *honghuo* and *re'nao* (red-hot sociality) in China. He argues that not only is the social world in China filled with sensory stimuli but also, most importantly, people actively produce the world sensorially. He claims that the role of the social, and not only how the senses receive and perceive the social but more importantly how social actors actively construct their social worlds in sensorially rich manners, and how moments of sensorialized sociality become *institutionalized* ... we sensorialize our world, especially through engaging in intense social activities. (2008: 488–90, italics added)

To Chau, 'a "mindful-body" or an "attentive body" is simply the precondition for any person's action-full life world' (492), and the sensory sociality is epitomized into aesthetics.

Following his ideas, I contend that the significance of 'emotion' for my Chinese interlocutors exactly lies in this institutionalized and epitomized sensorialized sociality. Most of the time, their interaction with Zambians is cut off because they could not sense and are not able to co-produce the 'emotion' embedded in social relations, situations and social institutions. To push it further, one could argue that the community in China is formed centring on the unison of 'hearts' and the resonance of 'emotion' (for 'community of sentiment', see Appadurai 1990), which they actively reproduce in practice. To view 'emotion' in this way, the relevance of emotion in China may have been totally mistaken by Potter. Arguably, 'emotion' in China is the first-order factor of the social and it is the foundation of sociality and community. Every social fact – social institution and structure included – has a dimension of embedded 'emotion' that enables it to function, and to know is to resonate with a sensitive heart – this is perhaps the most valuable contribution that my Chinese interlocutors could offer to anthropology in general.

Notes

Introduction

1 This term is used by Chinese migrants in Zambia to refer to the senior Chinese immigrants who came to Zambia around the 1990s. *Lao* means 'senior'; 'Zambia' here does not denote nationality.
2 The Chinese term for anthropology may be translated literally as 'human-kind study'. Morphologically, the term places more emphasis on the biological aspects; hence, the response of Director Lu based on his understanding of evolution.
3 http://www.gov.cn/jrzg/2013-08/29/content_2476529.htm
4 The first contact between China and Africa can be traced back to the Ming Dynasty; nevertheless, since this book is focusing mainly on engagement by the PRC, previous fragmented Sino-African contacts have been selectively omitted. This omission does not deny the significance of this historical engagement for China's current involvement in Africa. Undeniably, this historical contact is constantly invoked by the Chinese government to demonstrate 'mutual reliable partnership' and to seek cooperation. For more details, see Snow (1988) and Alden, Large and Soares De Oliviera (2008).
5 http://politics.people.com.cn/GB/8198/384439/
6 Household registration (*hukou*) has long attracted scholarly attention. It was implemented during the Maoist period to regulate the distribution of the Chinese population, with impacts on the allocation of welfare, such as work, educational, medical, housing resources and so on. The system has been heavily criticized and subject to reform for a long time. For an overview, see Chan and Zhang (1999). For recent reform, see Chan and Buckingham (2008).
7 *Bang* is a Chinese colloquial term roughly equivalent to 'group' or 'gang' in English.
8 This is the key research question of Ching Kwan Lee's recent award-winning book *Specter of China* (2017), where she argues that the

involvement of Chinese state capital distinguishes China's investment in Africa from that of other countries.

9 In his study on the practice of gift exchange in the Chinese village of *Xiajia*, Yunxiang Yan (1996) points out that *guanxi* is not limited to instrumentalism but includes the dimensions of 'human emotion' (*renqing*) and 'feeling' (*ganqing*) in gift exchange. Andrew Kipnis (1997) argues in a similar line. As I will argue in detail in Chapter 2, I consider that this theoretical incorporation of *guanxi* and emotion may understate the significant role that emotion plays in the formation of social relationships in China and make emotion secondary in analysis.

10 Affect is often defined as a form of force, intensity and potentiality that exists prior to the subject and preconsciousness (Massumi 2002; Shouse 2005). It is portrayed as being autonomous, indeterminate and nonrepresentational, and is usually invoked in opposition to emotion, cognition and discourse (Harman 2012; Stewart 2007, 2017). As Massumi understands it – and many ethnographers draw their inspiration from him – affect should be equated with 'intensity', which is 'disconnected from the subjective, signifying, functional-meaning axis to which the more familiar categories of emotion belong' (2002: 441). In this book, however, I have no intention to separate affect from emotion. Borrowing from Wetherell, I will treat affect as an 'embodied meaning-making' process (2012: 4), which is ontogenetic and historical. Semantically, I take that affect entails emotion, and I am using both as interchangeable in this book. For the definition of 'affect', see Berlant 2006; Stewart 2007; Blackman 2012.

Chapter 1

1 Zambia is a multiparty system. Patriot Front and MMD (Movement for Multi-Party Democracy) are two majority parties. Politically, Patriot Front is a democratic socialist party, and during the election of 2006, the party leader, Sata, famously campaigned to chase foreigners, particularly Chinese migrants, out of Zambia. This was repeated in the 2011 election.

2 Kathleen Stewart, in her monograph *Ordinary Affect* (2007), has applied similarly writing styles while describing the 'affective dimension of everyday

life'. Although being well praised as 'touching', 'elegant' and containing the 'evocative power of descriptions', the work has been criticized as failing to 'exploit the analytical possibilities of affect' and it ignores the preset power relations while playing the refrains of 'familiar situations' (Pelkmans 2013). In this chapter, I will take the critiques into consideration while blending her writing styles with the ones in Chinese literature.

3 Prose (*sanwen*), along with poetry (*shige*), fiction (*xiaoshuo*) and drama (*xiju*) are categorized as four genres in Chinese literature. *Sanwen* is a traditional Chinese literary genre and has experienced several historical transformations. Contemporary *sanwen* was reinvented in the era of May-Four Movement (*wusi yundong*) by a series of writers such as Lu Xun and Zhu Ziqing. The main characteristics of *sanwen* are broadly considered to be (a) a loose structure and argument but coherence achieved by referring to the same 'spirit' (*shen*) or meaning (*xingsan'ershenbusan*); (b) the contents are normally organized into first-person narratives and authors endeavour to reach persuasion by invoking emotional resonance; and (c) emotional resonance is achieved through creating '*yijing*' (literally, settings of meaning) within texts to induce readers' imagination, which defines the aesthetic value (for more see *Zhongguo Xiandai Sanwenshi, The History of Chinese Contemporary Prose*, Yu Yuangui 1988; Shandong Wenyi Press).

4 Similarly, Schmitz has documented the widely spread rumours in Angola, both in the Chinese migrant community and in their host society. Chinese migrants are perceived as pirates as well as prisoners; whereas Angolans are regarded as thieves and robbers. Schmitz argues that rumours are produced due to the lack of mutual communications while it is the social foundation and process of transmission that interest me more in this chapter. See Schmitz (2014).

5 This allegory is from the Chinese classic *Huainanzi Renjianxun*. The message from the story is to tell the dialectic relations between good fortune and calamity – 'calamity begets fortune, and fortune begets calamity. This circle has no end, and its depths cannot be measured'. Nowadays, the story has been popularized as a Chinese idiom.

6 'According to the Western pattern, all members in an organization are equivalent, just as all straws in a bundle are alike. This is quite different from the Chinese pattern. Social relationships in China possess a self-

centred quality. Like the ripples formed from the stone thrown into a lake, each circle spreading out from the centre becomes more distant and at the same time more insignificant' (1992: 65).

Chapter 2

1. To say it was unconventional is because normally a middleman is required when two strangers try to do business in China. This is especially the case when individuals who are lower in the social hierarchy try to establish contacts with officials higher in the hierarchy. The middleman usually knows both parties previously, and his/her role is to act as guarantor for the initiator of the action. Without being introduced by a middleman, the initiator may risk being refused due to mistrust.
2. *Xiaoren* in Chinese is the opposite notion of *junzi* (man of honour), and they always appear as a pair. This pair of concepts is crucial in Confucian dogma as well as in Chinese morality. In the Confucian *Analects*, it is noted that '*juziyuyuyi, xiarenyuyuli*' (gentlemen distinguish themselves by upholding values, while petty men, by pursuing personal gains). As mentioned in the Introduction, value for Confucius not only contains rigid moral rules but also embraces propriety in mutual affection.

Chapter 4

1. In the anthropology of morality, scholars draw inspirations from Bernard Williams to intentionally distinguish ethics with morality. As Stafford (2010, 2013) points out, such conceptual differentiation is to equate morality with structure, ethics with agency. In this article, morality and ethics are used interchangeably. Following Keane (2015), I consider that ethics conceptually embraces morality.
2. In this chapter, 'Confucius moral philosophy' is not limited to mere Confucian doctrines but entails philosophical ideas from Daoism as well as Buddhism. In terms of the development of Chinese philosophy, three schools of thoughts have been synthesized for several times across different historical periods (see, Yu 2004).

Chapter 5

1. Seemingly, the daughter-in-law's action here is voluntary; however, it followed Mother Zou's 'soft command' – a point that I mentioned in Chapter 3. This efficiency of this communicative technique requires the cooperation of the other and heavily relies on the context. The command is within the 'unspoken'. In this case, by explicitly ordering Father Zou (husband) and Xiao Zou (son) to work, Mother Zou is imposing a pressure of sociality on the daughter-in-law; that is, Mother Zou could not order the daughter-in-law to do things as she is considered as 'outsider' in this context but, if the daughter-in-law does not help Mother Zou, she will face the danger of alienating Mother Zou then damage the familial relationships. This contextualized way, especially referring to situational relations, to communicate plays very important role in everyday social/moral evaluation. I will investigate this communicative technique later in this chapter.

Conclusion

1. Ways of communication are invented at my field site when Chinese and Zambians do not share the same language. The most common form of communication is gesture. For example, in the work place, if the Chinese manager removes the Zambian worker's safety helmet, the gesture means that the worker is fired. Pointing is used on a daily basis. Apart from gestures, mixed-language sentences are created. These are often based on Chinese grammar with insertion of random English words, such as, 'Tomorrow no come la' (*la* is a Chinese utterance particle).
2. This four-character idiom is abstracted from a poem by Tang Dynasty poet Li Shangyin. *Lingxi* is a spiritual, three-horned rhino in Chinese mythology. It is believed that if people possess the special horn, lovers' hearts would be tied together and beat in unison, and the romance would last forever regardless how far they were apart. The idiom nowadays is used to describe that close friends or lovers communicate with hearts and no words are needed to achieve mutual understanding.

Bibliography

Appadurai, A. (1990) 'Topographies of the Self: Praise and Emotion in Hindu India', in C. A. Lutz and L. Abu-Lughod (eds), *Language and the Politics of Emotion*, 92–113. Cambridge: Cambridge University Press.

Alden, C. (2007) *China in Africa*. London and New York: Zen Books.

Alden, C., Large, D. and Soares De Oliviera, R., eds. (2009) *China Returns to Africa: A Rising Power and a Continent Embrace*. London: Hurst.

Alden, L. and De Oliveira, R. S., ed. (2008) *China Returns to Africa: A Rising Power and a Continent Embrace*. C.Hurst & Co. Publishers Ltd.

Allport, G. W. and Postman L. (1965) *The Psychology of Rumor*. New York: Russell & Russell.

Ames, R. (2011) *Confucian Role Ethics: A Vocabulary*. Honolulu: University of Hawai'i Press.

Arsene, C. (2014) 'Chinese Employers and Their Ugandan Workers: Tensions, Frictions and Cooperation in an African City', *Journal of Current Chinese Affairs* 43 (1): 139–76.

Baah, A. and Jauch, H., eds. (2009) *Chinese Investments in Africa: A Labour Perspective*. Windhoek: African Labour Research Network.

Bargh, J., Chen, M. and Burrows, L. (1996) 'Automaticity of Social Behavior: Direct Effects of Trait Construct and Stereotype Activation on Action', *Journal of Personality and Social Psychology* 71 (2): 230–44.

Bell, E. (2011) *An Anthropological Study of Ethnicity and the Reproduction of Culture among Hong Kong Chinese Families in Scotland*, PhD Book, London School of Economics and Political Science.

Benton, G. and Pieke, F., eds. (1998) *The Chinese in Europe*. Basingstoke: Macmillan Press.

Berlant, L. (2006) 'Cruel Optimism', *Differences* 17 (3): 20–36.

Bernstein, B. (1986) 'A Sociolinguistic Approach to Socialization; with Some Reference to Educability', in J. Gumperz and D. Hymes (eds), *Directions in Sociolinguistics: The Ethnography of Communication*, 465–98. Oxford: Basil Blackwell.

Blackman, L. (2012) *Immaterial Bodies: Affect, Embodiment, Mediation*. London: Sage.

Bolt, M. (2013) 'The Dynamics of Dependence', *Journal of Royal Anthropological Institute* 19 (2): 243–45.

Bonacich, E. and Modell, J. (1980) *The Economics Basis of Ethnic Solidarity.* Berkeley: University of California Press.

Bourdieu, P. (1991) *Language and Symbolic Power: The Economy of Linguistic Exchanges*, edited and introduced by John B. Thompson, translated by Gino Raymond and Matthew Adamson. Cambridge: Polity in association with Basil Blackwell.

Bourdieu, P. (1977 [1972]) *Outline of a Theory of Practice.* Cambridge: Cambridge University Press.

Bräutigam, D. (2010) *The Dragon's Gift: The Real Story of China in Africa.* New York: Oxford University Press.

Bräutigam, D. and Tang, X. (2009) 'China's Engagement in African Agriculture: "Down to the Countryside"', *China Quarterly* 199: 686–706.

Brubaker, R. (2004) *Ethnicity without Groups.* Cambridge, MA: Harvard University Press.

Carsten, J., eds. (2000) *Cultures of Relatedness: New Approaches to the Study of Kinship.* Cambridge: Cambridge University Press.

Chan, A. (1986) *Employment Prospects of Chinese Youth in Britain: A Research Report.* London: Commission for Racial Equality.

Chan, K. W. and Buckingham, W. (2008) 'Is China Abolishing the *Hukou* System?' *China Quarterly* 195: 582–606.

Chan, K. W. and Zhang, L. (1999) 'The *Hukou* System and Rural-Urban Migration in China: Processes and Changes', *China Quarterly* 160: 818–55.

Chan-Fishel, M. and Lawson, R. (2007) 'Bankrolling the "Going Out" Strategy: China's Financing of African Aid and Investment, and Implications for Africa's Debt and Development', in M. Kitissou (ed.), *Africa in China's Global Strategy*, 108–31. London: Adonis and Abbey Publishers Ltd.

Chau, A. (2008) 'The Sensorial Production of the Social', *Ethnos* 73 (4): 485–504.

Chen, N., Clark, C., Gottschang, S. and Jeffery L., eds. (2001) *China Urban: Ethnographies of Contemporary Culture.* Durham: Duke University Press.

Christiansen, F. (2003) *Chinatown, Europe: An Exploration of Overseas Chinese Identity in the 1990s.* London: Routledge Curzon.

Chumley, L. H. and Harkness, N. (2013) 'Introduction: Qualia', *Anthropological Theory* 13 (1/2): 3–11.

Churchland, P. (2011) *Braintrust: What Neuroscience Tells Us About Morality.* Princeton: Princeton University Press.

Cialdini, R. B. (2001) 'The Science of Persuasion', *Scientific American* 284: 76–81.
Cohen, M. (1976) *House United, House Divided: the Chinese Family in Taiwan*. New York: Columbia University Press.
Crissman, L. W. (1967) 'The Segmentary Structure of Urban Overseas Chinese Communities', *Man* 2 (2): 185–204.
Dikötter, F. (1992) *The Discourse on Race in Modem China*. London: Hurst & Co.
Dikötter, F. (1994) 'Racial Identities in China: Context and Meaning', *China Quarterly* 138: 404–12.
Dittgen, R. (2010) *From Isolation to Integration? A Study of Chinese Retailers in Dakar*, Occasional Paper 57, Johannesburg: South African Institute of International Affairs.
Dobler, G. (2008) 'Solidarity, Xenophobia and the Regulation of Chinese Businesses in Namibia', in C. Alden, D. Large and Soares de Oliveria (eds), *China Returns to Africa: A Rising Power and a Continent Embrace*, 237–55. London: Hurst.
Dobler, G. (2009) 'Chinese Shops and the Formation of a Chinese Expatriate Community in Namibia', *China Quarterly* 199: 707–27.
Duara, P. (1991) 'Knowledge and Power in the Discourse of Modernity: The Campaigns against Popular Religion in Early Twentieth-Century China', *The Journal of Asian Studies* 50 (1): 67–83.
Duranti, A. (1997) *Linguistic Anthropology*. Cambridge and New York: Cambridge University Press.
Enfield, N. J. and Levinson, S. C. eds. (2006) *Roots of Human Sociality: Culture, Cognition and Interaction*. New York: Berg Publication.
Fang, I.-C. (2012) *Growing Up and Becoming Independent: An Ethnographic Study of New Generation Migrant Workers in China*, PhD Book, London School of Economics and Political Science.
Fassin, D. (2012) 'Toward a Critical Moral Anthropology', in D. Fassin (ed.), *A Companion to Moral Anthropology*. Malden: Wiley-Blackwell.
Faubion, J. (2001) 'Toward an Anthropology of Ethics: Foucault and the Pedagogies of Autopoiesis', *Representations* 74: 83–104.
Faubion, J. (2011) *An Anthropology of Ethics*. Cambridge: Cambridge University Press.
Fei, X. (1992 [1948]) *From the Soil: The Foundations of Chinese Society*, translation with an introduction and epilogue by Gary G. Hamilton and Wang Zheng. Berkeley: University of California Press.

Fei, X. (1998) *Xiangtu Zhongguo, Shengyu Zhidu* (From the Soil). Beijing: Beijing University Press.
Feng, Y. L. (2000) *The History of Chinese Philosophy (Zhongguo Zhexueshi)*. Shanghai: Chinese Eastern Normal University Press.
Ferguson, J. (1999) *Expectations of Modernity Myths and Meanings of Urban Life on the Zambian Copperbelt*. Berkeley: University of California Press.
Ferguson, J. (2006) *Global Shadows: Africa in the Neoliberal World Order*. Durham: Duke University Press.
Ferguson, J. (2013) 'Declarations of Dependence: Labour, Personhood, and Welfare in Southern Africa', *Journal of Royal Anthropological Institute* 19 (2): 223–42.
Ferguson, J. and Gupta, A. (1997) *Culture, Power, Place: Explorations in Critical Anthropology*. Durham: Duke University Press.
Ferguson, N. (2011) *Civilization: The West and the Rest*. London and New York: Allen Lane.
Feuchtwang, S. (2002) *An Anthropological Analysis of Chinese Geomancy*. Bangkok: White Lotus Press.
Feuchtwang, S. (2009) 'Social Egoism and Individualism: Surprises and Questions for a Western Anthropologist of China Reading Fei Xiaotong's Contrast between China and the West', in Ma Rong, Liu Shiding, Qiu Zeqi and Pan Naigu (eds), *Fei Xiaotong yu Zhongguo Shehuixui Renleixue* (Fei Xiaotong and Chinese Sociology and Anthropology), 18–32. Beijing: Social Science Academic Press.
Fong, V. L. (2004) *Only Hope: Coming of Age under China's One-Child Policy*. Stanford: Stanford University Press.
Fong, V. L. (2007) 'Parent-Child Communication Problems and the Perceived Inadequacies of Chinese only Children', *Ethos* 35 (1): 85–127.
Fortes, M. and Evans-Pritchard, E. E., eds. (1940) *African Political Systems*. London: Oxford University Press for the International African Institute.
Foucault, M. (1997) *Ethics, Subjectivity, and Truth: Essential Works of Foucault 1954–1980, Volume 2*, edited by James D. Faubion. New York: New Press.
Fukuyama, F. (1995) *Trust: The Social Virtues and the Creation of Prosperity*. London: Hamish Hamilton.
Giese, K. (2013) 'Same-Same But Different: Chinese Traders' Perspectives on African Labour', *China Journal* 69: 134–53.
Giese, K. and Marfaing, L., ed. (2019) *Chinese and African Entrepreneurs: Social Impacts of International Encounters*. Leiden and Boston: BRILL.

Giese, K. and Thiel, A. (2012) 'When Voicelessness Meets Speechlessness – Struggling for Equity in Chinese-Ghanaian Employment Relations', GIGA Working Paper, No. 194, May 2012, Hamburg: GIGA.

Giese, K. and Thiel, A. (2014) 'The Vulnerable Other – Distorted Equity in Chinese-Ghanaian Employment Relations', *Ethnic and Racial Studies* 37 (6): 1101–20.

Gluckman, M. (1958) *Analysis of a Social Situation in Modern Zululand*, Rhodes-Livingstone Papers No. 28. Manchester: University Press.

Gluckman, M. (1963) 'Gossip and Scandal', *Current Anthropology* 4 (3): 307–15.

Goffman, E. (1971) *The Presentation of Self in Everyday Life*. Harmondsworth: Penguin.

Grenfell, M. J., eds. (2010) *Bourdieu, Language and Linguistics*. London: Continuum.

Gumperz, J. and Hymes, D., eds. (1986) *Directions in Sociolinguistics: The Ethnography of Communication*. Oxford: Basil Blackwell.

Haglund, D. (2009) 'In It for the Long Term? Governance and Learning among Chinese Investors in Zambia's Copper Sector', *China Quarterly* 199: 627–46.

Haidt, J. (2012) *The Righteous Mind: Why Good People Are Divided by Politics and Religion*. London: Allen Lane.

Hall, D. and Ames, R. (1998) *Thinking from the Han: Self, Truth, and Transcendence in Chinese and Western Culture*. Albany: SUNY Press.

Hamilton, G. (1978) 'Pariah Capitalism: A Paradox of Power and Dependence', *Ethnic Groups: An International Periodical of Ethnic Studies* 2: 1–15.

Hankins, J. D. (2013) 'An Ecology of Sensibility: The Politics of Scents and Stigma in Japan', *Anthropological Theory* 13 (1–2): 49–66.

Hanks, W. (2006) 'Joint Commitment and Common Ground in a Ritual Event', in N. J. Enfield and S. C. Levinson (eds), *Roots of Human Sociality: Culture, Cognition and Interaction*. New York: Berg Publication.

Hansen, A. S. (2017) 'Guanhua! Beijing Students, Authoritative Discourse and the Ritual Production of Political Compliance', in S. Bregnbæk and M. Bunkenborg (eds), *Emptiness and Fullness: Ethnographies of Lack and Desire in Contemporary China*, 35–51. New York: Berghahn Books.

Hare, P. (2007) 'China and Zambia: The All-Weather Friendship Hits Stormy Weather', *The Jamestown Foundation China Brief* VII (5), 8 March: 7–9.

Harkness, N. (2013), 'Softer Soju in South Korea', *Anthropological Theory* 13 (1/2): 12–30.

Harman, G. (2012) *Weird Realism: Lovecraft and Philosophy*. Alresford: Zero Books.

Hirschkind, C. (2009) *The Ethical Soundscape: Cassette Sermons and Islamic Counterpublics*. New York: Columbia University Press.

Hochschild, A. (1983) *The Managed Heart: Commercialization of Human Feeling*. Berkeley and London: University of California Press.

Holland, D. W. and Throop, C. J., eds. (2011) *The Anthropology of Empathy: Experiencing the Lives of Others in Pacific Societies*. New York and Oxford: Berghahn Books.

Hsu, E. (2007) 'Zanzibar and Its Chinese Communities', *Population, Space and Place* 13: 113–24.

Human Rights Watch (HRW) (2011) '"You'll Be Fired if You Refuse:" Labor Abuses in Zambia's Chinese State-Owned Copper Mines', November 3.

Humphrey, C. (2012) 'Hospitality and Tone: Holding Patterns for Strangeness in Rural Mongolia', *JRAI* 18 (S1): 63–75.

Ivanhoe, P. J. (2000) *Confucian Moral Self Cultivation*, 2nd edn. Indianapolis: Hackett Publishing Company.

Ivanhoe, P. J. (2002) *Ethics in the Confucian Tradition*, 2nd edn. Indianapolis: Hackett Publishing Company.

Jacob, B. (1979) 'A Preliminary Model of Particularistic Ties in Chinese Political Alliances: Kan-ch'ing and Kuan-his in a Rural Taiwanese Township', *China Quarterly* 78: 237–73.

Jiang, W. (2009) 'Fuelling the Dragon: China's Rise and Its Energy and Resources Extraction in Africa', *China Quarterly* 199: 585–609.

Jullien, F. (1999) *The Propensity of Things: Toward a History of Efficacy in China*. New York: Zone Books.

Jullien, F. (2004) *Detour and Access: Strategies of Meaning in China and Greece*, translated by Sophie Hawkes. New York: Zone Books.

Jullien, F. (2009) *The Great Image Has No Shape*. Chicago: University of Chicago Press.

Kahneman, D. (2012) *Thinking, Fast and Slow*. London: Penguin.

Kajanus, A. (2015) *Chinese Student Migration, Gender and Family*. Basingstoke: Palgrave Macmillan.

Keane, W. (2014) 'Affordances and Reflexivity in Ethical Life: An Ethnographic Stance', *Anthropological Theory* 14 (1): 3–26.

Keane, W. (2015) *Ethical Life: Its Natural and Social Histories*. Princeton: Princeton University Press.

Kipnis, A. (1997) *Producing Guanxi: Sentiment, Self, and Subculture in a North China Village*. Durham: Duke University Press.

Kipnis, A. (2002) 'Practices of *Guanxi* Production and Practices of *Ganqing* Avoidance', in T. Gold and D. Guthrie and D. Wank (eds), *Social Connections in China: Institutions, Culture, and the Changing Nature of Guanxi*, 21–34. Cambridge: Cambridge University Press.

Laidlaw, J. (2002) 'For an Anthropology of Ethics and Freedom', *Journal of Royal Anthropological Institute* 8 (2): 311–32.

Laidlaw, J. (2010) 'Agency and Responsibility: Perhaps You Can Have Too Much of a Good Thing', in M. Lambek (ed.), *Ordinary Ethics: Anthropology, Language and Action*. New York: Fordham University Press.

Laidlaw, J. (2014) *The Subject of Virtue: An Anthropology of Ethics and Freedom*. Cambridge and New York: Cambridge University Press.

Laidlaw, J. (2017) 'Fault Lines in the Anthropology of Ethics', in C. Mattingly, et al. (eds), *Moral Engines: Exploring the Ethical Drives in Human Life*, 174–93. Oxford: Berghahn.

Lambek, M., ed. (2010) *Ordinary Ethics: Anthropology, Language and Action*. New York: Fordham University Press.

Lambek, M., ed. (2015) *The Ethical Condition: Essays on Action, Person, and Value*. Chicago: University of Chicago Press.

Lampert, B. and Mohan, G. (2014) 'Sino-African Encounters in Ghana and Nigeria: From Conflict to Conviviality and Mutual Benefit', *Journal of Current Chinese Affairs* 43 (1): 9–39.

Lan, S. S. (2016) 'The Shifting Meanings of Race in China: A Case Study of the African Diaspora Communities in Guangzhou', *City & Society* 28 (3): 298–318.

Large, D. (2008) 'Beyond "Dragon in the Bush": The Study of China–Africa Relations', *African Affairs* 107: 45–61.

Leavitt, J. (1996) 'Meaning and Feeling in the Anthropology of Emotions', *American Ethnologist* 23 (3): 514–39.

Lee, C. K. (2009) 'Raw Encounters: Chinese Managers, African Workers and the Politics of Casualization in Africa's Chinese Enclaves', *China Quarterly* 199: 647–66.

Lee, C. K. (2017) *The Specter of Global China: Politics, Labor, and Foreign Investment in Africa*. Chicago: University of Chicago Press.

Lemos, A. and Ribeiro, D. (2007) 'Taking Ownership or Just Changing Owners?' in F. Manji and S. Marks (eds), *African Perspectives on China*, 63–70. Oxford: Fahamu.

Liang, S. (1919) 'Dongxiwenhua Jiqi Zhexue' (Cultures and Philosophies of the East and the West), in Lai Chen (eds), *Liangshumin Xuanji* (Anthology of Liangshumin). Jilin: Jilin People's Press, 2010.

Lin, E. (2014) '"Big Fish in a Small Pond": Chinese Migration Shopkeepers in South Africa', *International Migration Review* 48 (1): 181–215.

Lin, Y. T. (1935) *My Country and My People*. New York: Reynal and Hitchcock, Inc.

Liu, X. (2010) *In One's Own Shadow: An Ethnographic Account of the Condition of Post-reform Rural China*. Berkeley: University of California Press.

Louie, V. S. (2004) *Compelled to Excel: Immigration, Education, and Opportunity among Chinese Americans*. Stanford: Stanford University Press.

Lu, X. and Perry, E. J., eds. (1997) *Danwei: The Changing Chinese Workplace in Historical and Comparative Perspective*. Armonk and New York: M. E. Sharpe.

Lutz, C. A. (1986) 'Emotion, Thought, and Estrangement: Emotion as a Cultural Category', *Cultural Anthropology* 1 (3): 287–309.

Lutz, C. A. (1988) *Unnatural Emotions: Everyday Sentiments on a Micronesian Atoll & Their Challenge to Western Theory*. Chicago: University of Chicago Press.

Lutz, C. A. and Abu-Lughod, L., eds. (1990) *Language and the Politics of Emotion*. Cambridge: Cambridge University Press.

Lutz, C. A. and Abu-Lughod, L., eds. (1993) *Language and the Politics of Emotion*. Cambridge: Cambridge University Press.

Lyon, M. L. (1995) 'Missing Emotion: The Limitations of Cultural Constructionism in the Study of Emotion', *Cultural Anthropology* 10 (2): 244–63.

Ma Mung, E. (2008) 'Chinese Migration and China's Foreign Policy in Africa', *Journal of Chinese Overseas* 4 (1): 91–109.

MacIntyre, A. (1981) *After Virtue: A Study in Moral Theory*. London: Duckworth.

Massumi, B. (2002) *Parables for the Virtual*. Durham and London: Duke University Press.

Mattingly, C. (2012) 'Two Virtue Ethics and the Anthropology of Morality', *Anthropology Theory* 12 (2): 161–84.

Mattingly, C. (2014) 'Moral Deliberation and the Agentive Self in Laidlaw's Ethics', *HAU: Journal of Ethnographic Theory* 4 (1): 473–86.

McNamee, T. (2012) *Africa in their Words: A Study of Chinese Traders in South Africa, Lesotho, Botswana, Zambia and Angola*. The Brenthurst Foundation Discussion Paper, 3.

Men, T (2014) 'Place-Based and Place-Bound Realities: A Chinese Firm's Embeddedness in Tanzania', *Journal of Current Chinese Affairs* 43 (1): 103–38.

Merleau-Ponty, M. (1962) *Phenomenology of Perception*. New Jersey: The Humanities Press.

Mohan, G. and Lampert, B (2013) 'Negotiating China: Reinserting African agency into China–Africa relations', *African Affairs* 112 (446): 92–110.

Monson, J. (2013) 'Remembering Work on the Tazara Railway in Africa and China, 1965–2011: When "New Men" Grow Old', *African Studies Review* 56 (1): 45–64.

Monson, J. and Rupp, S. (2013) 'Africa and China: New Engagements, New Research', *African Studies Review* 56 (1): 21–44.

Moore, H. and Long, N. (2012) 'Sociality Revisited: Setting a New Agenda', *Cambridge Anthropology* 30 (1): 40–7.

Moore, H. and Long, N. (2013) *Sociality: New Directions*. New York: Berghahn Book.

Moumouni, G. (2010) 'China's Relations with African Sub-regions: The Case of West Africa', *The Bulletin of Fridays of the Commission* 3 (1): 25–43.

Munn, N. (1986) *The Fame of Gawa: A Symbolic Study of Value Transformation in a Massim Society*. Cambridge: Cambridge University Press.

Mwanawina, I. (2008) *China-Africa Economic Relations: The Case of Zambia*. Nairobi: African Economic Research Consortium.

Osburg, J. (2013) *Anxious Wealth: Money and Morality among China's New Rich*. Stanford: Stanford University Press.

Oxfeld, E. (1992) 'Individualism, Holism, and the Market Mentality: Notes on the Recollections of a Chinese Entrepreneur', *Cultural Anthropology* 7 (3): 267–300.

Oxfeld, E. (1993) *Blood, Sweat, and Mahjong: Family and Enterprise in an Overseas Chinese Community*. Ithaca: Cornell University Press.

Oxfeld, E. (2010) *Drinking Water, but Remember the Source: Moral Discourse in a Chinese Village*. Berkeley: University of California Press.

Oxfeld, E. (2017) *Bitter and Sweet: Food, Meaning, and Modernity in Rural China*. Oakland: University of California Press.

Paine, R. (1967) 'What Is Gossip About? An Alternative Hypothesis', *Man* 2 (2): 272–85.

Park, Y. J. (2008) *A Matter of Honour: Being Chinese in South Africa*. Auckland Park: Jacana Press.

Park, Y. J. (2010) 'Boundaries, Borders and Borderland Constructions: Chinese in Contemporary South Africa and the Region', *African Studies* 69 (3): 457–79.

Park, Y. J. (2013) 'Perceptions of Chinese in Southern Africa: Constructions of the "Other" and the Role of Memory', *African Studies Review* 56 (1): 131–53.

Park, Y. J. and Huynh, Tu T. 2010. 'Introduction: Chinese in Africa', *African and Asian Studies* 9 (3): 207–12.

Peirce, C. (1997 [1890]) 'Ground, Object, and Interpretant', in C. Hartshorne and P. Weiss (eds), *The Collected Papers of Charles Sanders Peirce, Volume 1*, 227–29. Cambridge, MA: Harvard University Press.

Peirce, C. (1997 [1896]) 'The logic of mathematics: An attempt to develop my categories from within', in C. Hartshorne and P. Weiss (eds), *The Collected Papers of Charles Sanders Peirce, Volume 1*, 417–520. Cambridge, MA: Harvard University Press.

Peirce, C. (1998 [1903]) 'Nomenclature and Division of Triadic Relations, As Far As they Are Determined', in Peirce Edition Project (ed.), *The Essential Peirce, Selected Philosophical Writings: Volume 2 (1893–1913)*, 289–300. Bloomington: Indiana University Press.

Pelkmans, M. (2013) 'The Affect Effect', *Anthropology of This Century* (7), May 2013, aotcpress.com/articles/affect-effect/

Pieke, F. N. (2002) *Recent Trends in Chinese Migration to Europe: Fujianese Migration in Perspective, IOM Migration Research Series*, Vol. 6. Geneva: International Organization for Migration.

Pinker, S. (2007) *The Stuff of Thought: Language as a Window into Human Nature*. New York: Viking.

Pinker, S. (2008) *The Stuff of Thought: Language as a Window into Human Nature*. London: Penguin Books.

Potter, S. H. (1988) 'The Cultural Construction of Emotion in Rural Chinese Social Life', *Ethnos* 16: 181–208.

Potter, S. H. and Potter, J. M. (1990) *China's Peasants: The Anthropology of a Revolution*. Cambridge: Cambridge University Press.

Puett, M. and Gross-Loh, C. (2017) *The Path: A New Way to Think about Everything*. New York: Viking Publisher.

Qin, H. (1998) 'Dagongtongdi Benwei Yu Zhongguo Chuantong Shehui', *Shehuixue Yanjiu* (Sociological Studies) 5: 14–23.

Raine, S. (2009) *China's African Challenges*. Abingdon: Routledge for the International Institute for Strategic Studies.

Rapport, N. and Overing, J. (2000) *Social and Cultural Anthropology: The Key Concepts*. London and New York: Routledge.

Ren, Xuefei (2013) *Urban China*. Cambridge and Malden: Polity Press.

Robbins, J. (2004) *Becoming Sinners: Christianity and Moral Torment in a Papua New Guinea Society*. Berkeley: University of California Press.

Robbins, J. (2007) 'Between Reproduction and Freedom: Morality, Value and Radical Cultural Change', *Ethnos* 72 (3): 293–314.

Robbins, J. (2012) 'On Becoming Ethical Subjects: Freedom, Constraint, and the Anthropology of Morality', *Anthropology of This Century* (5). http://aotcpress.com/archive/issue-5/

Robbins, J. (2015) 'Ritual, Value, and Example: On the Perfection of Cultural of Cultural Representations', *Journal of the Royal Anthropological Institute* 21 (S1): 18–29.

Robbins, J. (2017) 'Where in the World are Values?' in C. Mattingly, R. Dyring, M. Louw and T. S. Wentzer (eds), *Moral Engines: Exploring the Ethical Drives in Human Life*, 155–73. New York and Oxford: Berghahn Books.

Robbins, J. (2018) 'Where in the World Are Values? Exemplarity, Morality and Social Process', in J. Laidlaw, B. Bodenhorn and M. Bolbraad (eds), *Recovering the Human Subject: Freedom, Creativity and Decision*, 174–93. Cambridge: Cambridge University Press.

Rofel, L. (1999) *Other Modernities: Gendered Yearnings in China after Socialism*. Berkeley: University of California Press.

Rosaldo, M. Z. (1980) *Knowledge and Passion: Ilongot Notions of Self and Social Life*. Cambridge: Cambridge University Press.

Rosaldo, R. (1982) 'The Things We Do With Words: Ilongot Speech Acts and Speech Act Theory in Philosophy', *Language in Society* 11: 203–37.

Rosnow, R. L. and Fine, G. (1976) *Rumor and Gossip: The Social Psychology of Hearsay*. New York and Oxford and Amsterdam: Elsevier.

Rotberg, R. I. (2008) *China into Africa: Trade, Aid and Influence*. Washington DC: Brookings Institution Press.

Sautman, B. (1994) 'Anti-Black Racism in Post-Mao China', *China Quarterly* 138: 413–37.

Sautman, B. and Yan, H. (2006) *East Mountain Tiger, West Mountain Tiger: China, the West, and 'Colonialism' in Africa*. Baltimore: Maryland Series in Contemporary Asian Studies.

Sautman, B. and Yan, H. (2008) 'Forests for the Trees: Trade, Investment and the China-in-Africa Discourse', *Pacific Affairs* 81 (1): 9–29.

Sautman, B. and Yan, H. (2009) 'African Perspectives on China-Africa Links', *China Quarterly* 199: 728–59.

Sautman, B. and Yan, H. (2011) 'Barking Up the Wrong Tree: Human Rights Watch and Chinese Copper Mining in Zambia', *Pambazuka News* 563 (December 14). https://www.pambazuka.org/governance/barking-wrong-tree

Sautman, B. and Yan, H. (2013) '"The Beginning of a World Empire"? Contesting the Discourse of Chinese Copper Mining in Zambia', *Modern China* 39 (2): 131–64.

Schacter, D., Gilbert, D. and Wegner, D. (2011) *Psychology: European Edition*. London: Palgrave Macmillan.

Schmidt, Steffen W., Scott, James C., Landé, C. and Guasti, L., eds. (1977) *Friends, Followers and Factions*. Berkeley: University of California Press.

Schmitz, C. M. T (2014) 'Significant Others: Security and Suspicion in Chinese-Angolan Encounters', *Journal of Current Chinese Affairs* 43 (1): 41–69.

Searle, J. (2010) *Making the Social World: The Structure of Human Civilization*. Oxford: Oxford University Press.

Shah, A. (2013) 'In Search of Certainty in Revolutionary India', in M. Pelkmans (ed.), *Ethnographies of Doubt: Faith and Uncertainty in Contemporary Societies*, 165–91. London and New York: I.B.Tauris.

Shaw, V. (1996) *Social Control in China: A Study of Chinese Work Units*. Westport: Praeger.

Sheridan, D. (2019) 'Weak Passports and Bad Behavior: Chinese Migrants and the Moral Politics of Petty Corruption in Tanzania', *American Ethnologist* 46 (2): 137–49.

Shouse, E. (2005) 'Feeling, Emotion, Affect', *M/C Journal* 8 (6). Retrieved from http://journal.media-culture.org.au/0512/03-shouse.php

Smart, A. (1999) 'Expressions of Interest: Friendship and *Guanxi* in Chinese Societies', in S. Bell and S. Coleman (eds), *The Anthropology of Friendship*. Oxford and New York: Berg Publication.

Snow, P. (1988) *The Star Raft: China's Encounter with Africa*. London: Weidenfeld and Nicolson.

Solinger, D. J. (1995) 'The Chinese Work Unit and Transient Labor in the Transition from Socialism', *Modern China* 21 (2): 155–83.

Sorace, C., Franceschini, I. and Loubere, N., eds. (2019) *Afterlives of Chinese Communism*. Canberra: ANU Press and Verso Books.

Stafford, C. (2000) 'Chinese Patriliny and the Cycles of *Yang* and *Laiwang*', in J. Carsten (ed.), *Cultures of Relatedness: New Approaches to the Study of Kinship*, 37–55. Cambridge: Cambridge University Press.

Stafford, C. (2007) 'What Is Going to Happen Next?' in R. Astuti, J. Parry and C. Stafford (eds), *Questions of Anthropology*. Oxford and New York: Berg Publication.

Stafford, C. (2009) 'Numbers and the Natural History of Imagining the Self in Taiwan and China', *Ethnos* 74 (1): 110–26.

Stafford, C. (2010) 'Some Qualitative Mathematics in China', *Anthropological Theory* 10: 81–5.

Stafford, C., ed. (2013) *Ordinary Ethics in China*. London: Bloomsbury.

Steinmuller, J. (2010) 'Communities of Complicity: Notes on State Formation and Local Sociality in Rural China', *American Ethnologist* 37 (3): 539–49.

Steinmuller, J. (2013) *Communities of Complicity: Everyday Ethics in Rural China*. New York: Berghahn.

Steinmuller, J. and Wu, F. (2011) 'School Killings in China: Society or Wilderness?', *Anthropology Today* 27 (1): 10–13.

Stewart, K. (2007) *Ordinary Affects*. Durham and London: Duke University Press.

Stewart, K. (2017) 'In the World that Affect Proposed', *Cultural Anthropology* 32 (2): 192–8.

Strauss, J. C. (2013) 'China and Africa Rebooted: Globalization(s), Simplification(s), and Cross-cutting Dynamics in "South-South" Relations', *African Studies Review* 56 (1): 155–70.

Strickland, M. (2010) 'Aid and Affect in the Friendships of Young Chinese Men', *JRAI* 16 (1): 102–18.

Sun, L. (1991) 'Contemporary Chinese Culture: Structure and Emotionality', *Australian Journal of Chinese Affairs* 26: 1–41.

Tan, T. (2010) *Qiaocun Youdao* (The Path in Village Qiao). Beijing: Sanlian Press.

Thrift, N. (2007) *Non-representational Theory: Space, Politics, Affect*. London: Routledge.

Toren, C. (2012) 'Imagining the World that Warrants Our Imagination', *Cambridge Anthropology* 30 (1): 64–79.

Tu, W. M. (1985) *Confucian Thought: Selfhood as Creative Transformation*. Albany: State University of New York Press.

Utomi, P. (2008) 'China and Nigeria', in J. Cooke (ed.), *U.S. and Chinese Engagement in Africa: Prospects for Improving U.S.-China-Africa Cooperation*, 49–59. Washington DC: Centre for Strategic and Interactional Studies.

Van Bracht, G. (2012) 'A Survey of Zambian Views on Chinese People and their Involvement in Zambia', *China Monitor: African and East-Asian Affairs* 1: 54–97.

Vygotsky, L. S. (1978) *Mind in Society: The Development of Higher Psychological Processes* Cambridge, MA: Harvard University Press.

Walder, A. G. (1983) 'Organized Dependency and Cultures of Authority in Chinese Industry', *Journal of Asian Studies* 43 (1): 51–76.

Walder, A. G. (1986) *Communist Neo-Traditionalism: Work and Authority in Chinese Industry*. Berkeley and Los Angeles: University of California Press.

Waldron, A., ed. (2008) *China in Africa*. Washington DC: Jamestown Foundation.

Wang, C. and Flam, D. (2007) 'Bridging the Gap: Experience and Attitudes in Sino-African Relations', *China Rights Forum* 2 (June): 196–208.

Wetherell, M. 2012, *Affect and Emotion: A New Social Science Understanding*. London: SAGE Publications Ltd.

Wickberg, E. (2007) 'Global Chinese Migrants and Performing Chineseness', *Journal of Chinese Overseas* 3: 177–93.

Williams, B. (1981) *Moral Luck*. Cambridge: Cambridge University Press.

Williams, B. (1985) *Ethics and the Limits of Philosophy*. London: Collins.

Yan, Y. (1996) *The Flow of Gifts: Reciprocity and Social Networks in a Chinese Village*. Stanford: Stanford University Press.

Yan, Y. (2003) *Private Life under Socialism: Love, Intimacy, and Family Change in a Chinese Village, 1949–1999*. Stanford: Stanford University Press.

Yan, Y. (2009a) *The Individualization of Chinese Society*. Oxford: Berg Publication.

Yan, Y. (2009b) 'Good Samaritan's New Trouble: A Study of Changing Moral Landscape in Contemporary China', *Social Anthropology* 17 (1): 9–14.

Yan, Y. (2010) 'The Chinese Path to Individualization', *The British Journal of Sociology* 61 (3): 489–512.

Yan, Y. (2011) 'How Far Away Can We Move From Durkheim? – Reflections on the New Anthropology of Morality', *Anthropology of This Century* (2). http://aotcpress.com/articles/move-durkheim-reflections-anthropology-morality/

Yan, Y. (2013) 'The Drive for Success and the Ethics of the Striving Individual', in C. Stafford (ed.), *Ordinary Ethics in China*, 263–93. London: Bloomsbury.

Yang, B. (2016) 'Understanding Mobility: Motivation, Recruitment, and Migration of Chinese Foremen to Zambia', *Cambridge Journal of China Studies* 11 (1): 129–40.

Yang, Mayfair Mei-hui (1988) 'The Modernity of Power in the Chinese Socialist Order', *Cultural Anthropology* 3 (4): 408–27.

Yang, M. M. H. (1994), *Gifts, Favors and Banquets: The Art of Social Relations in China*. Ithaca: Cornell University Press.

Yu, G. T. (1971) 'Working on the Railroad: China and the Tanzania-Zambia Railway', *Asian Survey* 11 (11): 1101–17.

Yu, J. (2007) *The Ethics of Confucius and Aristotle*. Oxford and New York: Routledge.

Yu, Y. G. ed. (1988) *The History of Chinese Contemporary Prose (Zhongguo Xiandai Sanwenshi)*. Shandong: Shandong Wenyi Press.

Yu, Y. (2004) *Collections of Yu Yin-shih's Writings (Yu Ying-shih Wenji)*. Guilin: Guangxi Normal University Press.

Yu, Y. (2012) *Zhongguo Wenhuashi Tongshi* (On the History of Chinese Culture). Beijing: Sanlian Book.

Zhang, H. (2010) *Windfall Wealth and Envy in Three Chinese Mining Villages*, PhD Book for London School Economics and Political Science.

Zhang, L. (2001) *Strangers in the City: Reconfigurations of Space, Power, and Social Networks within China's Floating Population*. Stanford: Stanford University Press.

Zhang, Y. (2007) *Transforming Emotions with Chinese Medicine: An Ethnographic Account from Contemporary China*. Albany: State University of New York Press.

Index

affect 132–4, 196, 201, 212 n.10, 213 n.2. *See also* speech capital
  situational 163, 172–8, 203, 204
affection, talking with 178–82. *See also* attentiveness and emotional labour
affective turn 28
Alden, C. 5, 211 n.4
Ames, R. 29–32, 135, 150, 155, 157, 178, 204
Angola 12
  shared suspicion in 46
Anhui Province 36
anthropology, of ethics 154
anxiety/fear (*Metagu*) 40, 43–6, 76, 133, 194–6, 202
  calamity and 68
  categorical binaries and 69
  caution and 51–6, 59–60
  Chinese embassy and 64–5, 67
  80 hou and 62
  linguistic registers of 49–50
  pervasiveness of 69, 71, 77
  rumour and 57–8
  significance of 47–8
  social ties and 48
  society as dangerous and 61–2
Arsene, C. 20
attentiveness and emotional labour 109–10
  'extra trouble to leader' principle and 123–9
  'to serve the leader' principle and 119–23
  work units and 111
  Zambian case 113–16

Bandung Summit (1955) 4
banquet speech manners 179–82, 186, 188–9
Barry (character) 119–22, 148, 152–3, 184–6
Bell, E. 12
Bernstein, B. 199
body (*ti*) 156
Bolt, M. 109
Boss Deng (character) 97–9
boss–worker dependency 109–10, 115–16, 118–20
  moral evaluation and 139–42
Botswana 12, 46
'bottleneck effect' in Chinese private business in Lusaka 85–90
Bourdieu, P. 161, 184
Buckingham, W. 211 n.6

calculation (*jisuan/suanji*)
  and affection, relationship between 93–4
  resentment of 94–6
casualization 106
  and informalization 107–8
Chan, K. W. 211 n.6
Chau, A. 182, 208–9
China-Aid Zambia Agriculture Technology Demonstration Centre (ATDC) 34–6, 80, 111, 112
  administrative hierarchy of 113
  and care of workers 112–13
  exclusivism at 63–4
Chinese migrants, categories of 9–10
Chinese sociality 25–8
  beyond social networking 33

categorization model related to 54, 69
and *lun* notion 29
reinterpretation of 29
commensality, idea of 181
community of complicity 162–3
company, keeping (*pei*) 120
Confucianism 153, 155–7, 82, 83, 205, 214 n.2
Confucian Role Ethics (Ames) 29
convivial affect 180–1
Crissman, L. W. 101
Cuba 13
cultural intimacy 162–3
cultural schema, of strangers 48–9, 70, 71

'Declarations of Dependence' (Ferguson) 107
Deng, X. 5
dependency
 affection and 131
 boss–worker 109–10, 115–16, 118–20
 organized 117
 significance of 107, 109
'differential mode of association' (*chaxugeju*) 25–7, 54, 76, 183
 Fei's model of 69–70
 negative effects of (*see* interactional affection (*jiaoqing*))
 reinterpretation of 28–34
Director Lu (character) 2–3
disunity (*butuanjie*) 76
Dobler, G. 10
Duranti, A. 173

embeddedness. *See also* ethical qualia
 of affect 192, 196
 of affection 132–4
 of Confucian values 20
 of emotion 32, 34, 41, 201–6
 in Chinese sociality 208–9
 of qualia 143, 149–50
 of socioeconomic conditions 20
 of speech capital 162
emotion (*ganqing*). *See also individual entries*
 dimensions of 32
 in China and critiques, hypothesis of 197–200
 Chinese contribution to anthropology of 206–8
 embedded significance, in Chinese sociality 208–9
 redefining 200–6
 significance of 91, 92, 133–4
emotional labour 103–10
 affective performance and 108–9
 attentiveness direction
  extra trouble to leader principle 123–9
  'to serve the leader' principle 119–23
  Zambian case 113–16
 case study 110–13
 meaning of 108
emotional proximity 33, 69
ethical qualia 135–7, 141
 effect on moral reflection and transformation 144–50
 meaning and significance of 142–4
Ethiopia 5
everyday sociality 21
 investigating, from Chinese perspective 21–5
exclusivism (*paiwai*) 48, 63–4, 70–1
eye strength to observe (*yanlijian'er*) 173
 significance of 177

face and speech, relationship between 167
factionalism 67, 76, 77

in action 85–90
and segmentation model
of overseas Chinese
communities
compared 101
familism 82–83
strong 89
family division (*fenjia*) 89
Fang, I.-C. 177–8
fate/karma (*yuanfen*) 98
Fei, X. 25, 33, 54
Ferguson, J. 15, 25, 107
Feuchtwang, S. 26, 49, 69
Forum on China-Africa Cooperation
(FOCAC) Summit 5
Foucault, M. 136
Freedman, M. 26
From the Soil (Xiaotong) 25
Fukuyama, F. 82–3, 85, 89

Ghana 19, 116
Giese, K. 19, 22, 116
Gluckman, M. 20–1
Going Out (*zouchuqu*), policy 5, 7–8
Grace (character) 185–6
group solidarity 66–7
Gupta, A. 25

Hamilton, G. 11
heart (*xin*) 207
Henan Province (China) 11
Hochschild, Arlie 108
Hsu, E. 9
Hu, J. 5
Hu family farm 89
human feelings (*renqing*) ethics 90
dimension of 91
and interactional affection
(*jiaoqing*) compared 92–3
significance of 96
human sociality 28
Humphrey, C. 46
Hunyh, T. T. 17

indirect speech, as communicative
preference 164–72
inner emotional state (*wuxing*) 205
interactional affection (*jiaoqing*) 40, 73–9, 202
anti-anti-affection as way of
cooperation and 90–9
faction in action and 85–90
mistrust and suspicion and 79–85
internalism and moral
evaluation 154
inter-personal relations and cultural
norms, significance
of 19–20
intersubjectivity 28, 29, 32, 78, 92, 108, 163, 196, 201–3, 205
ethical qualia and 134, 143, 144
intimacy, sense of (*qinmiganjue*) 33
irony, as linguistic style 163
'is-ought problem' 137

Ivanhoe, P. 155, 157
Jacobs, B. 83
Jiang, Z. 5
Jiangxi Construction
Cooperative 37
Jiangxi Province (China) 11
Jilin Province 35
Jullien, F. 203

Keane, W. 154, 214 n.1
Kenya 5
Kipnis, A. 27, 91, 199, 202, 212 n.9

labour conflicts and inter-personal
relations, in Ghanian
context 19
Laidlaw, J. 31
Lampert, B. 20
Lan, S. S. 70
Large, D. 16, 211 n.4
Lee, C. K. 18, 106, 107, 211–12 n.8
Lesotho 12, 18, 46

Li, K. 6
Li, Z. 118
linguistic capital 184
linguistic implicature 164
Litz, C. 47
Liu Wei (character) 95–6, 103–5, 129, 185–6
Long, N. 28
Lu, X. 111
Lutz, Catherine 206
Lyon, Margot 206–7

Ma, M. 9–10
McIntyre, A. 136
McNamee, T. 12, 46–7
macroscopic perspective, of Sino-African relationships 16–17
Manager Bao (character) 63–4, 79–82, 84, 114, 124, 164–6, 174–6, 185, 189
Manager Deng (character) 39, 43, 56, 57, 61, 64, 65, 87, 88, 160–1, 180, 181
Massumi, B. 212 n.10
Men, T. 20
mistrust and suspicion 79–85
Mohan, G. 20
money-lending practices 95–9
Mongolia 13
Monson, J. 17–18
Moore, H. 28
moral dilemma 151
moral evaluation (*buxiangyang'er*) 136, 137, 144, 153, 173, 215 n.1
  internalism and 154
  significance of 139–42
moral frustration 149
Mother Liu (character) 2, 3, 8, 36, 79–81, 86–7, 187–90
Munn, N. 135, 143

Nigeria 5
non-production work units (*shiye danwei*) 111
non-representational side, of ethics 154

obedience (*tinghua*) 128
'Old Zambians' (*laozanbiya*) 8, 14
'Open Door' policy 5
Osburg, J. 84, 92, 131
Oxfeld, E. 11, 207

pariah capitalism 11–12
Park, Y. J. 17, 18
pattern-recognition exercises 48
Peirce, C. 143
people from same region (*laoxiang*) 37, 52, 73, 84, 98, 186
performing (*biaoxian*) tactic 117
Perry, E. J. 111
Pinker, S. 164, 168
Potter, S. H. 42, 197–8
poverty and bitterness allowance (*jiankubuzhu*) 13
prose (*sanwen*) 213 n.3
'provincial assignment for project construction' (*duikouyuanjia*) 11

qualisign, significance of 143–4

racial discrimination 71
ritual (*li*) 156–7
role ethics 30–1, 133. *See also* ethical qualia
Rosaldo, M. Z. 191–2
rumour, as linguistic phenomenon 57–8
Rupp, S. 17–18

Sata, M. 7, 43, 212 n.1
Sautman, B. 15
Schmitz, C. M. T. 46, 213 n.4
Searle, J. 163, 191
seeing want others feel/want (*kanrenlianse*) 177–8

Index

segmentation, of overseas Chinese communities 101
self, as result of aggregating relations 157
self-cultivation (*xiuyang*) 136, 137, 143, 153
   ethical 144
   social roles and rituals and 156-7
   virtue and 155-6
self-problematization 136
sentiment (*qingcao*) 58, 91, 145, 204, 209
   anti-Chinese 7
   intersubjective 78
   moral 96
   negative 48-9, 185
   personal 45
   responsive 70
   shared 45, 57, 71
   social networking (*guanxi*) and 199
Shao, S. 162
shared suspicion 46
Sino-Hydro company (Kariba) 38-9
situation (*qingkuang*)
   sensitivity to 31-2
   social significance in China 31
situational affect 32, 163, 203-5
   as contextualization cue 172-8
Snow, P. 211 n.4
Soares De Oliviera, R. 211 n.4
social capital 187
social egoism 26, 198
social heat, sense of 182
sociality and speech, relationship between 167-8
social networking (*guanxi*) 27, 77, 78, 90, 100, 168, 199, 212 n.9
   ethnography of 90-1
   speech capital and 190
   views on 83-5

social roles
   as dyadic 31
   as embodiment process 30
   ritual and 157
   significance of 29-30, 144-50
South Africa 5, 12, 13, 18, 46
Speech and Eloquence (yanjiangyukoucai) (magazine) 162
speech capital 159-64
   indirect speech as communicative preference and 164-72
   and linguistic capital compared 184
   network and profits and 187-91
   situational affect as contextualization cue and 172-8
   talking with affection and 178-82
   work and favouritism and 183-7
spirit of structure 132
spontaneous sociality 83, 85, 91, 168
   lack of 89
Stafford, C. 48, 91-2, 93, 214 n.1
Steinmuller, H. 21, 62, 162-3
Stewart, K. 212 n.2
stranger (*shengren*) 54
   as cultural ideal 48
   cultural schema of 48-9, 70, 71
subjectivation 136
Sudan 13

Tanzania 18, 20
Tanzania-Zambia railway 6, 7, 18
Thiel, A. 116
Thomas (character) 2, 3, 127-8, 169-71, 174-7, 194
Toren, C. 28
'To serve the leader' (*weilingdaofuwu*) and attentiveness 119-23

extra trouble (*luan/mafan*) and   123–9
Trust (Fukuyama)   82

University of Zambia (UNZA)   34–6, 111
   farm   114

virtue, alternative   153–7
virtue ethics   154–5
virtuous leader   149

Walder, A.   83, 117
Wetherell, M.   212 n.10
white schools (*bairenxuexiao*)   14, 59
Williams, B.   136
work and working relationships, idea of   121–2
   extra trouble (*luan/mafan*) and   123–9
work unit (*danwei*)   111, 117
   characteristics of   111
Wu, F.   62

Xiang, Z. (character)   87
Xiao, F. (character)   60, 61, 63
Xiao, L. (character)   1, 2, 3, 37, 95–6, 124, 138–41, 148–9, 151, 175, 186
Xiao, Z.   190–1

Yan, H.   15

Yan, Y.   90–1, 130–1, 198, 199, 200, 212 n.9
Yang, M.   83–4
Yang, M. M. H.   27
yang and *laiwang* cycle   91–2

Zambia   6, 212 n.1
   anti-Chinese sentiment in   7
   China's role in development of   6
   Chinese provincial concentration in   10–11
   new Chinese arrivals in Africa and   4–15
Zambia Development Agency   6
Zambian Chinese Christian Fellowship   67
Zhang, L.   211 n.6
Zou family   37–9, 73–4, 96–8, 159, 215 n.1
   anxiety of   43–5
   caution and   51–6, 59–60
   Chinese National Day and   64–5
   rumour and   57–8
   society as dangerous and   61–2
   on borrowing money   97–9
   business with Sino-hydro company   74–5
   farm compound, structure of   51
   speech capital and   159–61, 164–7, 187–91
   talking with affection and   178–82

Printed in the United States
By Bookmasters